Utility and Production

Contributions to Economics

http://www.springer.de/cgi-bin/search_book.pl?series=1262

Georg Bol/Gholamreza Nakhaeizadeh/
Karl-Heinz Vollmer (Eds.)
Risk Measurements, Econometrics and Neural Networks
1998. ISBN 3-7908-1152-1

Joachim Winter
Investment and Exit Decisions at the Plant Level
1998. ISBN 3-7908-1154-8

Bernd Meyer
Intertemporal Asset Pricing
1999. ISBN 3-7908-1159-9

Uwe Walz
Dynamics of Regional Integration
1999. ISBN 3-7908-1185-8

Michael Carlberg
European Monetary Union
1999. ISBN 3-7908-1191-2

Giovanni Galizzi/
Luciano Venturini (Eds.)
Vertical Relationships and Coordination in the Food System
1999. ISBN 3-7908-1192-0

Gustav A. Horn/Wolfgang Scheremet/
Rudolf Zwiener
Wages and the Euro
1999. ISBN 3-7908-1199-8

Dirk Willer
The Development of Equity Capital Markets in Transition Economies
1999. ISBN 3-7908-1198-X

Karl Matthias Weber
Innovation Diffusion and Political Control of Energy Technologies
1999. ISBN 3-7908-1205-6

Heike Link et al.
The Costs of Road Infrastructure and Congestion in Europe
1999. ISBN 3-7908-1201-3

Simon Duindam
Military Conscription
1999. ISBN 3-7908-1203-X

Bruno Jeitziner
Political Economy of the Swiss National Bank
1999. ISBN 3-7908-1209-9

Irene Ring et al. (Eds.)
Regional Sustainability
1999. ISBN 3-7908-1233-1

Katharina Müller/Andreas Ryll/
Hans-Jürgen Wagener (Eds.)
Transformation of Social Security: Pensions in Central-Eastern Europe
1999. ISBN 3-7908-1210-2

Stefan Traub
Framing Effects in Taxation
1999. ISBN 3-7908-1240-4

Pablo Coto-Millán
Utility and Production
1999. ISBN 3-7908-1153-X

Frank Riedel
Imperfect Information and Investor Heterogeneity in the Bond Market
2000. ISBN 3-7908-1247-1

Kirsten Ralf
Business Cycles
2000. ISBN 3-7908-1245-5

Michele Bagella/Leonardo Becchetti (Eds.)
The Competitive Advantage of Industrial Districts
2000. ISBN 3-7908-1254-4

Frank Bohn
Monetary Union and Fiscal Stability
2000. ISBN 3-7908-1266-8

Jaime Behar
Cooperation and Competition in a Common Market
2000. ISBN 3-7908-1280-3

Michael Malakellis
Integrated Macro-Micro-Modelling Under Rational Expectations
2000. ISBN 3-7908-1274-9

Stefan Baumgärtner
Ambivalent Joint Production and the Natural Environment
2000. ISBN 3-7908-1290-0

Henri Capron, Wim Meeusen (Eds.)
The National Innovation System of Belgium
2000. ISBN 3-7908-1308-7

Tobias Miarka
Financial Intermediation and Deregulation
2000. ISBN 3-7908-1307-9

Chisato Yoshida
Illegal Immigration and Economic Welfare
2000. ISBN 3-7908-1315-X

continued on page 203

Pablo Coto-Millán

Utility and Production

Theory and Applications

Second Edition

With 26 Figures and 13 Tables

Physica-Verlag
A Springer-Verlag Company

Series Editors
Werner A. Müller
Martina Bihn

Author
Professor Pablo Coto-Millán
University of Cantabria
Department of Economics
Avda. Los Castros s/n.
39005 Santander
Spain
cotop@unican.es

ISSN 1431-1933
ISBN 3-7908-1423-7 Physica-Verlag Heidelberg New York
ISBN 3-7908-1153-X 1st edition Physica-Verlag Heidelberg New York

Cataloging-in-Publication Data applied for
Die Deutsche Bibliothek – CIP-Einheitsaufnahme
Coto-Millán, Pablo: Utility and production: theory and applications; with 13 tables / Pablo Coto-Millán. – 2nd. ed. – Heidelberg: Physica-Verl., 2003
(Contributions to economics)
ISBN 3-7908-1423-7

Physica-Verlag Heidelberg New York
a member of BertelsmannSpringer Science+Business Media GmbH

Softcover Design: Erich Kirchner, Heidelberg

SPIN 10845119 88/2202-5 4 3 2 1 0 – Printed on acid-free and non-aging paper

Preface to the Second Edition

This book is different from the first edition. There are three entirely new chapters: 2, 6 and 9. I have also included new sections in chapters 1, 4 and 8. Moreover, the remaining chapters, 3, 5 and 7, have been revised and updated.

In chapters 2 and 6 I felt it was necessary to include the main alternative theories of consumer and company behaviour along with the neo-classical models. The book contains four chapters of theory – 1, 2, 5 and 6 – and four chapters with theoretical and empirical applications – 3, 4, 7 and 8. Finally, chapter nine looks at choices made under conditions of uncertainty.

September 2002 P. Coto-Millán

Preface to the First Edition

Grateful acknowledgment is made to CICYT (Comisión Interministerial de Ciencia y Tecnología), National Plan R+D, Projects N-TXT96-2467 and N-TXT98-1453 for its financial support.

This text presents the economic theories on Utility and Production. In addition, such theories are used to explain the real problems of consumers and firms and several studies carried out by the author are displayed. Some collaboration by other professors of Economics is mentioned in the corresponding footnotes. The responsibility for errors and omissions, however, rests entirely upon the author.

In chapters 1 and 4 of the book I try to present the theory of Utility and Production.

Chapter 3 presents new functional forms and two empirical applications, on demand functions and systems.

In chapters 2 and 5, the main theorems and properties presented in chapters 1 and 4 are applied.

Chapter 6 presents new functional forms and two empirical applications, on production and cost functions respectively.

Chapters 1, 2, 4, and 5 have been used as class notes in advanced Microeconomics lectures from 1992 to 1997. Chapters 3 and 6 have been also discussed in different graduate courses in the 1992-1997 period. This allowed us to detect and correct many errors and mistakes. Of course I am sure that not all the errors have been removed. In any case I am the only one responsible for that.

August 1999 P. Coto-Millán

Table of Contents

Introduction

Microeconomics, also called the science of the markets, is the most productive branch of economics theory and it studies resources allocation and price theory. By economics theory we mean a language or device for deriving and obtaining operationally significant theorems, a way of understanding reality and the behaviour of society. This book actually aims to follow the tradition of other books about the theory of prices, in which prominent authors reflect on the different aspects of pricing in input and output markets. In this book, I have used advanced material for specialised graduate courses in microeconomic theory.

Microeconomics should not be defined in opposition to Macroeconomics, as its understanding constitutes the base and support for the study of the whole economy. All the fields and disciplines of economics should be grounded in Microeconomics; otherwise, we should suspect of their foundations. I even think that Microeconomics defines the profession, it is the ability to deal with this science that distinguishes an economist from a student of politics, an historian, a sociologist, an engineer or a mathematician with an interest in Economics. As a footballer shows his ability when dribbling with the ball, an economist is characterised by his ability in dealing with microeconomics. When economists say that a certain "expert" is not an economist, they mean that he does not use microeconomic concepts properly.

Microeconomics has successfully explained human behaviour. Thus, in this book, I explain the consumer and producer's behaviour and the theories and empirical treatment which try to describe and predict human behaviour.

Macroeconomics implies the study of unemployment and the general level of price (inflation). It is more controversial and less successful than Microeconomics. There is no widespread agreement among the economists about it. In conversations with colleagues in medicine and meteorology, I have heard the same complaints as those made by economists. They also must face people's preconceived ideas with respect to health or weather forecasting like the prejudices the economists must face. Almost every report in the media is wrong and is not supported by a thorough economic study. Therefore, it is pleasant to hear, generally in meetings with other professionals and in the calm of summer courses, about the same problems both as regards prejudices, and terminology. Especially in the latter question, there is a specific terminology for medicine, meteorology and economics, which can be considered artificial, sometimes exaggeratedly so, from articles in journals, for a lay audience. This is what generates tremendous confusion among the public and numerous prejudices against these sciences, which are sometimes based on ignorance, ideology and fanaticism.

Anyway, those who are determined to study Microeconomics obtain the advantage of understanding the behaviour of society.

We have referred to economics as the science that studies the way in which society solves economic problems. Economic theory can be considered as a language; i.e. what Marshall called "analysis mechanism", and its purpose, as when teaching a language, is to obtain as many substantive propositions as possible, like a language or a classification system or like a series of propositions with an empirical content. In Microeconomics, prices are a key element, hence, every prestigious economist has worked out a theory of prices.

Prices in this book are the incentives not only for consumers to use goods and services but also for them to produce goods and services. Moreover, prices efficiently provide the suitable information about these goods and services produced and consumed.

For prices to work as an incentive, one should be free to choose the goods and services to be used or produced. However, there must not be freedom to form coalitions and avoid competition. In fact, a review of the history of humanity provides empirical evidence supporting this proposition. The most incoherent and unbalanced economic systems have been frequently those not based on free choice.

There is an essential scientific principle, possibly referred to as the unification or generalisation principle: the existence of analogous key elements in different theories implies that all these theories are supported by a general theory that envelops and unifies them. Physics is searching at present for a theory to unify both quantum and relativity theories: without very much success as yet, unless we believe in the superstring theory. The unifying principle of generalisation by abstraction has been the static partial equilibrium for economists. It involves all the solutions to production and consumption problems with the same relationships and the same theorems, lemmas and corollaries. In fact, production and cost studies are developing in the same way as consumption and cost. Not only these analogies are remarkable but also those derived from the duals, which are the alternative outlines to optimisation problems, with the same properties and solutions. Moreover, very frequently, either primal or dual functions are not feasible from an empirical point of view, which leads us to change some functions into others, which have the same properties as the former ones; for instance, this is the case of distance functions.

What does this add to scientific knowledge? Probably, a wide range of possibilities to solve economic problems. Therefore, we have five groups of consumption and production functions: direct and indirect utility, cost, Marshallian and Hicksian (for consumption), and profit, cost, supply, input demand and input conditioned demand (for production). Thus, it seems that we can characterise consumption and production at least in five different ways although the problem is not completely solved from a formal point of view. What would be desirable to do with these five alternative functions?

(i) if we have a function, it would be desirable to have the procedures which would infer the remaining four groups of functions from it (correspondence problem);

(ii) if we have a dual function, it would be desirable to know if it corresponds with the primal (integrability problem);

(iii) the transformations of dual functions allow us to keep the properties of the non-changed functions (transformation problem).

In physics, the unifying principle would be Newtons' Universal Law of Gravity, as in the natural sciences, such a principle would be Darwin's Law of the Evolution of Species, while in economics, the principle which most resembles this would be Smith's Invisible Hand.

Could the rational individuals and therefore, the optimising behaviour and its primal and dual functions, be the driving of the economy? It seems that the unifying principle is the optimising behaviour of individuals that appears repeatedly when the economic problems are posed and solved.

Although the term dual has been used in the literature in different ways, by a dual we mean a function that allows us to obtain the same solution as its corresponding primal function so that the dual of another dual is the primal.

The field of the dual functions, the functions derived from the duals (for instance, the distance function), the optimisers with respect to the shadow variables rather than to the real variables, as well as the dual functions and those functions derived from the shadow optimisers, is a field in which the same problem is repeatedly posed. This means that every problem is likely to be characterised in terms of optimisers. However, their complexity and the fact that the individual's decisions may seem non-optimising or non-rational, do not mean that they are not really so. What we are actually supporting is the individual rationality as a philosophical principle, which underlies the dual functions.

Moreover, the dual functions and those derived from them can provide a broader empirical treatment and become a source of knowledge in future.

Duality implies an optimising behaviour and goods and service exchange. The microeconomics that includes the duality has provided a new approach to the exchange and distribution of resources as well as valuable means to predict the effects on the equilibrium results produced by the restrictions of the individuals who make decisions.

As mentioned above, the optimising behaviour is expected in an individual who can choose rationally. This is true in a particular institutional framework, which, in the economics theory, is specified for the consumer and the producer through institutional assumptions which can be summarised as follows:

(i) exchange in an unrestricted market;
(ii) complete information;
(iii) private ownership rights absolutely defined.

However, the rational behaviour has been questioned by some authors, being still a key topic of discussion based on the assumption that the individuals

(i) do not apply the transitive property properly;
(ii) do not have stable preferences;
(iii) are not computers which make optimising decisions by considering all the variables involved in a complex problem.

Point (i), is presented in numerous handbooks of microeconomic theory by an illustrative example such as the choice of apartments by students. As regards points (ii) and (iii), we all know individuals who, like ourselves, do not have stable preferences and who, in our opinion, do not optimise properly. Does this mean that the unifying dual principle is not useful? Or otherwise, should we forget about the optimising behaviour of consumers and producers?

Some authors state that the optimising behaviour assumption can be substituted by others such as the satisfaction assumption. One of the key elements of the New Institutional Economy (N.I.E.); the individuals' rationality is not unlimited but is restricted by their own aspirations, which makes consumers develop strategies to achieve their particular levels of satisfaction. Only when consumers feel that they have fallen short of their aspirations, they start revising their goals and design new strategies to achieve their purposes. As it can be seen, the process is more complex, can this process of making decisions be translated into optimising terms? It can probably but using some simplifying assumptions. Assume that the sequential optimising behaviours are developed and individuals do not revise their objectives until these have been achieved, then, part of the problem is solved. That is to say, the difficulty of the behaviours which seek for a particular level of aspirations as a target, rather than the broader set of all the possibilities, is twofold:

(i) the level of aspirations is not objective - as it was in the optimising possibility;

(ii) when does the mental process by which individuals revise their goals start?

From an orthodox view, the first problem is solved defining clearly a goal trying to achieve it from then onwards. This is the old problem of efficiency and efficacy. The second problem is that of assuming that revisions are made in sequences once the goals have been achieved.

From the N.I.E. approach, substituting satisfaction for optimisation means a fierce attack with the core of the neo-classic approach. In the neo-classic line, with the introduction of institutional elements from the N.I.E it is otherwise stated that the addition of new and institutional elements and problems such as transaction costs and ownership rights within the neo-classic structure, provides a richer and more powerful set of testing possibilities than that offered by the substitution of the optimising behaviour model for the satisfaction behaviour model.

From here we infer two approaches or institutional research programs: firstly, that supported by the optimising behaviour of individuals, that is, the principle of individual rationality called Neo-institutional Economics (N.E.), and secondly, the New Institutional Economies (N.I.E.), which proposes substitution of rationality for satisfaction. Apart from this, other factors are added such as restrictions to ownership rights and transaction costs. Any of these approaches may be adequate although I particularly prefer the orthodox branch of N.E., since dual functions work more definitely and objectively than the new research program of the N.I.E.

Anyway, the neo-classic model gains quality when transaction costs and variations in the structure of ownership rights are added. However, one runs into the cost of making the economic analysis more complex. Moreover, the economic analysis is useful not only to explain the exchange within a particular institutional framework of consumers and producers, but also to study the exchange and working of bureaucracy, political organisations, legislative assemblies and alternative economic systems. Results are explained in terms of agreements, institutions and economic systems of equilibrium. However, in this line, empirical hiring must be still developed.

PART I: UTILITY AND CONSUMER DEMAND ANALYSIS

1 Theory of Utility and Consumer Behaviour: A Comprehensive Review of Concepts, Properties and the Most Significant Theorems

In this section, we begin our study of consumer demand in the context of a market economy referred to as the system in which commodities (goods and services) are available to the consumer for purchase at known prices. Firstly, we study the primal problem of consumer utility maximisation. Secondly, we analyse the dual approach and, finally, we study indirect utility function, expenditure function, the theoretical restrictions of demand systems, Roy's Identity, Hotelling's Theorem, relationships between functions, the Slutsky equation and complementary and substitute goods, and the elasticities of substitution of goods. Finally, we offer basic references and further references and readings.

1.1 Theory of Utility

The term utility has been historically used by economists to refer to personal feelings such as pleasure, satisfaction, lack of pain, etc., led by consumption.

Some of the first formulations of this theory of utility were Jeremy Bentham and D. Bernouilli. Bentham put forward the different dimensions of utility: intensity, duration, certainty, proximity, etc, and provided a pathway towards the theory of economic behaviour relying on utility although it was not completely developed.

Bernouilli presented a different theory based on the 'moral hope' estimation in order to maximise utility, also introducing the concept of income marginal utility.

Following the above-mentioned authors, the economists Jevons, Menger and Walras successfully worked out the theory of utility in the late 19th century considering utility to be measurable in absolute quantities, that is to say, in the same way as we estimate production, for example, the physical amounts produced in kilos or tons. Such an approach, obsolete now, is called the cardinal theory approach.

At that time, there were already economists who were not convinced by the measurability condition of utility and the idea that personal feelings, which fall into the category of utility, are difficult to measure and therefore to be considered as absolute quantities, was gradually being introduced.

Finally, the ordinal theory approach replaced the cardinal approach. In the former, it is only necessary that individuals choose different combinations of goods with preference and indifference relationships, that is to say, we do not need to measure utility; the theory of utility can rely on two relatively simple and operationally relevant concepts: preference and indifference.

The classical school had a central logic of behaviour for employers, which relied on the idea of profit maximisation, but not for individuals as consumers. It is true that the classical school provided a theory for the value of goods produced and that worked out an income theory for non-produced goods, but there was no connection between these theories and the theory of employer's profit maximisation. After putting forward the theory of utility, economists had a joint explanation for economic behaviour; all individuals such as consumers and employers, are utility maximisers.

Moreover, whereas if in the beginning, in the cardinal theory economists used literary and numerical methods to explain utility, in the ordinal theory, they may use more sophisticated mathematical tools such as differential estimation.

1.2 Preference, Choice and Indifference Concept and Utility Function Existence

Assume a consumption bundles or consumption plans:

$$x_i = (x_1, x_2, \ldots x_n)$$

where x_i is a vector containing different quantities of each of the n commodities. In addition, $x_i \geq 0$, that is to say, the quantities, are always non-negative.

Assume now that due to preference and indifference relationships the consumers can choose between different pairs of plans.

Consider R for the relationships 'is at least as good as', $\succ$ for the relationship 'preferred to' and $\sim$ for the relationship 'indifferent to'. Consumers must be able to arrange the pairs in vector x_i. With this aim we use the criteria below to arrange preferences, therefore, these must be:

1. **complete**. Any pair of consumption plans x_1, x_2 can be expressed as

   $x_1 \, R \, x_2$ or $x_2 \, R \, x_1$ (or both)

   $x_1 \succ x_2$ or $x_2 \succ x_1$ (or both)

   $x_1 \sim x_2$ or $x_2 \sim x_1$ (or both);

2. **transitive**. For any three consumption plans x_1, x_2 and x_3 it is -verified that:

   if $x_1 \, R \, x_2$ and $x_2 \, R \, x_3$ then $x_1 \, R \, x_3$;

   and the same for indifference relationships $\sim$ and for preference relationships $\succ$;

3. **reflexive**. Any combination of consumption bundles 'is at least as good as' itself. That is to say:

   $x_1 \, R \, x_1$;

4. **nonsatiated**. Any pair of consumption bundles containing at least more than one good and not less of the other, is preferred. That is to say:

   if $x_1 \geq x_2$ and $x_1 \neq x_2$, then, $x_1 \succ x_2$ and x_1 R x_1;

5. **continuous**. For every x_1 in x_i, the groups { x_1: $x_1 \succ x_2$} and { x_2: $x_1 \succ x_2$}are also open to indifference relationships ~ and 'is at least as good as' relationships R. That is to say, the graph for an indifference group is a continuous area. In terms of the consumer behaviour; given a combination of two goods, the quantity owned of one of them can be reduced, and the other can increase, which compensate exactly for that reduction, so that the new combination is indifferent to the former;
6. **strictly convex**. Given a combination of x_i, for example a pair (x_1', x_2'), its best group would be strictly convex. In the figure 1.1:

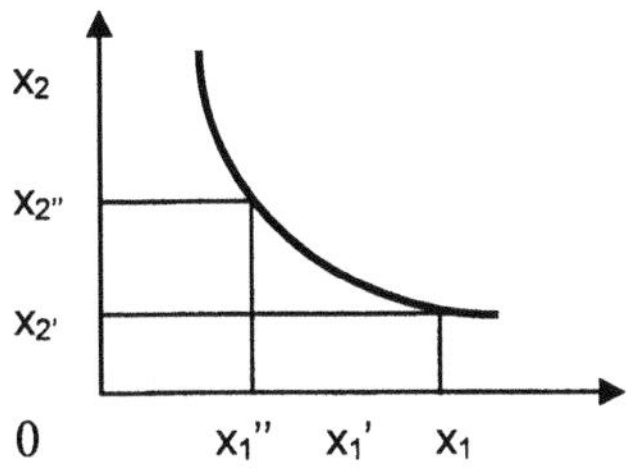

Fig. 1.1. Strictly convex

the best group for combination (x_1', x_2') is the set of points in the indifference curve I and in the shaded area, which, as can be observed, is strictly convex.

Otherwise, the straight line joining points (x_1', x_2') and (x_1'', x_2'') will be preferred to the combinations represented by these points.

Using the assumptions above on the consumer preferences, it is possible to arrange the groups of plans so that the utility function U(**x**) is guaranteed, which consists of assigning each combination of x_i a real number u.

Proposition 1: assuming that the binary relationships 'is at least as good as' are complete, reflexive, transitive, continuous, nonsatiated, these are represented by continuous utility function u:

$$R^k_+ \rightarrow R.$$

That is to say, we presume the existence of a utility function U(**x**) which numerically represents a range of preferences, and the utility functions developed from this are "regular", that is to say, strictly quasi-concave, increasing monotonic and continuous.

It can be proved, but not in this research, that preferences are strictly convex if, and only if, the utility function is strictly quasi-concave. It is also possible to give evidence that preferences are convex if, and only if, the utility function is quasi-concave.

In addition, we operationally assume that preferences are differentiable, which leads to the necessity of adding one more assumption:

7. differentiable. Utility functions are differentiable up to the degree desired.

Note that we refer to quasi-concave utility functions instead of concave ones, this is because we want to propose a framework with the minimum hypothesis. An additional reason, in the consumer theory, for using quasi-concave utility functions, is that transformed functions of quasi-concave functions are quasi-concave, while transformed functions of concave functions do not have to be concave.

1.3 Properties of the Utility Function

1.3.1 Additivity

A utility function is additive if it can be expressed as:

$$U(\mathbf{x}) = \Sigma F_i(x_i)$$

which implies that each good affects utility notwithstanding the quantity of it.

1.3.2 Homogeneity

A utility function is homogeneous of degree K if it satisfies

$$U(tx) = t^k U(\mathbf{x}); \ \forall t>0$$

from which it is derived

$$\frac{U_i(tx)}{U_j(tx)} = \frac{U_i(x)}{U_j(x)}; (i, j = 1,..., n).$$

1.3.3 Homotheticity

A utility function is homothetic if it can be expressed as

$$U(x) = F(f(x));$$

$$F(0) > 0;$$

$$f'(x) > 0.$$

1.3.4 Weak and Strong Separability

If there is a group of goods $(x_1, x_2,...x_r)/(r<n)$ which can be considered as only one good x_A $(x_1, x_2,...x_r)$, so that the utility function can be expressed as $U(x_A, x_{r+1},...x_n)$, it is assumed that the utility function presents Weak Separability in x_A.

Leontief Theorem on Weak Separability: for U(x) to be weakly separable, it must be satisfied that the MRS between two goods from a group is independent of the quantities of the two goods which do not belong to that group.

Strong Separability: this is a reinforcement of the Weak Separability condition and it is satisfied when the MRS between two goods belonging to different groups does not depend on the quantities of the goods which do not belong to any those groups. This implies a total independence between the different groups of goods and leads to additivity of the utility function for the groups of goods.

1.4 Basic Theory (Primal): Marshallian (or Walrasian) Demand Functions

We assume that the consumer preference relationships are rational and offer a complete and transitive ranking of the user's possible consumption choices. Moreover, the utility function is regular, that is to say, it has two properties: monotonicity and strict convexity. Assume there are three commodities, for example, maximising the utility function subject to the budget constraint is:

The augmented objective function is:

$$\left.\begin{array}{l}\text{Max } U(x) = U(x_1, x_2, x_3) \\ \text{S. to } y = p_1x_1 + p_2x_2 + p_3x_3\end{array}\right\} \tag{1.1}$$

$$\text{Max } L(x_1, x_2, x_3, \mu) = U(x_1, x_2, x_3) - \mu(p_1x_1 + p_2x_2 + p_3x_3 - y) \tag{1.2}$$

where μ is the Lagrange multiplier (or the marginal utility of income), y is the income and p_i is the price of commodities.

The first-order (necessary) conditions for maximisation are:

$$\partial L/\partial x_1 = L_1 = U_1(x_1, x_2, x_3) - \mu\, p_1 = 0$$

$$\partial L/\partial x_2 = L_2 = U_2(x_1, x_2, x_3) - \mu\, p_2 = 0$$

$$\partial L/\partial x_3 = L_3 = U_3(x_1, x_2, x_3) - \mu\, p_3 = 0$$

$$\partial L/\partial \mu = L_\mu = - p_1x_1 - p_2x_2 - p_3x_3 + y = 0. \tag{1.3}$$

The first-order conditions in (1.3) can be divided into groups of two which would allow us to obtain an equality between the marginal ratio of substitution and the price ratio of goods. This equality postulates that consumers should distribute their income so that the marginal utility of the last monetary unit spent on the goods x_1, x_2 and x_3 must be equal.

From the equation system (1.3) we obtain the income marginal utility, μ:

$$U_1(x^*)/P_1 = U_2(x^*)/P_2 = U_3(x^*)/P_3 = \mu \tag{1.4}$$

$$U_1(x^*)/U_2(x^*) = P_1/P_2\,,\; U_1(x^*)/U_3(x^*) = P_1/P_3\,,\; U_3(x^*)/U_2(x^*) = P_3/P_2 \tag{1.5}$$

$$\left|\overline{H_2^u}\right| = \left|H_3^L\right| = \begin{vmatrix} U_{11} & U_{12} & -p_1 \\ U_{21} & U_{22} & -p_2 \\ -p_1 & -p_2 & 0 \end{vmatrix} = \begin{vmatrix} 0 & -p_1 & -p_2 \\ -p_1 & U_{11} & U_{12} \\ -p_2 & U_{12} & U_{22} \end{vmatrix} > 0,$$

$$\left|\overline{H_3^u}\right| = \left|H_4^L\right| = \begin{vmatrix} U_{11} & U_{12} & U_{13} & -p_1 \\ U_{21} & U_{22} & U_{23} & -p_2 \\ U_{31} & U_{32} & U_{33} & -p_3 \\ -p_1 & -p_2 & -p_3 & 0 \end{vmatrix} = \begin{vmatrix} 0 & -p_1 & -p_2 & -p_3 \\ -p_1 & U_{11} & U_{12} & U_{13} \\ -p_2 & U_{21} & U_{22} & U_{23} \\ -p_3 & U_{31} & U_{32} & U_{33} \end{vmatrix} < 0. \tag{1.6}$$

Solving the equation system (1.3) yields the following Marshallian (or Walrasian) demand functions:

$$\left.\begin{aligned} x_1 &= x_1(p_1, p_2, p_3, y) \\ x_2 &= x_2(p_2, p_1, p_3, y) \\ x_3 &= x_3(p_3, p_1, p_2, y) \end{aligned}\right\} \tag{1.7}$$

1.4.1 Properties of the Marshallian (or Walrasian) Demand Functions

The Marshallian (or Walrasian) demand presents the following properties:

1. Homogeneity of degree zero in (**p**, y).
2. Walras' law: **p x** = y for all $x \in x$ (**p**,y).
3. Convexity: if U(**x**) is quasi-concave, then x (**p**,y) is a convex set.

1.5 Consumer Equilibrium (Dual): Hicksian (or Compensated) Demand Functions

As an alternative to the above assumption, consumer equilibrium can be obtained, given the prices of goods, by reaching a level of utility minimising expenditure as follows:

$$\left.\begin{aligned} &\min g(p,x) = px = p_1x_1 + p_2x_2 + p_3x_3 \\ &\text{S.to } U(x) = U(x_1, x_2, x_3) = u \end{aligned}\right\} \tag{1.8}$$

The objective function is:

$$S(x_1, x_2, x_3; \lambda) = p_1x_1 + p_2x_2 + p_3x_3 - \lambda\,[U(x_1, x_2, x_3) - u] \tag{1.9}$$

The first-order conditions (1.9) for minimisation are:

$$\left.\begin{aligned}
\frac{\partial S}{\partial x_1} &= S_1 = p_1 - \lambda U_1(x_1, x_2, x_3) = 0 \\
\frac{\partial S}{\partial x_2} &= S_2 = p_2 - \lambda U_2(x_1, x_2, x_3) = 0 \\
\frac{\partial S}{\partial x_3} &= S_3 = p_3 - \lambda U_3(x_1, x_2, x_3) = 0 \\
\frac{\partial S}{\partial \lambda} &= S_\lambda = -U(x_1, x_2, x_3) + u = 0
\end{aligned}\right\} \tag{1.10}$$

The second-order conditions (1.9) for minimisation are:

$$\left|H_3^S\right| = \begin{vmatrix} 0 & -U_1 & -U_2 \\ -U_1 & -\lambda U_{11} & -\lambda U_{12} \\ -U_2 & -\lambda U_{21} & -\lambda U_{22} \end{vmatrix} < 0, \left|H_4^S\right| = \begin{vmatrix} 0 & -U_1 & -U_2 & -U_3 \\ -U_1 & -\lambda U_{11} & -\lambda U_{12} & -\lambda U_{13} \\ -U_2 & -\lambda U_{21} & -\lambda U_{22} & -\lambda U_{23} \\ -U_3 & -\lambda U_{31} & -\lambda U_{32} & -\lambda U_{33} \end{vmatrix} < 0 \tag{1.11}$$

Since conditions (1.3)-(1.6) of the primal are identical to conditions (1.10)-(1.11) of the dual, both assumptions lead to the same equilibrium. This is due to the fact that (1.1) or (1.2) are the primal and (1.8) or (1.9) are the dual of the problem of the consumer. All this is known as the Fundamental Theorem of Consumption Duality.

If (1.10) and (1.11) are verified, the following Hicksian (or compensated) demand functions are derived:

$$\left.\begin{aligned}
x_1 &= h_1\ (p_1, p_2, p_3, u) \\
x_2 &= h_2\ (p_2, p_1, p_3, u) \\
x_3 &= h_3\ (p_3, p_1, p_2, u)
\end{aligned}\right\} \tag{1.12}$$

1.5.1 Properties of the Hicksian (or Compensated) Demand Functions

The Hicksian (or compensated) demand presents the following properties:

1. Homogeneity of degree zero in **p**.
2. Non-excess utility: for any $x \in h(\mathbf{p},u)$, $U(\mathbf{x}) = u$.
3. Convexity: if $U(\mathbf{x})$ is quasi-concave, then $h(\mathbf{p},u)$ is a convex set.

1.6 Indirect Utility Function

Indirect utility function $V = V(\mathbf{p}, y)$ provides the maximum utility for given prices and income. This is obtained by substituting the ordinary or Marshallian demand functions obtained above (1.7) in the utility functions of such goods, that is to say:

$$V = V(\mathbf{p},y) = U(x_1(\mathbf{p},y), x_2(\mathbf{p},y), x_3(\mathbf{p},y)) = \max_x \{U(x) / \mathbf{px} = y\}.$$

The properties of the indirect utility function $V = V(\mathbf{p},y)$ are:

1. Homogenous of degree zero in (p, y).
2. Strictly increasing in y and nonincreasing in p.
3. Quasi-convex in p.
4. Continuous in p and y.

1.7 Expenditure Function

Expenditure function $G = G(\mathbf{p},u)$ provides the minimisation of the expenditure for the given price and utility. This is obtained by substituting the compensated or Hicksian demand function obtained from (1.12), that is to say:

$$G = G(\mathbf{p},u) = g(\mathbf{p}, h_1(\mathbf{p},u), h_2(\mathbf{p},u), h_3(\mathbf{p},u)) = \min_x \{g(\mathbf{p},u) / U(x) = u\}.$$

The properties of the expenditure function $G = G(\mathbf{p},u)$ are

1. Homogenous of degree one in p.
2. Strictly increasing in u and nondecreasing in p.
3. Concave in p.
4. Continuous in p and u.

1.8 Restrictions of the Demand Systems

The consumer theory implies that consumer demand systems must satisfy a range of restrictions (or conditions) derived from the adjustment to budget constraints and/or the consumer's total optimisation process. From an empirical point of view, such restrictions are used to find out whether the estimations agree with the axiomatic consumer theory. There are five common restrictions (or conditions).

1.8.1 Engel Aggregation Condition

With a shift in income, the quantities of the goods demanded will be modified until the whole income is absorbed. It is known that, if the budget constraint is satisfied then we have:

$$y = p_1 x_1(\mathbf{p},y) + p_2 x_2(\mathbf{p},y) + p_3 x_3(\mathbf{p},y) \tag{1.13}$$

and differentiating with respect to income

$$dy = p_1 \frac{\partial x_1}{\partial y} dy + p_2 \frac{\partial x_2}{\partial y} dy + p_3 \frac{\partial x_3}{\partial y} dy = \sum_{i=1}^{3} p_i \frac{\partial x_i(\mathbf{p},y)}{\partial y} dy \tag{1.14}$$

and dividing both members from (1.14) by *dy* and multiplying and dividing the contents in

$$\left[\sum_{i=1}^{3} p_i \frac{\partial x_i(p,y)}{\partial y} dy\right]$$ by (y/x_i), we obtain

$$1 = \sum_{i=1}^{3}\left[\frac{p_i x_i}{y}\right]\cdot\left[\frac{y}{x_i}\frac{\partial x_i(p,y)}{\partial y}\right].$$

Stating the expenditure share of good x_i:s_i=$p_i x_i/y$ and taking into account that the expression in parenthesis is just the income elasticity of good x_i, which we will show as ε_{iy}, we finally obtain the following restriction:

$$s_1\,\varepsilon_{1y} + s_2\,\varepsilon_{2y} + s_3\,\varepsilon_{3y} = 1;$$

$$\sum_{i=1}^{3} s_i\,\varepsilon_{iy} = 1.$$

1.8.2 Cournot Aggregation Condition

For the budget constraint to be held, it must be satisfied that when the price of a good changes, the quantities demanded are adjusted until expenditure remains the same. Differentiating (1.13) with respect to p_j:

$$y = p_1 x_1(p,y) + p_2 x_2(p,y) + p_3 x_3(p,y)$$

$$0 = p_1\frac{\partial x_1}{\partial p_j}dp_j + p_2\frac{\partial x_2}{\partial p_j}dp_j + p_3\frac{\partial x_3}{\partial p_j}dp_j + x_j dp_j = \sum_{i=1}^{3} p_i\frac{\partial x_i}{\partial p_j}dp_j + x_j dp_j$$

Multiplying and dividing in Σ by p_j and x_j respectively:

$$0 = \sum_{i=1}^{3}\frac{p_i x_i}{p_j}\left(\frac{p_j}{x_i}\frac{\partial x_i}{\partial p_j}\right)dp_j + x_j dp_j$$

and multiplying the whole expression by $(p_j/dp_j y)$ and rearranging the term, we obtain:

$$\sum_{i=1}^{3}\frac{p_i x_i}{y}\left(\frac{p_j}{x_i}\frac{\partial x_i}{\partial p_j}\right) + \frac{p_j x_j}{y} = 0.$$

If the share of income spent in goods i and j are s_i and s_j respectively, and the expression in parenthesis is represented by cross-price elasticity ε_{ij}, we have the following restriction:

$$s_1\varepsilon_{1j} + s_2\varepsilon_{2j} + s_3\varepsilon_{3j} + s_j = \sum_{i=1}^{3} s_i\varepsilon_{ij} + s_j = 0.$$

1.8.3 Homogeneity Condition

One of the equilibrium properties held by the primal problem of optimisation analysed in point 1.1, is the homogeneity of degree zero of the demand functions $x_i = x_i(\mathbf{p}, y)$ in prices and income. Applying Euler's Theorem this implies that

$$\frac{\partial x_j}{\partial p_1}p_1 + \frac{\partial x_j}{\partial p_2}p_2 + \frac{\partial x_j}{\partial p_3}p_3 + \frac{\partial x_j}{\partial y}y = \sum_{i=1}^{3}\frac{\partial x_j}{\partial p_i}p_i + \frac{\partial x_j}{\partial y}y = 0$$

and dividing the expression above by x_j:

$$\frac{\partial x_j}{dp_1}\frac{p_1}{x_j} + \frac{\partial x_j}{\partial p_2}\frac{p_2}{x_j} + \frac{\partial x_j}{\partial p_3}\frac{p_3}{x_j} + \frac{\partial x_j}{\partial y}\frac{y}{x_j} = \sum_{i=1}^{3}\frac{\partial x_j}{\partial p_i}\frac{p_i}{x_j} + \frac{\partial x_j}{\partial y}\frac{y}{x_j} = \sum_{i=1}^{3}\varepsilon_{ji} + \varepsilon_{iy} = 0$$

which in terms of elasticity yields

$$\varepsilon_{j1} + \varepsilon_{j2} + \varepsilon_{j3} + \varepsilon_{jy} = \sum_{i=1}^{3}\varepsilon_{ji} + \varepsilon_{jy} = 0.$$

1.8.4 Symmetry or Integrability Condition

Net cross-substitution effects must be equal since both Hotelling's and Young's Theorems on the expenditure function are satisfied

$$S_{ij} = \frac{\partial h_i}{\partial p_j} = \frac{\partial}{\partial pj}\left(\frac{\partial G}{\partial p_i}\right) = \frac{\partial^2 G}{\partial p_i \partial p_j} = \frac{\partial^2 G}{\partial p_j \partial p_i} = \frac{\partial}{\partial p_i}\left(\frac{\partial G}{\partial p_j}\right) = \frac{\partial h_j}{\partial p_i} = S_{ji}$$

which in terms of the Slustky equation can be expressed as:

$$\frac{\partial h_i}{\partial p_j} = \frac{\partial x_i}{\partial p_j} + x_j\frac{\partial x_i}{\partial y} = \frac{\partial x_j}{\partial p_i} + x_i\frac{\partial x_j}{\partial y} = \frac{\partial h_j}{\partial p_i}.$$

1.8.5 Negativity Condition

Since expenditure function is concave (see section 1.5) the matrix produced by cross substitution effects should be a semidefinite negative matrix. In this case we have:

$$[S]=\begin{bmatrix} S_{11} & S_{12} & S_{13} \\ S_{21} & S_{22} & S_{23} \\ S_{31} & S_{32} & S_{33} \end{bmatrix} = \begin{bmatrix} \frac{\partial^2 G}{\partial p_1^2} & \frac{\partial^2 G}{\partial p_1 \partial p_2} & \frac{\partial^2 G}{\partial p_1 \partial p_3} \\ \frac{\partial^2 G}{\partial p_2 \partial p_1} & \frac{\partial^2 G}{\partial p_2^2} & \frac{\partial^2 G}{\partial p_2 \partial p_3} \\ \frac{\partial^2 G}{\partial p_3 \partial p_1} & \frac{\partial^2 G}{\partial p_3 \partial p_2} & \frac{\partial^2 G}{\partial p_3^2} \end{bmatrix}$$

[S] must be a semidefinite negative matrix, that is to say, it must satisfy:

$$|S_{ii}| = \frac{\partial^2 G}{\partial p_i^2} \leq 0, \ i=1,2,3; \quad \begin{vmatrix} S_{11} & S_{12} \\ S_{21} & S_{22} \end{vmatrix} = \begin{vmatrix} \frac{\partial^2 G}{\partial p_1^2} & \frac{\partial^2 G}{\partial p_1 \partial p_2} \\ \frac{\partial^2 G}{\partial p_2 \partial p_1} & \frac{\partial^2 G}{\partial p_2^2} \end{vmatrix} \geq 0;$$

$$\begin{vmatrix} S_{11} & S_{12} & S_{13} \\ S_{21} & S_{22} & S_{23} \\ S_{31} & S_{32} & S_{33} \end{vmatrix} = \begin{vmatrix} \frac{\partial^2 G}{\partial p_1^2} & \frac{\partial^2 G}{\partial p_1 \partial p_2} & \frac{\partial^2 G}{\partial p_1 \partial p_3} \\ \frac{\partial^2 G}{\partial p_2 \partial p_1} & \frac{\partial^2 G}{\partial p_2^2} & \frac{\partial^2 G}{\partial p_2 \partial p_3} \\ \frac{\partial^2 G}{\partial p_3 \partial p_1} & \frac{\partial^2 G}{d p_3 \partial p_2} & \frac{\partial^2 G}{\partial p_3^2} \end{vmatrix} \leq 0.$$

1.9 Roy's Identity

The Ordinary or Marshallian Demands can be obtained as mentioned above or by applying Roy's Identity.

Roy's Identity defines the optimal demand for a good as the negative quotient of the partial derivatives of the indirect utility function with respect to the price of that particular good and with respect to income.

Given the indirect utility function V(**p**, y) and the budget constraint, the Marshallian Demand Functions can be obtained as follows:

$$x_i = x_i\,(\mathbf{p}, y) = -\left[\frac{\frac{\partial V(\mathbf{p}, y)}{\partial p_i}}{\frac{\partial V(\mathbf{p}, y)}{\partial y}}\right], \quad (i = 1,2,3).$$

Proof:

$$\frac{\partial V}{\partial p_i} = \frac{\partial U(x(\mathbf{p}, y))}{\partial p_i} = \sum_{j=1}^{3} U_j \frac{\partial x_j}{\partial p_i} = \mu \sum_{j=1}^{3} p_j \frac{\partial x_j}{\partial p_i}$$

$$\frac{\partial V}{\partial y} = \frac{\partial U(x(\mathbf{p}, y))}{\partial y} = \sum_{j=1}^{3} U_j \frac{\partial x_j}{\partial y} = \mu \sum_{j=1}^{3} p_j \frac{\partial x_j}{\partial y},$$

given that:

$$y = p_1 x_1(\mathbf{p},y) + p_2 x_2(\mathbf{p},y) + p_3 x_3(\mathbf{p},y),$$

differentiating the above equation with respect to p_i, we have:

$$\frac{dy}{dp_i} = 0 = \frac{\partial x_1(\mathbf{p}, y)}{\partial p_i} p_1 dp_1 + \frac{\partial x_2(\mathbf{p}, y)}{\partial p_i} p_2 dp_2 + \frac{\partial x_2(\mathbf{p}, y)}{\partial p_i} p_3 dp_3 + x_i(\mathbf{p}, y)dp_i$$

$$= \sum_{j=1}^{3} \frac{\partial x_j(\mathbf{p}, y)}{\partial p_i} p_j \, dp_i + x_i(\mathbf{p}, y)dp_i \Rightarrow \sum_{j=1}^{3} \frac{\partial x_j(\mathbf{p}, y)}{\partial p_i} p_j dp_i = -x(\mathbf{p}, y)dp_i$$

and dividing the expression above by dp_i we will obtain:

$$\sum_{j=1}^{3} \frac{\partial x_j(\mathbf{p}, y)}{\partial p_i} p_j = -x(\mathbf{p}, y).$$

Substituting:

$$\frac{\partial V}{\partial p_i} = \mu \sum_{j=1}^{3} \frac{\partial x_j(\mathbf{p}, y)}{\partial p_i} p_j = -\mu x_i(\mathbf{p}, y)$$

and besides, differentiating with respect to the income level y, we have:

$$\frac{dy}{dy} = p_1 \frac{\partial x_1(\mathbf{p}, y)}{\partial y} dy + p_2 \frac{\partial x_2(\mathbf{p}, y)}{\partial y} dy + p_3 \frac{\partial x_2(\mathbf{p}, y)}{\partial y} dy + 0$$

and substituting:

$$1 = \sum_{j=1}^{3} p_j \frac{\partial x_j(\mathbf{p}, y)}{\partial y} \frac{dy}{dy} \quad \Rightarrow \frac{\partial V}{\partial y} = \mu \left[\sum_{j=1}^{3} p_j \frac{\partial x_j(\mathbf{p}, y)}{\partial y} \right] = \mu \cdot 1$$

and hence we obtain:

$$-\left[\frac{\frac{\partial V}{\partial p_i}}{\frac{\partial V}{\partial y}} \right] = -\left[-\frac{\mu \, x_i(p, y)}{\mu} \right] = x_i(p, y).$$

□

1.10 Hotelling's Theorem (or Shephard's Lemma for Consumers)

Compensated or Hicksian Demand can be obtained as mentioned above or by applying Hotelling's Theorem.

Hotelling defines Hicksian Demand of a good as the ratio of the partial derivatives of expenditure function with respect to the price of that particular good.

Given expenditure function G(**p**, u) and a level of utility, Hicksian Demand Functions can be obtained as follows:

$$x_i = h_i(\mathbf{p}, u) = \frac{\partial G(\mathbf{p}, u)}{\partial p_i}, \text{ for every } i = 1,2,3.$$

Proof:

$$T(p,x^0) = G(\mathbf{p},u^0) - \mathbf{p}x^0$$

$$\frac{\partial T(\mathbf{p}, x^0)}{\partial p_i} = \frac{\partial G(\mathbf{p}, u^0)}{\partial p_i} - h_1^0(p^0, u^0) = 0, \ \forall_i = 1,2,3,$$

$$\frac{\partial G(p, x^0)}{\partial p_i} = h_i(p^0, u^0) = x_i^0 \ , \forall_i = 1,2,3. \qquad \square$$

1.11 Relationships between the UMP and the EMP

The following figure 1.2 outlines sections from 1.4 to 1.9 of this chapter.

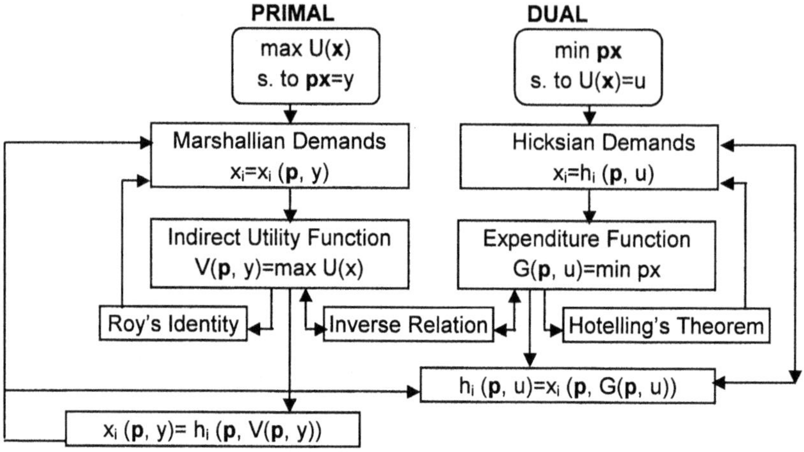

Fig. 1.2. Consumer behaviour

1.12 The Slutsky Equation

Although the compensated demand function is not directly observed, the Slutsky equation is a relationship which lets us easily obtain its derivative (with respect to a price) from the Marshallian demands. Since these demands, prices and the level of income are observed, the structure of Hicksian demand (unobserved) can be indirectly derived. The Slutsky equation is formally expressed as follows:

$$\frac{\partial x_i(\mathbf{p},y)}{\partial p_j} = \frac{\partial h_i(\mathbf{p},u)}{\partial p_j} - x_j(\mathbf{p},y)\frac{\partial x_i(\mathbf{p},y)}{\partial y} \tag{1.15}$$

Proof:
If the income effect has a negative variation rate, it can be written in discrete terms:

$$\Delta x_1 = \Delta x_1^s - \Delta x_1^r$$

dividing by Δp_2:

$$\frac{\Delta x_1}{\Delta p_2} = \frac{\Delta x_1^s}{\Delta p_2} - \frac{\Delta x_1^r}{\Delta p_2}; \text{since } \Delta y = x_2 \Delta p_2 \rightarrow \Delta p_2 = \frac{\Delta y}{x_2};$$

substituting:

$$\frac{\Delta x_1}{\Delta p_2} = \frac{\Delta x_1^s}{\Delta p_2} - \frac{\Delta x_1}{\Delta y} x_2$$

the last equation being known as the Slutsky Equation which, in continuous terms, can be written as:

$$\frac{\partial x_1}{\partial p_2} = \frac{\partial x_1^s}{\partial p_2} - \frac{\partial x_1}{\partial y} x_2$$

and in more general terms:

$$\frac{\partial x_i(\mathbf{p},y)}{\partial p_j} = \frac{\partial h_i(\mathbf{p},u)}{\partial p_j} - x_j(\mathbf{p},y)\frac{\partial x_i(\mathbf{p},y)}{\partial y};$$

the last expression can be given in elasticity terms following the steps below:

$$\frac{\partial x_i(\mathbf{p},y)}{\partial p_j}\frac{p_j}{x_i} = \frac{\partial h_i(\mathbf{p},u)}{\partial p_j}\frac{p_j}{x_i} - \frac{\partial x_i(\mathbf{p},y)}{\partial y} x_j(\mathbf{p},y)\frac{p_j}{x_i}$$

$$\varepsilon_{ij} = \varepsilon^S{}_{ij} - \frac{\partial x_i(p,y)}{\partial y} p_j \frac{x_j}{x_i}(p,y);\ \forall_i = 1,2,\ldots,n$$

where ε_{ij} and ε_{ij}^s represent the price elasticities of the Marshallian and Hicksian demand, respectively, of the good i before possible variations of p_j.

$$\frac{x_j(p,y)}{x_i}\frac{\partial x_i(p,y)}{\partial y} p_j = \frac{\partial x_i(p,y)}{\partial y}\frac{y}{x_i}\frac{x_j(p,y)}{y} p_j,$$

$$\frac{x_j(p,y)}{x_i}\frac{\partial x_i(p,y)}{\partial y} p_j = \varepsilon_{iy} S_j;\ \text{where}\ S_j = \frac{x_j(p,y)}{y} p_j,$$

which is the total expenditure rate of the good j, an ε_{iy} is the income elasticity of the good i; that is to say:

$$\varepsilon_{ij} = \varepsilon^S{}_{ij} - \varepsilon_{iy} S_j.$$ □

This expression is the same as (1.15). The left hand side term shows how the Marshallian demand of x_i changes as the price of good x_i changes (level of income remaining constant), which, due to (1.15), is the same as Hicksian demand variation of x_i when p_i changes (the level of utility being constant) plus the variation undergone by the Marshallian demand for x_i due to income changes multiplied by the demand for x_j.

1.13 Complementary and Substitutive Relationships

Two goods are complementary when they satisfy the same necessity, and the marginal utility of one of them will increase when the quantity available of the other increases. However, two goods are substitutive when the marginal utility of one of them decreases as the quantity available of the other, which satisfies the same necessity, increases.

The utility sign U_{ij} (**x**) shows the change direction of the marginal utility of x_i when the quantity consumed of x_j changes, that is to say:

$$U_{ij}(x)\begin{cases} = 0 \text{ independence} \\ > 0 \text{ complementary} \\ < 0 \text{ substitutive} \end{cases}$$

Another criterion for the characterisation of complementary or substitutive relationships is observing the cross elasticity sign of the demand for two goods. Since the cross elasticity has the same sign as $\partial x_i/\partial p_j$, the criterion will be as follows:

$$\frac{\partial x_i}{\partial p_j}\begin{cases} = 0\; x_i \text{ independant on } x_j \\ < 0\; x_i \text{ gross complementary of } x_j \\ > 0\; x_i \text{ gross substitute of } x_j \end{cases}$$

which are considered as gross relationships, since the sign of the previous derivative depends on the income and substitution effects in the Slutsky equation, that is to say:

$$\frac{\partial x_i(\mathbf{p}, y)}{\partial p_j} = \frac{\partial h_i(,\mathbf{p}, u)}{\partial p_j} - x(\mathbf{p}, y)\frac{\partial x_i(\mathbf{p}, y)}{\partial y}.$$

It is obvious that the sign of the income effect is not in any way related to the complementary or substitutive relationships of the goods.

To suppress the former criteria, Hicks proposed the concept of net relationships

which relies on the sign of the cross substitution effect $\frac{\partial h_i(\mathbf{p}, u)}{\partial p_j}$:

$$\frac{\partial h_i(p, u)}{\partial p_j}\begin{cases} = 0\; x_i \text{ and } x_j \text{ are independent} \\ < 0\; x_i \text{ and } x_j \text{ are net complementary} \\ > 0\; x_i \text{ and } x_j \text{ are net substitutes} \end{cases}$$

With the concepts of gross and net, the following relationships can be established:

1. if x_i and x_j are net substitutes and x_j is an inferior good, the later is gross substitute of x_i. That is to say,

   $$\text{if } \frac{\partial h_i(p,u)}{\partial p_j} > 0, \text{with} \frac{\partial x_j}{\partial y} < 0, \text{then} \frac{\partial x_j}{\partial p_i} > 0.$$

   However,

$$\text{if } \frac{\partial h_i(p,u)}{\partial p_j} > 0, \text{ with } \frac{\partial x_j}{\partial y} > 0, \text{ then } \frac{\partial x_j}{\partial p_i} \begin{cases} = 0 & x_i \text{ independent on } x_j \\ < 0 & x_i \text{ gross complementary of } x_j \\ > 0 & x_i \text{ gross substitute of } x_j. \end{cases}$$

2. if x_i and x_j are net complementary and x_j is normal good, the latter is gross complementary of x_i. That is to say,

$$\text{if } \frac{\partial h_i(p,u)}{\partial p_j} < 0, \text{ with } \frac{\partial x_j}{\partial y} > 0, \text{ then } \frac{\partial x_j}{\partial p_i} < 0.$$

However,

$$\text{if } \frac{\partial h_i(p,u)}{\partial p_j} < 0, \text{ with } \frac{\partial x_j}{\partial y} < 0, \text{ then } \frac{\partial x_j}{\partial p_i} \begin{cases} = 0 & x_i \text{ independent on } x_j \\ < 0 & x_i \text{ gross complementary of } x_j \\ > 0 & x_i \text{ gross substitute of } x_j. \end{cases}$$

Basic References

Gravelle, H., Rees, R.: Microeconomics, 3rd edn. Longman Group UK Limited 1994
Mas-Collel, A., Whinston, M. D., Green, J. R.: Microeconomic theory. New York: Oxford University Press 1995
Varian, H.: Microeconomic analysis, 3rd edn. W.W. Norton & Company1992

References and Further Reading

Arrow, K.: Rational choice functions and orderings. Econometrica 26, 121-127 (1959)
Debreu, G.: Theory of value. New York: Wiley 1959
Hicks, J.: Value and capital.Oxford: Clarendon Press 1939
Hicks, J.: A Revision of demand theory. Oxford: Oxford 1956
Hurwicz, L., Uzawa: On the integrability of demand functions. In: Chipman, J., Hunwier, L., Sonnenschein H.: Preferences, utility and demand. New York: Harcourt Brace, Jovanovich 1971
Marshall, A.: Principles of economics. London: MacMillan 1920
Shelling, T.: Micromotives and macrobehavior. New York: Norton 1979
Samuelson, P.: Foundations of economic analysis. Cambridge, Mass.: Harvard University Press 1947

2 Alternative Theories of Consumer Behaviour

2.1 Introduction

This chapter sets out alternative consumer behaviour models. First, we shall look at the discrete choice model and time allocation models. Next, we shall examine a model synthesising discrete choice and time allocation. Then we shall turn to the characteristics model. This model has been improved by including work and travel time in the utility function and finding a relationship between goods and leisure. Finally, we address a model under conditions of incomplete information and revealed preference theory.

2.2 Discrete Choice Models

Discrete choice models as applied to Biology and Medicine appeared in 1930, when probabilities were estimated for a patient to recover health once he had been subjected to a given treatment or surgery. Later, in 1950, discrete choice models began a long tradition in economic applications. These applications were associated with abstract models of rational consumer choice theory, for example, whether or not to demand (whether or not to consume) a given product subject to certain budget constraints.

In disaggregate and behavioural transport demand, the pioneering work is Stanley Warner's (1962), although the main advances in economic and statistical ideas on which recent studies are based are to be found in two papers by McFadden (1973, 1974) and a monograph by Domencich and McFadden (1975).

The discrete choice model can be set out as follows:

$$\left.\begin{array}{l} \text{Max } U(x) \\ \text{subject to: } \Sigma\, p_i\, x_i \leq I \end{array}\right\}$$

from which we get $x_i^*(\vec{p}\,; I)$, i.e., observable Marshallian demands. However, I am assuming here that goods are continuous, i.e., that $\vec{x}$ represents a vector of continuous goods. If we are faced with discrete goods – for instance, we must take a bus or not, or buy a car or not – then we must include the set of discrete alternatives of the non-continuous goods. Let M be that set of alternatives and let Q_i be the vector of characteristics that matter for each discrete alternative, such as comfort, time and safety. Finally, C_i will be the price of the alternative. The discrete choice model can now be expressed as:

$$\left.\begin{array}{l} \text{Max } U(x, Q_i) \\ \text{subject to: } \Sigma\, p_j\, x_j + c_i \leq I \\ \qquad\qquad i \in M \end{array}\right\}$$

We shall solve this problem in two steps. In the first step, we assume a chosen discrete alternative, which means we have a continuous problem. I.e., when i is known the problem is a classical problem of the type:

$$\left.\begin{array}{l} \text{Max } U(x, Q_i) \\ \text{subject to: } \Sigma\, p_j\, x_j \leq I - c_i \end{array}\right\}$$

From here we can obtain the Marshallian demands of the type:

$$x_j^* \,(p_j;\, I - c_i;\, Q_i)$$

And, substituting in the direct utility function, we get

$$U\,[x^*\,(I - c_{ij}\, p_j;\, Q_i),\, Q_i\,] \equiv V\,(p;\, I - c_i;\, Q_i)$$

The conditional indirect utility function.

In the second step we move on to

$$\begin{array}{l} \text{Max } V_i \\ i \in M \end{array}$$

Where the statistical modelling of V_i is:

$$V_i = \overline{V}_i + \varepsilon_i$$

$\overline{V}_i$ being the mean of V_i, a known component, and ε_i the random component.

Choosing alternative i implies:

$$V_i > V_j \quad \forall\, i \neq j$$

As the probability of choosing i is P_i:

$$P_i = \text{Prob}\,(\overline{U}_i + \varepsilon_i > \overline{U}_j + \varepsilon_j;\ \forall\, j \neq i) = \text{Prob}\,(\varepsilon_j - \varepsilon_i \leq \overline{U}_i - \overline{U}_j;\ \forall\, j \neq i)$$

If we assume that ε follows a given distribution (Gumbel, for example) w then we have the logit models and can use the demand model covering qualities and prices.

$$P_i = \frac{e^{U_i}}{\sum_j e^{\overline{U}_j}}\,.$$

2.3 Time Allocation Models

2.3.1 Hicks Model

Let us assume that the consumer utility function depends on the set of consumed goods $\vec{x}$ and the leisure time quantity L, taking the latter to be the time not devoted to work (W).

$$U = U(\vec{x}, L)$$

If we assume that more leisure is preferred to less, then $\frac{\partial U}{\partial L} > 0$, i.e., the marginal utility of leisure is always positive.

Moreover, the consumer is under two constraints. First, we have a budget constraint:

$$\sum_{i}^{n} p_i x_i = Y$$

where Y represents the budgetary yield, or constraint, which can be expressed as

$$Y = w W + \overline{Y}$$

where w is wages per work unit, W is the quantity of work and the variable $\overline{Y}$ represents non-wages yield, generated by company profits, interest, etc.

Second, the consumer faces a time constraint:

$$T = W + L$$

That is to say, time is divided into work and leisure. The consumer's problem, therefore, is:

$$\left.\begin{aligned} &\text{Max } U(x_i, L) = U \\ &\text{subject to } \Sigma p_i x_i = w W + \overline{Y} \\ &\qquad T = W + L \end{aligned}\right\}$$

$$\mathrm{L}(x_i, L, \lambda, \mu) = U(x, L) + \lambda (p_1 x_1 + ... + p_n x_n - w W - \overline{Y}) + \mu (T - W - L)$$

$$\partial \mathrm{L} / \partial x_1 = U_1 - \lambda p_1 = 0$$

$$\partial \mathrm{L} / \partial x_n = U_n - \lambda p_n = 0$$

$$\partial \mathrm{L} / \partial L = U_L - \mu = 0$$

$$\partial \mathrm{L} / \partial \lambda = p_1 x_1 + ... + p_n x_n - w W - \overline{Y} = 0$$

$$\partial \mathrm{L} / \partial \mu = T - W - L = 0$$

The first-order conditions give us the Marshallian demands of $\vec{x}$ y and L:

$$x^* = x^*(p_1, p_2, \ldots, p_n, w, W, \overline{Y})$$

$$L^* = L^*(p_1, p_2, \ldots, p_n, w, W, \overline{Y})$$

Furthermore, on the basis of this goods-leisure model we can construct the yield-leisure model, enabling us to get the following result: 'the relationship of substitution of yield by leisure is equal to salary'.

2.3.2 Yield-Leisure Model

The first transformation we must perform is to assume that goods prices remain constant. In this case,

$$x^* = x^*(W, \overline{Y}, w)$$

and given that $Y = \overline{Y} + w\,W$, substituting:

$$x^* = x^*(W, Y)$$

as $T = L + W$ and $T = \overline{T}$; $x^* = x^*(L, Y)$.

Where, let us recall, L represents leisure and the variable Y represents yield. Both leisure and yield are desirable goods. The substitution relationship between yield and leisure is

$$\frac{dY}{dL} = \frac{U_L}{U_Y}.$$

where $U = U(L, Y)$ and the budget restriction $Y = \overline{Y} + w\,W$. The first-order conditions for the Lagrangian:

$$\mathrm{L}(L, Y) = U(L, Y) + \lambda\,(Y - \overline{Y} - w\,W)$$

are:

$$\partial \mathrm{L} / \partial L = U_L - \lambda\, w = 0;\; W + L = T$$

$$\partial \mathrm{L} / \partial Y = U_Y - \lambda = 0$$

$$\partial \mathrm{L} / \partial \lambda = Y - \overline{Y} - w\,W = 0$$

hence

$$\frac{U_Y}{U_L} = \frac{\lambda}{\lambda w};\; \frac{U_L}{U_Y} = w$$

From this, we can obtain the consumer's yield demand:

$$Y^* = Y^*(\overline{Y}, w, W)$$

and the optimum leisure demand:

$$L^* = L^*(\overline{Y}, w, W)$$

but we can also define indirect utility

$$U = V[Y^*(\overline{Y}, w, W); L^*(\overline{Y}, w, W)]$$

hence

$$\frac{\partial U}{\partial W} = -V_L + V_Y w = 0$$

$$V_L = V_Y w$$

$$\frac{V_L}{V_Y} = w$$

and

$$\frac{U_L}{U_Y} = \frac{V_L}{V_Y} = w$$

That is to say, the quotient of marginal work and yield utilities is equal to salary.
Graphically:

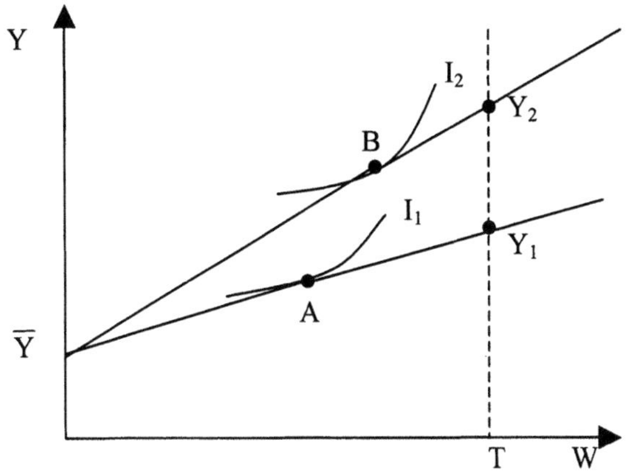

Figure 2.1

The yield constraint with salary w is the straight line $\overline{Y}\,Y_1$, given by $Y = \overline{Y} + w\,W$. On the other hand, we must impose the condition that a negative quantity of work cannot be offered, i.e., $W \geq 0$, and that more work cannot be offered than the total time period, i.e., $W \leq T$. The gradient of the salary straight line will be:

$$\frac{dY}{dW} = w$$

As salary increases, the gradient of the salary straight line increases. The indifference curves I_1, I_2 show the combinations of Y and L that provide the same utility level. Given that L = T – W, with a set T, for each value of L there exists a corresponding value of W.

The gradient of the indifference curve M, L is

$$\frac{dY}{dL} = -\frac{U_L^*}{U_Y^*};\ \frac{dY}{dW} = -\frac{U_W}{U_Y}$$

Consumer equilibrium will be attained on reaching the highest indifference curve given the constraint of the salary straight line, which establishes yield as a function of the consumer's offer of work. I.e., when the indifference curve touches the salary straight line:

$$-\frac{U_W}{U_Y} = w = -\frac{U_L^*}{U_Y^*}$$

The consumer is ready to accept, for the loss of one unit of leisure (the marginal relationship between yield and leisure) w, the amount of money that she receives for reduction of leisure by one unit (increase in time devoted to work). On that basis, we can obtain the work offer curve

$$W = W(w);\ \text{with}\ \frac{dW}{dw} > 0$$

If preferences were different, then $\frac{dW}{dw} < 0$, since the work offer curve doubles back.

2.3.3 Extended Yield-Leisure Model

The yield-leisure model we have set out can be extended by introducing the quality or characteristic β, which reflects the degree of comfort in work employment. The utility function is now

$$U = U(Y, L, \beta)$$

where it is assumed that

$$\frac{\partial U}{\partial Y} > 0;\ \frac{\partial U}{\partial L} > 0;\ \frac{\partial U}{\partial \beta} > 0$$

The consumer's constraints are now:

$$Y = \overline{Y} + W\,w$$

$$L = T - W$$

$$\beta = W\,w_\beta$$

where w_β is salary per unit of comfort.

From this, we can obtain demand functions for yield, Y, leisure, L, and work comfort, β:

$\beta = \beta(Y, \overline{Y}, W, w_\beta)$

The basic point is that one must choose between yield, Y, and comfort, β. Graphically:

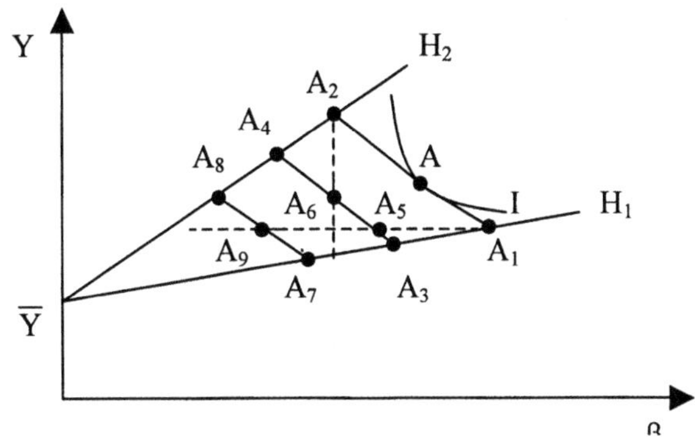

Figure 2.2

The individual will choose either job H_1, combination A_1, or job H_2, combination A_2, or alternatively a combination of both jobs, such as combination A^*. Let us assume that the individual must travel to each job. This makes yield-comfort combinations move toward origin.

For example, the displacement of the possibilities boundary will move to A_4A_3, thus the individual will choose any of the points lying between A_5A_6. If the time required to travel to work is greater, the boundary moves to A_7A_8; then the individual ends up specialising in job H_1 in combination A_9, as no possible combination exists for job H_2.

Therefore, we have added another variable, travel time to the workplace, t_v. On choosing to offer work, the determining variables will be the amount of leisure, L, comfort at work, β, non-salary yield, $\overline{Y}$, salary yield, Ww, and travel time to the workplace, t_v. If we consider the fixed leisure quantity $\overline{L}$ and the fixed non-monetary yield $\overline{Y}$, then the work offer:

$$W = W(w, \beta, t_v)$$

where $\dfrac{\partial W}{\partial w} > 0$; $\dfrac{\partial W}{\partial \beta} > 0$; $\dfrac{\partial W}{\partial t_v} < 0$.

However, the travel-time variable t_v cannot be deduced from the above optimisation program. Therefore, we shall posit a new, extended program.

2.3.4 Goods-Leisure Model with Time Allocation to Goods Consumption

2.3.4.1 Becker's Model

Becker's model (1965) introduces the idea that the consumer requires time to consume goods. In addition, time is scarce. Therefore, the consumer is under a budget constraint and a consumption-time constraint.

The model is now:

$$\left.\begin{array}{l} \text{Max } U = U(x_i) \\ \text{subject to } \overline{Y} + w\,W = \Sigma\, p_i\, x_i \\ \qquad\qquad T = \Sigma\, T_i + W \end{array}\right\}$$

To simplify, we shall assume that there is a proportional relationship between the quantity of the i-th good consumed and the time used for that consumption, i.e.:

$$T_i = t_i\, x_i$$

Where t_i is the price of good x_i in terms of time, i.e., the number of time units required to consume one unit of good x_i.

On substituting, the model can be set out as:

$$\left.\begin{array}{l} \text{Max } U(x_i) = U \\ \text{subject to (i) } \Sigma\, p_i\, x_i = \overline{Y} + w\,W \\ \qquad\qquad \text{(ii) } \Sigma\, T_i + W = T \end{array}\right\}$$

Under this model, $T_i = \Sigma\, t_i\, x_i$ and W are not choice variables, as a consequence of the proportionality assumption, which assumes that the choice of a set of goods determines the time of consumption for each good, and thus determines work time, since $W = T - \Sigma\, t_i\, x_i$.

If in the first constraint we substitute

$$\Sigma\, p_i\, x_i = \overline{Y} + w\,(T - \Sigma\, t_i\, x_i)$$

or

$$\Sigma\, p_i\, x_i + w\, \Sigma\, t_i\, x_i = \overline{Y} + w\,T$$

hence

$$\Sigma\, x_i\,(p_i + w\, t_i) = \overline{Y} + w\,T$$

Here $w_i\, t_i$ is the opportunity cost of the time devoted to consumption of one unit of good x_i.

As p_i is the monetary price of good x_i, if we add to it the opportunity cost $w_i\, t_i$, we shall have the 'real' price of good x_i. I.e., the sum of the explicit price of good x_i and the implicit price in terms of time of a unit of good i.

If the entirety of yield were dedicated to goods consumption, and assuming for the sake of simplicity that only two goods exist, then we can set out:

$$(p_1 + wt_1)\, x_1 + (p_2 + wt_2)\, x_2 = \overline{Y} + w\, W$$

Solving for x_2,

$$x_2 = [\, \overline{Y} + w\, T - (p_1 + wt_1)\, x_1] \,/\, (p_2 + wt_2)$$

deriving with respect to x_1

$$dx_2 \,/\, dx_1 = -(\, p_1 + wt_1) \,/\, (p_2 + wt_2)$$

Consumer equilibrium is given by:

$$U_1 \,/\, U_2 = (p_1 + wt_1) \,/\, (p_2 + wt_2)$$

That is to say, the consumer's marginal substitution relationship is equal to the reason of 'real prices'. Hence, the optimum combination of goods chosen will depend, given consumer preferences, on 'real prices', i.e., monetary prices and consumption time, salary and non-salary yield:

$$x_i = x_i\, (p_1, p_2, t_1, t_2, w, \overline{Y}\,)$$

or, in terms of 'real prices'

$$x_i = D_i\, (p_1 + wt_1;\, p_2 + wt_2;\, \overline{Y} + w\, T)$$

where $Y = \overline{Y} + wT$ is the full or maximum yield that an individual would get if he worked all the available time.

2.4 Train-McFadden Synthesis Model

An attempt to synthesise the discrete-choice and time-allocation models is found in the paper by Train and McFadden (1978). These authors work with aggregate variables. Hence G represents goods consumed by their respective prices, i.e., it is a scalar variable that synthesises all goods into monetary units. Variable L represents leisure, i.e., time not devoted to work or travel to work, c_i represents the price of transport option i, t_i is the travel time for option i, W is work time in hours, w, is the wage rate, T is total time available, M is the set of discrete alternatives of a good not contained in G and, finally, E is non-salary income.

The model now takes the form:

$$\left.\begin{array}{l} \text{Max } U\,(G, L) \\ \text{subject to } \;(i)\; G + c_i = w\, W + E \\ \qquad\qquad\quad (ii)\; L + W + t_i = T \end{array}\right\}$$

$$i \in M$$

Solving for the constraints we get:

$$G = w\, W + E - c_i$$

$$L = T - W - t_i$$

Substituting these values in the target function we get:

$$U\,[(w\,W + E - c_i); (T - W - t_i)]$$

Therefore, the problem can now be viewed as:

$$\text{Max } U\,[(w\,W + E - c_i); (T - W - t_i)]$$

We shall solve this problem in two steps.

In the first phase, we optimise the continuous variable W for a given transport option i, i.e.,

$$\frac{dU}{dW} = \frac{\partial U}{\partial G} w - \frac{\partial U}{\partial L} = 0 \Rightarrow \frac{\partial U / \partial L}{\partial U / \partial G} = w$$

from which we obtain the optimum quantity of work:

$$W^* = W^*[(E - c_i); (w); (T - t_i)]$$

This result shows that an individual will choose the quantity of the work good such that the marginal utility of leisure is equal to the marginal utility of work.

In the second phase we take the continuous variable 'optimum work quantity', W^*, and substitute in the direct utility function, thus obtaining the conditional indirect utility function, i.e.:

$$U\,[(w\,W^* + E - c_i); (T - W^* - t_i)] \equiv V(E - c_i; w; T - t_i) \equiv V_i^*$$

From which we obtain the subjective time value VS_t,

$$VS_t = \frac{\dfrac{\partial U}{\partial G} w \dfrac{\partial W^*}{\partial t_i} - \dfrac{\partial U}{\partial L}\left(\dfrac{\partial W^*}{\partial t_i} + 1\right)}{\dfrac{\partial U}{\partial G}\left(w \dfrac{\partial W^*}{\partial t_i} - 1\right) - \dfrac{\partial U}{\partial L}\dfrac{\partial W^*}{\partial t_i}}$$

$$\left(\frac{\partial U}{\partial G} w - \frac{\partial U}{\partial L}\right)\frac{\partial W^*}{\partial t_i} - \frac{\partial U}{\partial L} = \frac{\partial V}{\partial t_i}$$

$$\left(\frac{\partial U}{\partial G} w - \frac{\partial U}{\partial L}\right)\frac{\partial W^*}{\partial c_i} - \frac{\partial U}{\partial G} = \frac{\partial V}{\partial c_i}$$

hence,

$$VS_t = \frac{\partial U / \partial L}{\partial U / \partial G}$$

furthermore, we have seen that this quotient is equal to the wage rate, therefore:

$$VS_t = \frac{\partial U / \partial L}{\partial U / \partial G} = w$$

That is to say, on the Train and McFadden model with endogenous income, the subjective time value is equal to the wage rate. To simplify, Train and McFadden assumed a Cobb-Douglas function. The model is thus:

$$\left.\begin{array}{l} \max\limits_{G,L}\ U = A\, G^{1-\beta} L^{\beta} \\ \qquad G + B\, c_i = w\, W \\ \qquad L + W + B\, t_i = T \\ \qquad i \in M \end{array}\right\}$$

substituting,

$$U = A(E + w\,W - B\,c_i)^{1-\beta}\,(T - W - Bt_i)^{\beta}$$

$$V = V[(E - Bc_i);\ w;\ (T - Bt_i)]$$

where the subjective time value,

$$\frac{\partial V / \partial t_i}{\partial V / \partial c_i} = w$$

Note that the choice of mode depends only on the variables (t_i, c_i, w), i.e., time, time cost and salary.

To estimate a cardinal utility we can use the following model:

$$\overline{U}_i = \alpha_i + \gamma \frac{c_i}{w} + \theta t_i + \ldots$$

Thus Train and McFadden have been able to incorporate the time variable as a variable explaining utility, while transport cost or travel alternative, c_i, and the salary rate also appear as explanatory variables.

However, the Train-McFadden model has the following limitations:

- It assumes that work hours, W, do not affect utility.
- It assumes that employees can choose work hours, W, whereas most people work an eight-hour day.

2.5 Lancaster's Consumption Technology Model

On the conventional theory of consumer behaviour, for a given set of preferences one chooses a combination of goods to maximise utility subject to budget constraints. Lancaster posits that individuals choose a combination of qualities or characteristics of goods to maximise utility subject to budget constraints and to the acquisition of goods as factors within a consumption process that transforms acquired goods into a set of qualities or characteristics.

Formally, the individual maximises:

$$\left.\begin{array}{l} \underset{x_1, x_2, \ldots, x_n}{\text{Max}}\ U = U(\alpha_1, \alpha_2, \ldots, \alpha_k) \\ \text{subject to (i) } \Sigma\, p_j\, x_j = Y;\ x_j \geq 0\ (\forall\ j = 1, \ldots, n) \\ \qquad\qquad\quad \text{(ii) } \alpha_i = \alpha_i\ (x_1, x_2, \ldots, x_n);\ (\forall\ i = 1, \ldots, k) \end{array}\right\} \tag{2.3}$$

the individual's preferences are represented by a utility function such as:

$$U = U(\alpha_1, \alpha_2, \ldots, \alpha_k)$$

This utility function has the same properties with respect to vector α_i as the utility function $U = U(x_1, x_2, \ldots, x_n)$. However, the quantity of each characteristic will depend on the set of goods chosen, which is represented as:

$$\alpha_i = \alpha_i\ (x_1, x_2, \ldots, x_n);\ (\forall\ i = 1, \ldots, k)$$

In general, it is to be expected that there will exist more goods than characteristics, i.e., $n > R$. Nevertheless, each good can have more than one characteristic. Meat or fish have characteristics such as calories, vitamins, protein, taste, etc.

The utility maximisation program (2.3) can be solved for an optimum set of goods $\vec{x}^*$, which responds to changes in prices, income and consumption technology. To simplify analysis, we assume that consumption technology is linear. In other words, a unit of good j produces γ_{ij} units of characteristic i, γ_{ij} being constant, irrespective of the quantity of good j or any other good.

The quantity of characteristic i, obtained from a set of goods, is the sum of the quantities of i produced by each good:

$$\alpha_i = \gamma_{i1}\, x_1, + \gamma_{i2}\, x_2 + \ldots + \gamma_{in}\, x_n = \sum_j \gamma_{ij} x_j$$

$$(\forall\ i = 1, \ldots, k) \tag{2.4}$$

Now we substitute (2.4) in (2.3)

$$\left.\begin{array}{l} \underset{x_1, x_2, \ldots, x_n}{\text{Max}}\ U = U(\alpha_1, \alpha_2, \ldots, \alpha_k) \\ \text{subject to (i) } \Sigma\, p_j\, x_j = Y;\ x_j \geq 0\ (\forall\ j = 1, \ldots, n) \\ \qquad\qquad\quad \text{(ii) } \alpha_i = \gamma_{i1}\, x_1, + \gamma_{i2}\, x_2 + \ldots + \gamma_{in}\, x_n;\ (\forall\ i = 1, \ldots, k) \end{array}\right\}$$

The result of this optimisation program, as in its equivalent in the conventional theory, will depend on preferences, goods prices and monetary yield. However, unlike the conventional model, consumer choice is affected by the consumption technology that determines the combination of characteristics obtained from a given set of goods. From first-order conditions, we obtain the optimum consumer demand functions in the form:

$$x_i^* = x_i^*\ (p_1, p_2, \ldots, p_n, Y, \alpha_{11}, \ldots, \alpha_{kn})$$

$$(\forall\ i = 1, \ldots, k)$$

That is, the demand for the good is explained by variations in price, yield and technology with regard to the demand for characteristics.

Furthermore, Lancaster's approach (1966) enables us to calculate the subjective value of characteristic i. Thus,

$$VS_i = \frac{\partial V / \partial q_i}{\partial V / \partial c_i}$$

Where VS_i is the subjective value of characteristic i, V is the indirect utility function, q_i is the quantity of characteristic i, and c_i is the cost of characteristic i. In the same way we can define the subjective value of the set of characteristics α_i:

$$VS_{\alpha_i} = \frac{\partial V / \partial q_{\alpha_i}}{\partial V / \partial c_i}$$

Where the variables are defined as before, but now with reference to α_i.

For example, the consumer buys different types of food and combines them to obtain a range of characteristics: tastes, calories, vitamins, carbohydrates, etc. Let us say that rational consumers look for an optimum combination of characteristics which they believe are appropriate for their diet. The same is true when a consumer buys different kinds of clothes and combines them to obtain a set of characteristics: comfort, elegance, warmth, etc. Or when one chooses a mode of transport or several consecutive modes or an intermodal option, in order to obtain a set of characteristics: comfort, speed, safety, etc. Even when an individual offers her productive capacity, i.e., when she constructs her offer of work, she is interested in a salary and a certain work time but also a range of characteristics such as comfort, promotion opportunities, integration, etc. We see, therefore, the wealth of the characteristics approach is reflected not only in demand but also in supply in some cases.

2.6 Jara-Díaz Model

2.6.1 Jara-Díaz and Farah Model (1987)

Jara-Díaz and Farah (1987) modified the Train-McFadden model (1978) with an alternative approach, considering individuals' fixed income, on taking into account fixed working hours at a given wage rate. The model posited by Jara-Díaz and Farah (1987) is as follows:

$$\left.\begin{aligned} &\max_{G,L}\ U = A\,G^{1-\beta} L^{\beta} \\ &\text{subject to}\ \ G + B\,c_i = I \\ &\qquad L + W + B\,t_i = T \\ &\qquad i \in M \end{aligned}\right\}$$

That is to say,

$$\underset{G,L}{\text{Max}}\; A(I - Bc_i)^{1-\beta}\,(T - W - B_i)^{\beta}$$

If everything is fixed, where is the compromise between goods and leisure? The answer is that the compromise is in the transport mode chosen by the individual: the discrete choice between different travel modes – fast and expensive or cheap and slow, for instance.

Graphically, the choice between taking a taxi or a bus can be represented as follows:

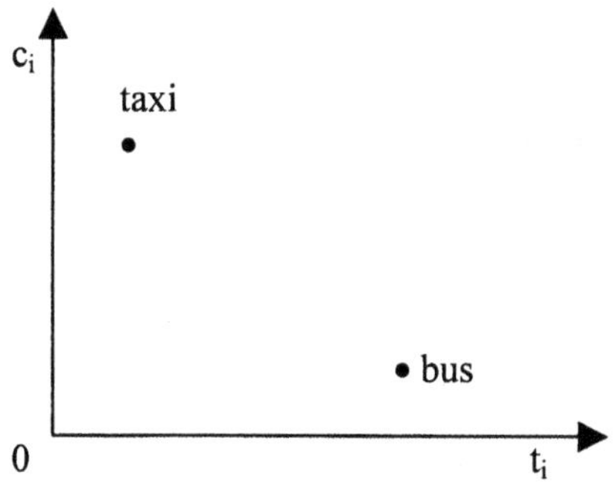

Fig. 2.3

On adding G and L to the above graph, the representation looks like:

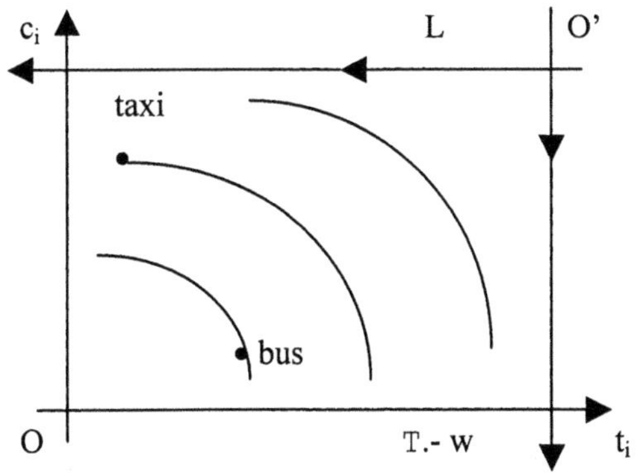

Fig. 2.4

Performing a Taylor expansion, the expense rate depends on income I, divided by total time minus work time, i.e.:

$$I / (T - W) = q$$

Dependent only on

$$-(1 - \beta)\frac{c_i}{w} - Bt_i$$

This expression shows that the relationship between travel cost and salary rate explains the choice of travel mode. This model supersedes the Train-McFadden model (1978) in that it overcomes its second limitation; however, it still assumes that working hours W do not influence utility.

2.6.2 Jara-Díaz Model (1998)

To overcome the limitation in the previous model, we have the 1998 Jara-Díaz model:

$$\left.\begin{aligned} &\text{Max } U = U(G, L, W, t_i) \\ &\text{subject to } \; G + c_i = w\,W \\ &\qquad\qquad L + W + t_i = T \\ &\qquad\qquad i \in M \end{aligned}\right\}$$

This model, the explanatory variables of which have already been used in prior models, is reminiscent of Becker's model (1965) and De Serpa's model (1971).

We shall solve the problem in two phases.

In the first phase we solve the continuous problem conditional on W, assuming a given travel mode i and substituting G and L in U from the constraints. This leads to:

$$\underset{W}{\text{Max}}\ U\,[(w\,W - c_i);\ (T - W - t_i);\ W;\ t_i]$$

The first-order condition is

$$\frac{dU}{dW} = 0 = \frac{\partial U}{\partial G} w - \frac{\partial U}{\partial L} + \frac{\partial U}{\partial W}$$

From where we get the optimum work quantities.

$$W^* = W^*\,(-c_i\,;\ w;\ T - t_i\,;\ t_i)$$

Substituting W^* in the direct utility function or target function of the optimisation programme, we obtain the conditional indirect utility function:

$$V_t = V_t\,[(w\,W^* - c_i);\ (T - W^* - t_i);\ W^*;\ t_i] = V\,(c_i,\ t_i)$$

Here the subjective time value VS_t can be obtained in the usual way:

$$\frac{\partial V_i \,/\, \partial t_i}{\partial V_i \,/\, \partial c_i} = VS_t$$

$$\frac{\partial V_i}{\partial t_i} = \frac{\partial U}{\partial G} w \frac{\partial W^*}{\partial t_i} - \frac{\partial U}{\partial L}\left(\frac{\partial W^*}{\partial t_i} + 1\right) + \frac{\partial U}{\partial W^*}\frac{\partial W^*}{\partial t_i} + \frac{\partial U}{\partial t_i}$$

$$\frac{\partial V_i}{\partial t_i} = -\frac{\partial U}{\partial G} w - \frac{\partial U}{\partial W} + \frac{\partial U}{\partial t_i}$$

$$\frac{\partial V_i}{\partial c_i} = \frac{\partial U}{\partial G}\left(w \frac{\partial W^*}{\partial c_i} - 1\right) - \frac{\partial U}{\partial L}\frac{\partial W^*}{\partial c_i} + \frac{\partial U}{\partial W}\frac{\partial W^*}{\partial c_i} = -\frac{\partial U}{\partial G}$$

Substituting, we get:

$$VS_t = \frac{\partial V_i \,/\, \partial t_i}{\partial V_i \,/\, \partial c_i} = w + \frac{\partial U \,/\, \partial W}{\partial U \,/\, \partial G} - \frac{\partial U \,/\, \partial t_i}{\partial U \,/\, \partial G}$$

That is, the subjective time value turns out to be equal to the sum of the salary rate and the subjective value of work, minus the subjective travel-time value.

The case of exogenous income means that the individual cannot decrease working hours any further than what the contract stipulates, but nobody is stopping him from working more if he likes, despite not receiving any monetary reward for it. The general formulation is now:

$$\left.\begin{array}{l} \text{Max } U\,(G,\ L,\ W,\ t_i) \\ \text{subject to } \ G + c_i = w\,W = I \\ \qquad\qquad L + W + t_i = T \\ \qquad\qquad i \in M \\ \qquad\qquad W \geq W_F \end{array}\right\}$$

That is to say, $wW = I$ and W must be at least equal to a fixed quantity of work hours W_F.

Substituting G and L in the equality constraints we obtain:

$$\max_{W;i\in M} U[(I - c_i); (T - W - t_i); W; t_i] \, / \, W - W_F \geq 0$$

Solving in W conditional on i, only leisure and work contribute to the variation of U due to a change in W. The first-order conditions are:

$$-\frac{\partial U}{\partial L} + \frac{\partial U}{\partial W} + \mu = 0$$

$$\mu (W - W_F) = 0$$

$$\mu \geq 0$$

If in the optimum conditional the individual chooses to work more than required ($W^* > W_F$), then the multiplier μ is zero and the marginal utility of leisure is equal to the marginal utility of work, which must be positive. Hence $\frac{\partial U}{\partial W} > 0$. Further, we determine the optimum work quantity:

$$W^* = W^* [(I - c_i); (T - t_i); t_i]$$

Substituting in the direct utility function we obtain the conditional indirect utility function conditioned for $W > W_F$, which is:

$$Vi = U [(I - c_i); (T - W^* - t_i); W^*; t_i]$$

Now we wish to obtain VS_t, which is calculated assuming that $\mu = 0$ on the basis of:

$$VS_t = \frac{\partial V_i / \partial t_i}{\partial V_i / \partial c_i} = \frac{-\partial U / \partial W + \partial U / \partial t_i}{-\partial U / \partial G}$$

$$VS_t = \frac{\partial U / \partial W}{\partial U / \partial G} - \frac{\partial U / \partial t_i}{\partial U / \partial G}$$

If $\mu > 0$, then $W^* = W_F$, hence $\frac{\partial W^*}{\partial t_i} = 0$, implying that:

$$VS_t = \frac{\partial V_i / \partial t_i}{\partial V_i / \partial c_i} = \frac{\partial U / \partial L}{\partial U / \partial G} - \frac{\partial U / \partial t_i}{\partial U / \partial G}$$

The subjective travel-time value is always equal to the money value of leisure minus the monetary value of travel-time in the direct utility function. A general result for the fixed or exogenous income model is:

$$VS_t = \frac{\partial U / \partial W}{\partial U / \partial G} + \frac{\mu}{\partial U / \partial G} - \frac{\partial U / \partial t_i}{\partial U / \partial G}$$

2.7 Models of Consumer Behaviour with Incomplete Information

The models we have looked at up to now assume that the consumer has full information on the prices and qualities of the goods he buys. But most of the time consumers act under conditions of uncertainty or incomplete information. Uncertainty can be technological – relating to the quality, safety, operation and durability of goods – or market uncertainty, relating to the various terms of sale, basically the different prices at which the product is sold.

Uncertainty can have a range of effects. In particular, it can affect the consumer's present and future decision. This sort of uncertainty is suitably treated in the context of expected-utility theory, so we shall not be concerned with it here. Another approach to uncertainty is to say that the information improvements that the consumer gets on making his decision reduce uncertainty and thus enable him to make a better choice. If this is the case, the consumer will be prepared to pay for information. Information can be acquired ready-made from others, such as from the media or specialised information, or the consumer can acquire it on his own.

Below I shall set out a model based on De Serpa (1971), Train and McFadden (1978), Jara-Díaz and Farah (1987) and Jara-Díaz and Tudela (2000):

$$\mathrm{Max} U = U(G, L)$$

subject to

$$G + B \cdot \theta_i \cdot c_i = I = wW$$

$$L + W + B \cdot t_i = \tau$$

$$i \in M$$

where:

U represents the utility level
G is the product of the prices by the quantities of the continuous goods
L is the time available (leisure) for spending
I is income in the time period τ
W is the number of hours worked in that period τ
C_i is the cost of travel in the alternative transport mode i
T_i is travel time in the i-th mode on each journey
B is the number of journeys in the time period in question τ
θ_i is a parameter that penalises the cost of the i-th mode, such that if $\theta_i = 1$, then the actual cost or fare paid by the individual coincides with the real cost of the i-th alternative. On the other hand, if $\theta_i < 1$, then the actual cost paid by the consumer is less than the real cost; finally, if $\theta_i > 1$, the actual cost or fare paid by the consumer is greater than the real cost.

Solving for the constraints we have:

$$G = I - B \cdot \theta_i \cdot c_i = wW - B \cdot \theta_i \cdot c_i$$

$$L = \tau - W - B \cdot t_i$$

Substituting these values in the target function we get:

$$U[(wW - B \cdot \theta_i \cdot c_i);(\tau - W - B \cdot t_i)]$$

Therefore, the problem can now be viewed as:

$$\underset{i \in M}{\text{Max}} U[(wW - B \cdot \theta_i \cdot c_i);(\tau - W - B \cdot t_i)]$$

This problem is solved in two phases:

In the first phase we optimise the continuous variable W with respect to an alternative i,

$$\frac{dU}{dW} = 0 = \frac{\partial U}{\partial G} w - \frac{\partial U}{\partial L} \Rightarrow \frac{\partial U / \partial L}{\partial U / \partial G} = w$$

In the second phase, we take the optimum continuous variable, W^*, and we replace it in the direct utility function, thus obtaining the indirect utility function:

$$V = V[(wW^* - B \cdot \theta_i \cdot c_i);(\tau - W^* - B \cdot t_i)]$$

From here we obtain the subjective time value:

$$VS_{t_i} = \frac{\partial V / \partial t_i}{\partial V / \partial c_i} = \frac{\partial U / \partial L}{\partial U / \partial G} = w$$

If we use a Cobb-Douglas function, the model would be:

$$\underset{G,L}{\text{Max}}\ U = A \cdot (Ww - B \cdot c_i \cdot \theta_i)^{\alpha} \cdot (\tau - W - B \cdot t_i)^{\beta}$$

were the coefficients α, β are positive and less than 1.

The indirect utility function would be:

$$V_i = V_i[(Ww - B \cdot c_i \cdot \theta_i);(\tau - W - B \cdot t_i)]$$

particularly for the Cobb-Douglas functional phase:

$$V_i = A \cdot (wW - B \cdot c_i \cdot \theta_i)^{\alpha} \cdot (\tau - W - B \cdot t_i)^{\beta}$$

So that this indirect utility function satisfies the second-order optimality conditions, it must allow second-order continuous partial derivatives, or be expressible as a Taylor series around the point (wW; τ-W). That is to say:

$$V_i = A \cdot (wW)^{\alpha} \cdot (\tau - W)^{\beta - 1} \cdot \left[(\tau - W) - \alpha \frac{B \cdot \theta_i \cdot c_i}{g} - \beta \cdot B \cdot t_i \right]$$

where $g = \frac{wW}{\tau - W}$ is the spend rate.

Note that the choice of mode only depends on the variables (g; c_i; θ_i; t_i), i.e., the travel time t_i, the travel cost c_i, the uncertainty factor θ_i and the spend rate.

An approximation of V_i could be as follows:

$$\hat{V}_i = -\alpha \frac{\theta_i c_i}{g} - \beta \cdot t_i$$

An immediate conclusion is that the choice of mode depends on the value θ_i; if $\theta_i = 1$, then the result is the same as with perfect information. But if $\theta_i > 1$, the actual cost paid by the consumer is greater than the real cost, while if $\theta_i < 1$, the actual cost paid is less than the real cost.

On the basis of this expression we can obtain the subjective time value:

$$VS_{t_i} = \frac{\partial V_i / \partial t_i}{\partial V_i / \partial c_i}$$

If we calculate the derivatives with respect to $\hat{V}_i$

$$\partial \hat{V}_i / \partial t_i = -\beta$$

$$\partial \hat{V}_i / \partial c_i = -\frac{\alpha \theta_i}{g}$$

then

$$VS_{t_i} = \frac{-\beta}{-\alpha \frac{\theta_i}{g}} = \frac{\beta \cdot g}{\alpha \cdot \theta_i}$$

Therefore, the subjective time value is affected by the uncertainty factor: if $\theta i < 1$, the subjective time value is greater than if $\theta i > 1$.

Therefore the degree of information affects consumers' decisions. A lack of information favours alternatives with an actual cost below the real cost. Hence individuals use private cars as a mode of transport versus public transport, because the subjective time value is greater than it would be if information were perfect.

2.8 Revealed Preference Theory

All the results and predictions of consumer utility maximisation theory can be derived from revealed preference theory. This theory was begun by Samuelson (1947 and 1948) and was carried on by Houthakker (1950). Revealed preference theory postulates that individuals' preferences are not directly observable and thus we cannot know whether a consumer's behaviour is based on a utility maximisation criterion. Alternatively, instead of taking individuals' preferences as the starting-point, we can start from certain instances of individual behaviour where the individual needs to choose one option among several. These instances are relatively simple and give rise to the 'weak axiom of revealed preference' (hereinafter, WARP) and the 'strong axiom of revealed preference' (hereinafter, SARP).

The instances are as follows:

First, it is assumed that the consumer faces a given price vector, p, with a fixed monetary income Y, and that the consumer spends his entire monetary income.

Second, the consumer chooses just one set of goods, X, for each combination of prices and income. In other words, the consumer will always choose the same set of goods for a specific set of prices and income.

Third, it is assumed that there is one, and only one, combination of prices and income for which each set of goods is chosen.

Fourth, it is assumed that consumer choices are consistent, i.e., if he chooses set X^0 when he might have chosen set X^1, when set X^1 is chosen then X^0 is not a viable alternative. Let p^0 be the price vector at which X^0 is acquired. If in this action X^1 is a viable combination, its cost, $p^0 X^1$, must not be greater than the cost of X^0, p^0X^0. The latter is also the monetary income of the consumer, $M_0 = p^0X^0$ when X^0 is chosen.

Now let p^1 be the price vector at which X^1 is chosen; then X^0 will not be viable at the prices p^1, because, if it were, it would have been chosen. I.e., its cost p^1X^0 must exceed the cost of X^1, p^1X^1, which is equal, when X^1 is chosen, to the consumer's monetary income. This instance can be set out as:

$p^0X^0 \geq p^0X^1$ implies that $p^1X^1 < p^1X^0$ (WARP) when X^0 is chosen at p^0, M^0 and X^1 at p^1, M_1; then if X^0 is chosen when X^1 can be acquired, we say that X^0 is revealed as preferred to X^1. In other words, if a consumer directly reveals that she prefers basket (X_1^1,X_2^1) to basket (X_1^0, X_2^0), and if those baskets are not the same, it cannot happen that she reveals directly a preference for (X_1^0, X_2^0) before (X_1^1,X_2^1). I.e., if she buys basket (X_1^1, X_2^1) at the prices p^1 and the basket (X_1^0, X_2^0) at the prices p^0, then:

$$p^1(X_1^1+X_2^1) \geq p^1(X_1^0+X_2^0) \Rightarrow p^0(X_1^0+X_2^0) < p^0(X_1^1+X_2^1)$$

If basket X^1 can be acquired when X^0 is acquired, then when X^1 is acquired X^0 must not be viable.

Furthermore, if a consumer directly or indirectly reveals that she prefers (X_1^1, X_2^1) to (X_1^0, X_2^0), and those baskets are not the same, it cannot happen that she reveals directly or indirectly that she prefers (X_1^0, X_2^0) to (X_1^1, X_2^1). This is the Strong Axiom of Revealed Preference (SARP).

On the basis of these instances and the two axioms we can generate all the predictions based on utility and relating to consumer demand functions.

The two above axioms can be defined even more simply. Thus the WARP can be stated as, 'If a subject can choose between two options, A and B, and expresses a preference for A at a given time, in any other situation in which she must choose between A and B she will choose A.' When there are more than two goods – for instance, when there are n goods – the weak axiom becomes the strong axiom.

The revealed preference approach enables us to derive regular demand functions, i.e., with the usual properties of neo-classical demand functions, on the basis of fairly simple behavioural axioms. In a way, the revealed preference approach is analogous to integratability. In integratability, after all, if a subject's demand functions are known, one may infer from such functions – provided that they have certain regular properties – the utility or preference structure that generated them. This equivalence was pointed out by Kihlstrom, Mas-Colell and Sonnenscheim (1976), who unified both approaches by placing the revealed preference axioms in relation to the axioms of the Slutsky matrix.

References

Becker, G.: A Theory of the Allocation of Time. *The Economic Journal* 75, 493-517 (1965)

De Serpa, A.: A Theory of the Economics of Time. *The Economic Journal* 81, 828-846 (1971)

Domencich, T., McFadden, D.: *Urban Travel Demand: a Behavioral Analysis*. Amsterdam, Holland, North-Holland 1975

Evans, A.: On the Theory of the Valuation and Allocation of Time. *Scottish Journal of Political Economy*, Febr., 1-17 (1972)

Gronau, R.: Home Production, a Survey. In: Ashenfelter, O., Layard, R. (eds.) *Handbook of Labor Economics*, vol 1, 273-304. North-Holland 1986

Houthakker, H. S.: Revealed Preference and the Utility Function. *Economica* 17, 159-174 (1950)

Jara-Díaz, S. R.: Time and Income in Travel Demand: towards a Microeconomic Activity Framework. In: Garling, T., Laitia, T., Westin, K. (eds.) *Theoretical Foundations of Travel Choice Modelling*. Elsevier 1997

Jara-Díaz, S. R.: Interpretación Microeconómica del Valor Subjetivo del Tiempo de Viaje Calculado a Partir de Modelos de Elección Modal Discreta. *X Congreso Panamericano de Ingeniería de Tránsito y Transporte*, 85-95 (1998)

Jara-Díaz, S. R., Farah, M.: Transport Demand and User's Benefit with Fixed Income: the Goods/Leisure Trade-Off Revisited. *Transportation Research* 21B, 165-170 (1987)

Jara-Díaz, S. R., Martínez, F., Zurita, I.: A Microeconomic Framework to Understand Residential Location. *2nd European Transport Forum*, Proceedings Seminar H., 115-128 (1994)

Johnson, B.: Travel Time and the Price of Leisure. *Western Economic Journal*, Spring, 135-145 (1966)

Juster, F. T.: Rethinking Utility Theory. *Journal of Behavioral Economics* 19, 155-179 (1970)

Kihlstrom, R., Mas-Collel, A., Sonnenscheim: The Demand Theory of the Eeak Axiom of Revealed Preference. *Econometrica* 44, 971-978 (1970)

Lancaster, K.: *Consumer Demand: a New Approach*. New York, Columbia University Press 1971

McFadden, D.: Conditional Logit Analysis of Qualitative Choice Behavior. In: Zarembka, P. (ed.) *Frontiers in Econometrics*. NY & London, Academic Press 1973

McFadden, D.: The Measurement of Urban Travel Demand. *Journal of Public Economics*, 303-328 (1974)

McFadden, D.: Cost, Revenue and Profit Functions. In: Fuss, M., McFadden, D. (eds.) *Production Economics*. Amsterdam, Holland, North-Holland 1978

McFadden, D.: Modelling the Choice of Residential Location. In: Karlquiot, A., Lundquist, F., Snikars, F., Weibull, J. (eds.) *Spatial Interaction Theory and Planning Models*. Amsterdam, Holland, North-Holland 1978

McFadden, D., Talvitie, Antii and Associates: *Urban Travel Demand Forecasting Project. Final Report*. Institute of Transport Studies, U.C. Berkeley 1977

McFadden, D., Winston, C.: Joint Estimation of Discrete and Continuous Choices in Freight Transportation. Presented at the *Meeting of the Econometric Society* 1981

Oort, C.: The Evaluation of Travelling Time. *Journal of Transport Economics and Policy*, September, 279-286 (1969)

Samuelson, P.: *Foundations of Economic Analysis*. Harvard University Press, Cambridge, Mass 1947

Samuelson, P.: Consumption Theory in Terms of Revealed Preference. *Economica* 15, 243-253 (1948)

Train, K., McFadden: The Goods/Leisure Trade-Off and Disaggregate Work Trip Mode Choice Models. *Transportation Research* 12, 349-353 (1978)

Warner, S. L.: *Stochastic Choice of Mode in Urban Travel: A Study in Binary Choice*. Evanston, IL: Northwestern U. Press 1962

Winston, G. C.: Activity Choice: a New Approach to Economic Behavior. *Journal of Economic Behavior and Organization* 8, 567-585 (1987)

3 Main Forms of Utility Functions

This chapter has been divided into three big sections in which we present the main functional forms of the utility functions: Cobb-Douglas, CES and quasi-linear. Each of these functional forms, and therefore, each section, has been developed according to the exposure in the previous chapter. Thus, firstly, we obtain the Marshallian and Hicksian demand functions in every functional specification, to follow with the indirect and cost utility functions. Moreover, in the Cobb-Douglas functional form, we obtain expenditure-share functions, Engel curves and elasticities. In the CES functional form, we go even further and prove CES demand system restrictions. And finally, in the quasi-linear functional form, a similar exposure to that developed for the CES is presented.

The purpose of this chapter is instrumental rather than theoretical. We do not provide new concepts, but we only specify utility functional forms in order to further use the optimisation theory and the significant theorems to obtain the relevant functions in the theory of the consumer behaviour.

At the end of this chapter, we recommend a range of readings with more practical work.

3.1 The Cobb-Douglas Utility Function

Assume the following function:

$$u(x) = u(x_1, x_2, \ldots, x_n) = \prod_{i=1}^{h} x_i^{\beta_i} \tag{3.1}$$

In (3.1) β_i is a non-negative parameter. On the other hand, searching for more simplicity, we will study the Cobb-Douglas utility function only for two goods, thus:

$$u(x) = u(x_1, x_2) = x_1^{\beta_1} \; x_2^{\beta_2} \tag{3.2}$$

and, on the other hand, raising (3.2) to $1/\beta_i+\beta_2$ and denoting $\alpha=\beta_i/\beta_i+\beta_2$ we have:

$$u(x) = u(x_1, x_2) = x_1^{\alpha} \, x_2^{1-\alpha}. \tag{3.3}$$

3.1.1 Properties

As can be observed, the Cobb - Douglas utility function is increasing monotonic and quasi-concave. As far as the first property is concerned, this is completely satisfied if the values of β_i are positive. If the Cobb - Douglas utility function is quasi-concave then the corresponding indifference curves must be strictly convex. Making the derivate of (3.3) equal to zero we have:

$$du = \frac{\partial u}{\partial x_1} dx_1 + \frac{\partial u}{\partial x_2} dx_2 = 0 \tag{3.4}$$

where

$$\frac{\partial u}{\partial x_1} = u_1 = \alpha\, x_1^{\alpha-1}\, x_2^{1-\alpha} = \frac{\alpha}{x_1} u(x) \tag{3.5}$$

$$\frac{\partial u}{\partial x_2} = u_2 = (1-\alpha) x_1^{\alpha}\, x_2^{-\alpha} = \frac{(1-\alpha)}{x_2} u(x) \tag{3.6}$$

which are the marginal utilities of the goods x_1 and x_2 respectively.

Substituting in (3.4) we have:

$$\alpha \frac{u(x)}{x_1} dx_1 + (1-\alpha) \frac{u(x)}{x_2} dx_2 = 0;$$

solving dx_2/dx_1 we have the MRS_1^2 with the sign shifted:

$$\frac{dx_2}{dx_1} = \frac{\alpha}{1-\alpha} \frac{x_2}{x_1} \tag{3.7}$$

which has the expected sign since α, by hypothesis, is always lower than the unit. It can be observed that the slope of the indifference curves is constant along any ray-vector from the origin (See figure 3.1). This property is not exclusively of the Cobb - Douglas function but common to all the homothetic utility functions, and therefore, to those homogeneous.

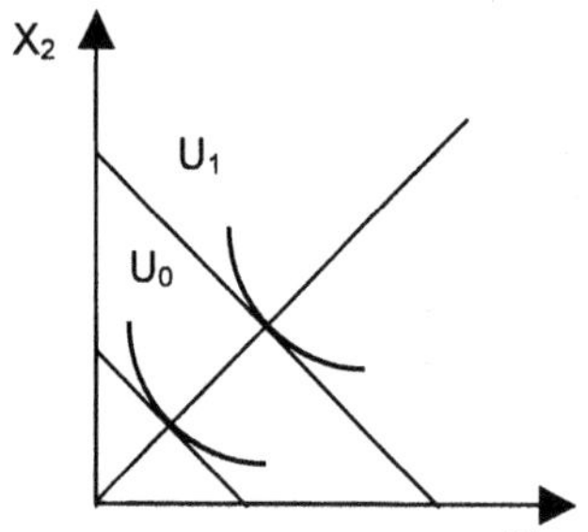

Fig. 3.1. Indifference curves of a homothetic utility function

Deriving (3.7):

$$\frac{d^2x_2}{dx_1^2} = \frac{\alpha}{1-\alpha}\frac{-x_2}{x_1^2}.$$

3.1.2 Marshallian or Ordinary Demands (Primal)

The rational behaviour of consumers can be expressed as a maximisation problem of a utility function (objective function) subject to a budget constraint. In other words:

$$\left.\begin{array}{l} \max.u(x) \\ \text{s. to } \mathbf{px} = y \end{array}\right\}. \tag{3.8}$$

Then, the Lagrangian function of (3.8) will be:

$$L(x_1,x_2, \mu) = u(x_1,x_2) + \mu(y-p_1x_1- p_2x_2),$$

and the fist-order conditions for maximisation are:

$$\left.\begin{array}{l} \frac{\partial L(x_1,x_2,\mu)}{\partial x_1} = \frac{\alpha\ u(x)}{x_1} - \mu p_1 = 0 \\ \\ \frac{\partial L(x_1,x_2,\mu)}{\partial x_2} = \frac{(1-\alpha)\,u(x)}{x_2} - \mu p_2 = 0 \\ \\ \frac{\partial L(x_1,x_2,\mu)}{\partial \mu} = y - p_1x_1 - p_2x_2 = 0 \end{array}\right\},$$

where μ is the Lagrange multiplier and can be assumed as the marginal utility of income. Note that the first two first-order conditions account for the known equilibrium result, where the indifference curve slope (MRS) is tangent to the budget constraint:

$$MRS_1^2 = \frac{\alpha}{1-\alpha}\frac{x_2}{x_1} = \frac{p_1}{p_2} \tag{3.9}$$

Taking into account (3.9) and the last first-order condition, it is possible to obtain

$$x_1(\mathbf{p}, y) = x_1(p_1, p_2, y) = \frac{\alpha y}{p_1} \tag{3.10}$$

$$x_2(\mathbf{p}, y) = x_2(p_1, p_2, y) = \frac{(1-\alpha)y}{p_2}\ . \tag{3.11}$$

Besides, for (3.10) and (3.11) to develop a utility maximising combination, the second-order condition must be satisfied, i.e., the Hessian of the matrix must be strictly negative definite:

$$\begin{vmatrix} \frac{\partial u}{\partial x_1} & -p_1 \\ -p_1 & 0 \end{vmatrix} = -p_1^2 < 0;$$

which is satisfied for any positive price.

$$\begin{vmatrix} u_{11} & u_{12} & -p_1 \\ u_{21} & u_{22} & -p_2 \\ -p_1 & -p_2 & 0 \end{vmatrix} = u_{12}\, p_1\, p_2 + u_{21}\, p_1\, p_2 - u_{11}\, p_2^2 - u_{22} p_1^2 > 0$$

is also satisfied since from (3.5) and (3.6), and provided that $0<\alpha<1$, we have:

$$u_{11} = \alpha\, (\alpha-1) x_1^{\alpha-2} x_2^{1-\alpha} < 0$$

$$u_{22} = -\alpha\, (1-\alpha) x_1^{\alpha} x_2^{-\alpha-1} < 0$$

$$u_{21} = u_{12} = \alpha\, (1-\alpha) x_1^{\alpha-1} x_2^{-\alpha} > 0.$$

3.1.3 The Indirect Utility Function

Once the demanded amounts of the different goods, which solve the maximisation problem, have been obtained (3.8), we will know the maximum level of utility, which can possibly be reached at given prices and income. This information is given by the indirect utility function, V (**p**,y);

$$V(\mathbf{p}, y) = \max u(x) = \max \left\{x_1^{\alpha} x_2^{1-\alpha}\right\} \text{so that } \mathbf{px} = y.$$

The expression of the indirect utility function is obtained by substituting in the utility function (3.2) the Marshallian demands (3.10) and (3.11), which are the demanded amounts of both goods which maximise the level of satisfaction of the individual given the budget constraint, i.e.,

$$V(\mathbf{p}, y) = \{x_1(\mathbf{p}, y)\}^{\alpha} \{x_2(\mathbf{p}, y)\}^{1-\alpha} = \left(\frac{\alpha\, y}{p_1}\right)^{\alpha} \left(\frac{(1-\alpha) y}{p_2}\right)^{1-\alpha},$$

Rearranging the terms we have:

$$V(\mathbf{p}, y) = \left(\frac{\alpha}{p_1}\right)^{\alpha} \left(\frac{1-\alpha}{p_2}\right)^{1-\alpha} y.$$

3.1.4 Hicksian or Compensated Demands (Dual)

The consumer equilibrium can be also presented as the solution of the following problem:

$$\left.\begin{array}{l} \min\ y = \mathbf{px} \\ \text{s.to}\ \ u = x_1^{\alpha} x_2^{1-\alpha} \end{array}\right\} \tag{3.12}$$

The Lagrangian function of (3.12) is

$$S(x_1, x_2, \lambda) = p_1 x_1 + p_2 x_2 - \lambda \left[u(x_1, x_2) - u\right]$$

and the following first-order conditions are

$$\left.\begin{array}{l} \dfrac{\partial S}{\partial x_1} = S_1 = p_1 - \lambda \dfrac{\alpha\, u(x)}{x_1} = 0 \\ \dfrac{\partial S}{\partial x_2} = S_2 = p_2 - \lambda \dfrac{(1-\alpha)\, u(x)}{x_2} = 0 \end{array}\right\} \rightarrow MRS_1^2 = \frac{\alpha}{1-\alpha}\frac{x_2}{x_1} = \frac{p_1}{p_2}$$

$$\frac{\partial S}{\partial \lambda} = S_\lambda = -x_1^{\alpha} x_2^{1-\alpha} + u = 0.$$

Solving for example, x_1 in S_λ and substituting in the expression MRS we obtain:

$$MRS_1^2 = \frac{\alpha}{1-\alpha} \frac{x_2}{\left(\dfrac{u}{x_2^{1-\alpha}}\right)^{\frac{1}{\alpha}}} = \frac{p_1}{p_2}. \tag{3.13}$$

Rearranging (3.13) and with the aim of obtaining an expression for the Hicksian demand for the good x_2 we will follow these steps:

$$x_2 = \frac{p_1}{p_2} \frac{1-\alpha}{\alpha} \left(\frac{u}{x_2^{1-\alpha}}\right)^{\frac{1}{\alpha}},$$

and solving x_2 we will have

$$x_2^{\frac{1}{\alpha}} = \frac{p_1}{p_2} \frac{1-\alpha}{\alpha} u^{\frac{1}{\alpha}};$$

then finally, the Hicksian demand for the good x_2 is given by the following expression:

$$x_2 = h_2(\mathbf{p}, u) = \left(\frac{1-\alpha}{\alpha} \frac{p_1}{p_2}\right)^{\alpha} u \tag{3.14}$$

We obtain a Hicksian demand of the good x_1 similar to the one above:

$$x_1 = h_1(\mathbf{p}, u) = \left(\frac{\alpha}{1-\alpha}\frac{p_2}{p_1}\right)^{1-\alpha} u. \tag{3.15}$$

3.1.5 The Expenditure Function

As it is already known, the expenditure function shows the minimum amount, which must be necessarily spent in order to achieve a particular level of utility of the prices given. This function can be easily obtained by substituting the amounts listed in the objective function of the optimisation dual problem (3.12) into the Hicksian demands (3.14) and (3.15). Then,

$$G(\mathbf{p}, u) = p_1\left(\frac{\alpha}{1-\alpha}\frac{p_2}{p_1}\right)^{1-\alpha} u + p_2\left(\frac{1-\alpha}{\alpha}\frac{p_1}{p_2}\right)^{\alpha} u.$$

an expression which subject to the steps below undergoes great simplification:

$$G(\mathbf{p}, u) = u\left[\left(\frac{\alpha}{1\text{-}\alpha}\right)^{1-\alpha} p_2^{1\text{-}\alpha} p_2^{1\text{-}1+\alpha} + \left(\frac{1\text{-}\alpha}{\alpha}\right)^{\alpha} p_1^{\alpha} p_2^{1\text{-}\alpha}\right]$$

$$G(\mathbf{p}, u) = u p_1^{\alpha} p_2^{1\text{-}\alpha}\left[\left(\frac{\alpha}{1\text{-}\alpha}\right)^{1-\alpha} + \left(\frac{1\text{-}\alpha}{\alpha}\right)^{\alpha}\right] =$$

$$u p_1^{\alpha} p_2^{1\text{-}\alpha}\left[\frac{\alpha^{1-\alpha}\alpha^{\alpha} + (1-\alpha)^{\alpha}(1-\alpha)^{1-\alpha}}{(1-\alpha)^{1-\alpha}\alpha^{\alpha}}\right]$$

$$G(\mathbf{p}, u) = u p_1^{\alpha} p_2^{1\text{-}\alpha}\left[\frac{1}{(1-\alpha)^{1-\alpha}\alpha^{\alpha}}\right].$$

Finally, the expenditure function will result as follows:

$$G(\mathbf{p}, u) = u\left(\frac{p_1}{\alpha}\right)^{\alpha}\left(\frac{p_2}{1\text{-}\alpha}\right)^{1-\alpha} \tag{3.16}$$

Once we have the indirect utility function it is possible to obtain the expenditure function much more simply, by just solving the income. From

$$V(\mathbf{p}, y) = \left(\frac{\alpha}{p_1}\right)^{\alpha}\left(\frac{1-\alpha}{p_2}\right)^{1-\alpha} y$$

and solving the income

$$G(\mathbf{p},u)=y=V(\mathbf{p},y)\left(\frac{p_1}{\alpha}\right)^{\alpha}\left(\frac{p_2}{1-\alpha}\right)^{1-\alpha}=u\left(\frac{p_1}{\alpha}\right)^{\alpha}\left(\frac{p_2}{1-\alpha}\right)^{1-\alpha}$$

3.1.6 Elasticities, Engel Curves and Expenditure Share Functions

If we distinguish the Marshallian demand functions from the prices and the level of income, we will have the own price (ε_{ii}), cross price (ε_{ij}) and income elasticities (ε_{iy}):

$$\varepsilon_{11}=\frac{\partial x_1(\mathbf{p},y)}{\partial p_1}\frac{p_1}{x_1}=\frac{\partial}{\partial p_1}\left[\frac{\alpha y}{p_1}\right]\frac{p_1}{x_1}=\frac{\alpha y}{p_1^2}\frac{p_1}{\frac{\alpha y}{p_1}}=-1$$

$$\varepsilon_{12}=\frac{\partial x_1(\mathbf{p},y)}{\partial p2}\frac{p_2}{x_1}=\frac{\partial}{\partial p_2}\left[\frac{\alpha y}{p_2}\right]\frac{p_2}{x_1}=0$$

$$\varepsilon_{1y}=\frac{\partial x_1(\mathbf{p},y)}{\partial y}\frac{y}{x_1}=\frac{\partial}{\partial y}\left[\frac{\alpha y}{p_1}\right]\frac{y}{x_1}=\frac{\alpha}{p_1}\frac{y}{\frac{\alpha y}{p_1}}=1.$$

The correspondent own price, cross-price and income elasticities of the good x_2 are identical to those obtained for the good x_1. The values obtained need a brief comment since they show the restrictions presented in the Cobb-Douglas utility function:

1. Since the price elasticity (ε_{ii}) is negative it confirms a decrease in the demand with an increase in the price. However, a unitary price elasticity is quite restrictive.
2. The income elasticities (ε_{iy}) are all unitary. All the goods are normal, i.e., the Cobb-Douglas utility function does not allow the existence of inferior goods, which is highly restrictive.
3. All the cross-price elasticities (ε_{ij}) are null, showing that all the goods are gross and independent from each other. In other words, the demand for each good is only affected by its own price.
4. Since all the goods are gross and independent from each other and, furthermore, they are all normal, it follows that, all the goods are net substitutes. In other words, the Slutsky equation expressed in terms of elasticities is given by

$$\varepsilon_{ij}=\varepsilon_{ij}^{S}-S_j\varepsilon_{iy}$$

where

$$\varepsilon_{ij}^{S} = \frac{\partial h_i(p,u)}{\partial p_j}\frac{p_j}{x_i}$$

and since s_j, the expenditure share of the good x_j, is always non-negative, ε_{ij} is null and ε_{iy} is positive then ε_{ij}^{j} is always positive.
The Engel function associates the amount demanded for a good with the level of income, assuming that the level of prices is constant. The income elasticity of any good is just the quotient between the slope of the Engel function and the slope of any ray-vector which joins this function with the origin (see figure 3.2). As in this case, all the income elasticities are unitary. Thus, the Engel curve is represented by a line starting from the origin (see figure 3.3). The unitary condition of the income elasticity for all the goods represents also a restrictive characteristic of the Cobb-Douglas function, since it precludes the existence of luxury goods, i.e., goods with an income elasticity higher than the unit.

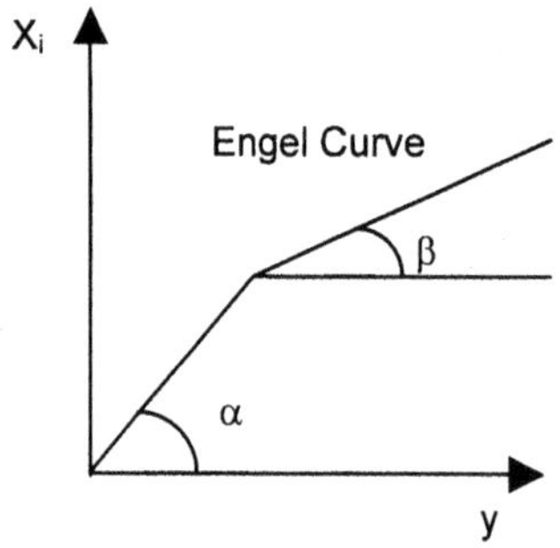

Fig. 3.2. Income elasticity (α / β)

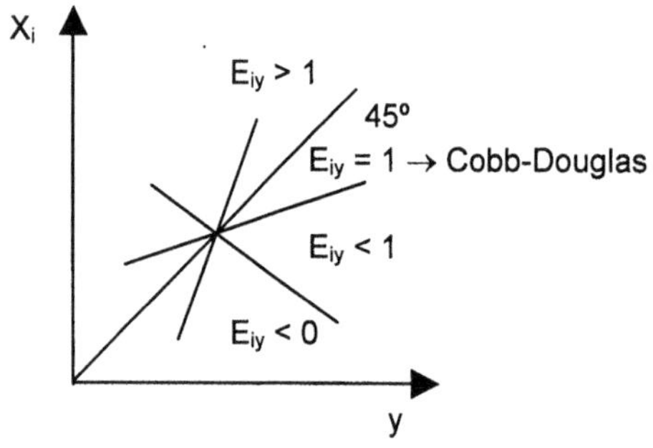

Fig. 3.3. Engel curve

Since the demand for all the goods increases proportionally to the income, the expenditure share functions of all the goods are constant and independent from the income. Such functions are obtained by multiplying the Marshallian demand for a good by its price and dividing it by the level of income:

$$s_i = \frac{p_i \, x_i(p,y)}{y} \quad \begin{cases} s_1 = \dfrac{p_1}{y} \dfrac{\alpha \, y}{p_1} = \alpha \\ \\ s_2 = \dfrac{p_2}{y} \dfrac{(1-\alpha)\, y}{p_2} = (1-\alpha). \end{cases}$$

3.2 The Utility Function of the Constant Elasticity of Substitution (CES)

Assume the following utility function:

$$u(x_1,...,x_n) = x_1^a + x_2^a + ... + x_n^a,$$

although its most traditional formulation is as follows:

$$f(x_1,...,x_n) = A\left[b_1 \, x_1^a + b_2 \, x_2^a + ... + b_n \, x_n^a\right]^{\frac{1}{a}},$$

which is a more complex expression. However, this can be avoided when using it as the utility function if we develop the following monotone increasing transformation:

$$u = \left(\frac{f}{A}\right)^a = b_1 \, x_1^a + ... + b_n \, x_n^a,$$

which, in order to be simplified, we develop into $b_1 = b_2 = ... = b_n = 1$.

3.2.1 Marshallian Demands

In order to simplify the analysis, assume we have only two goods (x_1, x_2), for which the maximisation problem can be posed as follows:

$$\left.\begin{array}{ll} \max u(x_1, x_2) = x_1^a + x_2^a \\ \text{s. to} \quad p_1 x_1 + p_2 x_2 = y \end{array}\right\}.$$

The first-order conditions are:

$$L = x_1^a + x_2^a - \mu \left[p_1 x_1 + p_2 x_2 - y\right]$$

$$\left.\begin{array}{l} \dfrac{\partial L}{\partial x_1} = a \, x_1^{a-1} - \mu \, p_1 = 0 \\ \dfrac{\partial L}{\partial x_2} = a \, x_2^{a-1} - \mu \, p_2 = 0 \end{array}\right] \rightarrow \left(\frac{x_1}{x_2}\right)^{a-1} = \frac{p_1}{p_2} \Rightarrow \frac{x_1}{x_2} = \left(\frac{p_1}{p_2}\right)^{\frac{1}{a-1}}$$

$$\frac{\partial L}{\partial \mu} = p_1 x_1 + p_2 x_2 - y = 0$$

and we have

$$\text{MRS} = \left(\frac{x_1}{x_2}\right)^{a-1}.$$

The MRS is decreasing and the indifference curves convex if a>1.
Depending on the value of the parameter "a", the CES function can result in different ways:

a) when a = 1 the utility function is linear: $u(x_1, x_2) = x_1^a + x_2^a$ and the goods are perfect substitutes:

   MRS = 1= constant.

   The CES becomes a Cobb-Douglas
b) when a = 0 CES indifference curves are very similar to Cobb-Douglas indifference curves. In the following Cobb-Douglas function $u(x_1,x_2) = x_1^a x_2^a$ the indifference curves satisfy that MRS = x_1/x_2, i.e., it does not depend on the absolute values of x_1 and x_2 but on the proportion between them. In a CES function the MRS is

$$\text{MRS} = \left(\frac{x_1}{x_2}\right)^{0-1} = \left(\frac{x_1}{x_2}\right)^{-1} = \frac{x_2}{x_1}.$$

   Then it also presents the indifference curves, which depend only on the proportion between x_1 and x_2.
c) when a = - ∞ the CES function is similar to a Leontief function, thus, the goods are perfect complements:

$$\text{MRS} = \left(\frac{x_1}{x_2}\right)^{-\infty-1} = \left(\frac{x_1}{x_2}\right)^{-\infty} = \left(\frac{x_2}{x_1}\right)^{\infty};$$

   then, if $x_2 > x_1 \Rightarrow \text{MRS} = \infty$ and if. $x_2 < x_1 \Rightarrow \text{MRS} = 0$.

On the whole, the Marshallian demands will be:

$$\left(\frac{x_1}{x_2}\right)^{a-1} = \text{MRS} = \frac{p_1}{p_2} \rightarrow \left(\frac{x_2}{x_1}\right)^{1-a} = \frac{p_1}{p_2}.$$

From here we can obtain

$$x_2 = \left(\frac{p_1}{p_2}\right)^{\frac{1}{1-a}} x_1;$$

with s = 1/(1-a) we have:

$$x_2 = \left(\frac{p_1}{p_2}\right)^s x_1 = \left(\frac{p_1}{p_2}\right)^s \left[\frac{y}{p_1} - \frac{p_2}{p_1} x_2\right] = \left(\frac{p_1}{p_2}\right)^s \frac{y}{p_1} - \left(\frac{p_1}{p_2}\right)^{s-1} x_2;$$

then,

$$x_2 \left[1 + \left(\frac{p_1}{p_2}\right)^{s-1}\right] = \left(\frac{p_1}{p_2}\right)^s \frac{y}{p_1}$$

and solving x_2:

$$x_2 = \frac{\left(\frac{p_1}{p_2}\right)^s \frac{y}{p_1}}{\frac{p_2^{s-1} + p_1^{s-1}}{p_2^{s-1}}} = \frac{y\, p_2^{-s}}{\frac{p_2^{s-1} + p_1^{s-1}}{p_2^{s-1}\, p_1^{s-1}}} = \frac{y\, p_2^{-s}}{\frac{1}{p_1^{s-1}} + \frac{1}{p_2^{s-1}}} = \frac{y\, p_2^{-s}}{p_1^{1-s} + p_2^{1-s}};$$

we have the following:

$$x_2 = x_2(\mathbf{p}, y) = \frac{y\, p_2^{-s}}{\sum_{i=1}^{n} p_i^{1-s}},$$

which is the Marshallian demand for x_2.

The term Σp_i^{1-s} can be taken as a "price index" associated to the set of goods. Denoting this term P, we will have:

$$x_2 = \frac{y\, p_2^{-s}}{P}.$$

The same can be said to happen with respect to the Marshallian demand function for x_1:

$$x_1 = x_1(\mathbf{p}, y) = \frac{y\, p_1^{-s}}{\sum_{i=1}^{n} p_i^{1-s}} = \frac{y\, p_1^{-s}}{P}.$$

3.2.2 The Indirect Utility Function

Substituting the demands in the utility function:

$$V(\mathbf{p}, y) = u\left(x_1^*, x_2^*\right) = \left[\frac{y\, p_1^{-s}}{P}\right]^a + \left[\frac{y\, p_2^{-s}}{P}\right]^a = \frac{y^a}{P^a}\left(p_1^{-sa} + p_2^{-sa}\right) =$$

$$= y^a \frac{p_1^{-\left(\frac{1}{1-a}\right)a} + p_2^{-\left(\frac{1}{1-a}\right)a}}{\left(p_1^{-\frac{a}{1-a}} + p_2^{-\frac{a}{1-a}}\right)^a} = \frac{y^a}{\left(p_1^{-\frac{a}{1-a}} + p_2^{-\frac{a}{1-a}}\right)^{a-1}} =$$

$$= y^a \frac{1}{\left(p_1^{1-s} + p_2^{1-s}\right)^{a-1}} = \frac{y^a}{P^{a-1}} = \frac{y^a}{P^{-\frac{1}{s}}} = V(\mathbf{p}, y).$$

3.2.3 Hicksian Demands

Applying Hotelling's Theorem,

$$h_1(\mathbf{p}, u) = \frac{\partial G}{\partial p_1} = u^{\frac{s}{s-1}} \frac{1}{1-s}\left[p_1^{1-s} + p_2^{1-s}\right]^{\frac{1}{1-s}-1} (1-s) p_1^{-s}$$

$$h_1 = u^{\frac{s}{s-1}} p_1^{-s} p^{\frac{s}{1-s}}$$

We have the Hicksian demand for of the good x_1.

For the good x_2 the following relationship can be applied:

$$x_2[p, G(\mathbf{p}, u)] = h_2(\mathbf{p}, u)$$

$$x_2 = \frac{y p_2^{-s}}{P} = \frac{\left[u^{\frac{s}{s-1}} p^{\frac{1}{1-s}}\right] p_2^{-s}}{P} = u^{\frac{s}{s-1}} p^{\frac{s}{1-s}} p_2^{-s} = h_2,$$

which is the Hicksian demand for the good x_2.

3.2.4 The Expenditure Function

Solving $y = G$ $(V = u)$:

$$G = \left[u P^{-\frac{1}{s}}\right]^{\frac{1}{a}}$$

$$G = u^{\frac{s}{s-1}} p^{\frac{1}{1-s}} = u^{\frac{s}{s-1}} \left[p_1^{1-s} + p_2^{1-s}\right]^{\frac{1}{1-s}};$$

then we have the expenditure function.

3.2.5 Application to the Particular CES Utility Function

Obtain each type of function for the particular case of a =1/2, then,

$$u\left(x_1, x_2\right) = x_1^{\frac{1}{2}} + x_2^{\frac{1}{2}}.$$

In this case s = 1/(1-a) = 2; therefore, we have that the Marshallian demands are

$$x_1(p, y) = \frac{y\, p_1^{-2}}{p_1^{-1} + p_2^{-1}},$$

which is the Marshallian demand for x_1, and

$$x_2(p_1, p_2, y) = \frac{y\, p_2^{-2}}{p_1^{-1} + p_2^{-1}}$$

is the Marshallian demand for x_2.

3.2.5.1 *The Indirect Utility Function*

$$V(P, y) = \frac{y^{\frac{1}{2}}\, p_1^{-1}}{\left(p_1^{-1} + p_2^{-1}\right)^{\frac{1}{2}}} + \frac{y^{\frac{1}{2}}\, p_2^{-1}}{\left(p_1^{-1} + p_2^{-1}\right)^{\frac{1}{2}}} = \frac{y^{\frac{1}{2}}}{\left(p_1^{-1} + p_2^{-1}\right)^{-\frac{1}{2}}} = V.$$

3.2.5.2 *The Expenditure Function*

$$G(P, u) = u^2 \left(p_1^{-1} + p_2^{-1}\right)^{-1} = \frac{u^2}{p_1^{-1} + p_2^{-1}} = G.$$

3.2.5.3 *Hicksian Demands*

$$h_2 = \frac{\left[u^2 \left(p_1^{-1} + p_2^{-1}\right)^{-1}\right] p_2^{-2}}{p_1^{-1} + p_2^{-1}} = \frac{u^2\, p_2^{-2}}{\left(p_1^{-1} + p_2^{-1}\right)^2} = h_2.$$

The same for h_1..

3.2.5.4 *The Own, Cross and Income Elasticity of the CES Demand System*

We can observe that the restrictions for ordinary demand functions are satisfied when a = ½. The corresponding elasticities are:

$$\varepsilon_{11} = \frac{-2\,y\,p_1^{-3}\,p_1^{-1} - 2\,y\,p_1^{-3}\,p_2^{-1} + p_1^{-2}\,y\,p_1^{-2}}{P^2} \frac{p_1}{\frac{y\,p_1^{-2}}{P}}$$

$$\varepsilon_{11} = \frac{-y\,p_1^{-4} - 2\,y\,p_1^{-3}\,p_2^{-1}}{P} \frac{p_1^{+3}}{y}$$

$$\varepsilon_{11} = \frac{-p_1^{-1} - 2\,p_2^{-1}}{P} = \frac{-2p_1^{-1} - 2\,p_2^{-1} + p_1^{-1}}{P} = -2 + \frac{p_1^{-1}}{P}$$

$$\varepsilon_{11} = -2 + \frac{p_1^{-1}}{p_1^{-1} + p_2^{-1}} \Rightarrow \varepsilon_{22} = -2 + \frac{p_2^{-1}}{P}.$$

The cross elasticity is

$$\varepsilon_{12} = y\,p_1^{-2}\,(-1)\left[p_1^{-1} + p_2^{-1}\right]^{-2}(-1)\,p_2^{-2}\,\frac{p_2}{\frac{y\,p_1^{-2}}{P}}$$

$$\varepsilon_{12} = \frac{y\,p_1^{-2}\,p_2^{-2}}{P^2} \frac{p_2}{\frac{y\,p_1^{-2}}{P}} = \frac{p_2^{-1}}{P} = \varepsilon_{12} \Rightarrow \varepsilon_{21} = \frac{p_1^{-1}}{P}$$

and the income elasticity is

$$\varepsilon_{1y} = \frac{p_1^{-2}}{P} \frac{y}{\frac{y\,p_1^{-2}}{P}} = 1 = \varepsilon_{1y} = \varepsilon_{2y}.$$

3.2.5.5 Restrictions of CES Demand Systems

Engel Aggregation Condition

$$s_1\,\varepsilon_{1y} + s_2\,\varepsilon_{2y} = 1$$

$$\frac{p_1\,x_1}{y}1 + \frac{p_2\,x_2}{y}1 = \frac{p_1\,x_1 + p_2\,x_2}{y} = 1.$$

The condition is satisfied.

Cournot Aggregation Condition

$$s_1\,\varepsilon_{12}+\varepsilon_{21}\,s_2=-s_2 \Rightarrow s_1\,\varepsilon_{12}+s_2(\varepsilon_{21}+1)=0$$

$$\frac{p_1\,x_1}{y}\frac{p_2^{-1}}{P}+\frac{p_2\,x_2}{y}\left(-1+\frac{p_2^{-1}}{P}\right)=\frac{p_2^{-1}}{P}\left(\frac{p_1\,x_1+p_2\,x_2}{y}\right)-\frac{p_2\,x_2}{y}=$$

$$=\frac{p_2^{-1}}{P}-\frac{p_2}{y}\frac{y\,p_2^{-2}}{P}=\frac{p_2^{-1}}{P}-\frac{p_2^{-1}}{P}=0.$$

The condition is satisfied.

Homogeneity Condition

$$\varepsilon_{11}+\varepsilon_{12}+\varepsilon_{1y}=0$$

$$\left(-2+\frac{p_1^{-1}}{P}\right)+\frac{p_2^{-1}}{P}+1=-1+\frac{p_1^{-1}+p_2^{-1}}{P}=-1+1=0.$$

The condition is satisfied.

Cross-Effect Symmetry or Integrability Condition

$$s_{12}=s_{21}\Rightarrow\frac{\partial h_1}{\partial p_2}=\frac{\partial h_2}{\partial p_1}.$$

Through the Slutsky equation:

$$s_{21}=\frac{\partial h_2}{\partial p_1}=\frac{\partial x_2}{\partial p_1}+x_1\frac{\partial x_2}{\partial y}=\frac{y\,p_1^{-2}\,p_2^{-2}}{P^2}+\frac{y\,p_1^{-2}}{P}\frac{p_2^{-2}}{P}=\frac{2\,p_1^{-2}\,p_2^{-2}\,y}{P^2}$$

$$s_{12}=\frac{\partial h_1}{\partial p_2}=\frac{\partial x_1}{\partial p_2}+x_2\frac{\partial x_1}{\partial y}=\frac{y\,p_1^{-2}\,p_2^{-2}}{P^2}+\frac{y\,p_2^{-2}}{P}\frac{p_1^{-2}}{P}=\frac{2\,p_1^{-2}\,p_2^{-2}\,y}{P^2}.$$

Therefore, the condition is satisfied.

Negativity Condition

The matrix of the substitute terms must be negative semidefinite

G (p,u) = concave.

$$\frac{\partial h_1}{\partial p_1}=\frac{\partial x_1}{\partial p_1}+x_1\frac{\partial x_1}{\partial y}=\frac{-y\,p_1^{-4}-2y\,p_1^{-3}\,p_2^{-1}}{P^2}+\frac{y\,p_1^{-2}}{P}\frac{p_1^{-2}}{P}$$

$$s_{11} = \frac{\partial h_1}{\partial p_1} = -\frac{2y\, p_1^{-3}\, p_2^{-1}}{P^2}$$

$$s_{22} = \frac{\partial h_2}{\partial p_2} = -\frac{2y\, p_2^{-3}\, p_1^{-1}}{P^2}.$$

We have

$$S_{11} \le 0,$$

which is satisfied, and

$$s = \begin{vmatrix} s_{11} & s_{12} \\ s_{21} & s_{22} \end{vmatrix} \ge 0,$$

which is also satisfied.

3.3 Quasi-linear Utility Functions

The following is the functional form of a quasi-linear utility function:

$$u(x_1, x_2) = f(x_1) + c\, x_2.$$

3.3.1 Marshallian Demands

In order to find optimal solutions, we must solve the following Lagrange equation:

$$L(x_1, x_2, \mu) = f(x_1) + c\, x_2 - \mu\, [p_1 x_1 + p_2 x_2 - y]$$

The first-order conditions are:

$$\frac{\partial L}{\partial x_1} = f'(x_1) - \mu\, p_1 = 0$$

$$\frac{\partial L}{\partial x_2} = c - \mu\, p_2 = 0 \rightarrow \frac{1}{\mu} = \frac{p_2}{c} \rightarrow \mu = \frac{c}{p_2}$$

$$\frac{\partial L}{\partial \mu} = p_1 x_1 + p_2 x_2 - y = 0.$$

As noted, the MU of the good x_2 is constant and equal to "c", while second-order conditions "make" the MU of the good x_1 decreasing at the prices given u_2/p_2, and therefore, the marginal income utility is obtained.

From the first-order conditions we have

$$\text{MRS} = \frac{u_1}{u_2} = \frac{f'(x_1)}{c} = \frac{p_1}{p_2},$$

where now the MRS does not depend on x_2, which makes the indifference curves be "vertically parallel". For a given value x_1, they have the same slope whatever the value x_2 may be. Then, the demand for the good x_1 will be

$$f'(x_1) = c\frac{p_1}{p_2}$$

$$x_1 = (f')^{-1}\left(c\frac{p_1}{p_2}\right)$$

which is the Marshallian demand for the good x_1, and where $(f')^{-1}$ is the inverse function of f'.

It can be observed that x_1 does not depend on the income but only on the prices and the parameters.

In the particular case of $f(x_1) = x_1^{1/2}$, it is satisfied that

$$f'(x_1) = \frac{1}{2x_1^{\frac{1}{2}}} = \frac{c\,p_1}{p_2},$$

where the function demand is obtained by solving x_1:

$$x_1 = \left(\frac{p_2}{2\,c\,p_1}\right)^2.$$

The Marshallian demand for x_2 is developed by substituting x_1 in the budget constraint:

$$y = p_1\left(\frac{p_2^2}{4\,c^2\,p_1^{\,2}}\right) + p_2 x_2 = \frac{p_2^2}{4\,c^2\,p_1} + p_2 x_2;$$

solving x_2:

$$p_2 x_2 = y - \frac{p_2^2}{4\,c^2\,p_1} \Rightarrow x_2 = \frac{y}{p_2} - \frac{p_2}{4\,c^2\,p_1};$$

which is the Marshallian demand for the good x_2.

3.3.2 The Indirect Utility Function

It is obtained by substituting the Marshallian demands in the utility function:

$$V(\mathbf{p},y)=u\left(x_1^*,x_2^*\right)=\frac{p_2}{2\,c\,p_1}+c\left[\frac{y}{p_2}-\frac{p_2}{4\,c^2\,p_1}\right]=\frac{p_2}{2\,c\,p_1}+\frac{cy}{p_2}-\frac{p_2}{4\,c\,p_1}$$

$$V(\mathbf{p},y)=\frac{p_2}{4\,c\,p_1}+\frac{c\,y}{p_2}.$$

3.3.3 The Expenditure Function

It can be obtained by solving $y = G$ (for duality) in the indirect function V (since $u = V$)

$$u=V(\mathbf{p},y)=\frac{p_2}{4\,c\,p_1}+\frac{c\,y}{p_2}$$

$$u-\frac{p_2}{4\,c\,p_1}=\frac{c\,y}{p_2}\rightarrow G(\mathbf{p},u)=\frac{u\,p_2}{c}-\frac{p_2^2}{4\,c^2\,p_1}$$

3.3.4 Roy's Identity

We can prove Roy's identity:

$$\left.\begin{array}{l}\dfrac{\partial V}{\partial p_1}=\dfrac{-p_2}{4\,c\,p_1{}^2}\\[2ex] \dfrac{\partial V}{\partial y}=\dfrac{c}{p_2}\end{array}\right\}\rightarrow-\frac{\dfrac{\partial V}{\partial p_1}}{\dfrac{\partial V}{\partial y}}=\frac{\dfrac{p_2}{4\,c\,p_1{}^2}}{\dfrac{c}{p_2}}=\frac{p_2{}^2}{4\,c^2\,p_1{}^2}=x_1(\mathbf{p},y).$$

3.3.5 Hotelling's Theorem: Hicksian Demand Functions

Through Hotelling's Theorem we have the following Hicksian demand functions:

$$h_1(\mathbf{p},u)=\frac{\partial G(\mathbf{p},u)}{\partial p_1}=\frac{-p_2^2}{4\,c^2}\frac{-1}{p_1^2}=\frac{p_2^2}{4c^2\,p_1^2}=h_1=x_1.$$

It can be observed that the Hicksian demand for the good x_1 coincides with its Marshallian demand since the income effect on this good is null $\partial x_1/\partial y = 0$.

Besides, the Hicksian demand for the good x_2 is

$$h_2(\mathbf{p},u)=\frac{\partial G}{\partial p_2}=\frac{u}{c}-\frac{p_2}{2\,c^2 p_1}=h_2(\mathbf{p},u).$$

3.3.6 Application to the Particular Quasi-linear Utility Function

Observe that the demand function restrictions are satisfied in the particular case

$$f(x_1) = \ln x_1.$$

3.3.6.1 The Marshallian Demand

The Marshallian demand for x_1 is

$$f'(x_1) = \frac{1}{x_1} = \frac{c\,p_1}{p_2} \rightarrow x_1(\mathbf{p}, y) = \frac{p_2}{c\,p_1},$$

with respect to x_2

$$y = \left(\frac{p_2}{c}\right) + p_2 x_2 \rightarrow x_2(\mathbf{p}, y) = \frac{y}{p_2} - \frac{1}{c}.$$

3.3.6.2 Restrictions of the Quasi-linear Demand System

Homogeneity Condition

The corresponding elasticities are

$$\left.\begin{aligned} \varepsilon_{11} &= \frac{\partial x_1}{\partial p_1}\frac{p_1}{x_1} = \frac{-p_2}{c\,p_1^2}\frac{p_1}{\frac{p_2}{c\,p_1}} = -1 \\ \varepsilon_{12} &= \frac{\partial x_1}{\partial p_2}\frac{p_2}{x_1} = \frac{1}{c\,p_1}\frac{p_2}{\frac{p_2}{c\,p_1}} = 1 \\ \varepsilon_{1y} &= \frac{\partial x_1}{\partial y}\frac{y}{x_1} = 0 \end{aligned}\right\} \rightarrow \varepsilon_{11} + \varepsilon_{12} + \varepsilon_{1y} = 0,$$

which satisfy the Homogeneity Condition:

$$\left.\begin{aligned} \varepsilon_{22} &= \frac{-y}{p_2^2}\frac{p_2}{\frac{y c - p_2}{c\,p_2}} = \frac{-y}{y - \frac{p_2}{c}} \\ \varepsilon_{21} &= 0 \\ \varepsilon_{2y} &= \frac{1}{p_2}\frac{y}{\frac{c y - p_2}{p_2 c}} = \frac{y}{y - \frac{p_2}{c}} \end{aligned}\right\} \rightarrow \varepsilon_{22} + \varepsilon_{21} + \varepsilon_{2y} = 0.$$

The Homogeneity Condition is therefore satisfied.

Engel Aggregation Condition

$$s_1\,\varepsilon_{1y}+s_2\,\varepsilon_{2y}=1$$

$$\frac{p_1x_1}{y}0+\frac{p_2x_2}{y}\frac{y}{y-\frac{p_2}{c}}=\frac{p_2\frac{yc-p_2}{p_2\,c}}{y-\frac{p_2}{c}}=\frac{y-\frac{p_2}{c}}{y-\frac{p_2}{c}}=1.$$

The property is satisfied.

Cournot Aggregation Condition

$$s_1\varepsilon_{12}+s_2\,\varepsilon_{22}=-s_2\Rightarrow s_1\,\varepsilon_{12}+s_2(\varepsilon_{22}+1)=0$$

$$\frac{p_1x_1}{y}1+\frac{p_2x_2}{y}\left[1-\frac{y}{y-\frac{p_2}{c}}\right]=\frac{p_1x_1+p_2x_2}{y}-\frac{p_2x_2}{y-\frac{p_2}{c}}=$$

$$=1-\frac{p_2\left(\frac{yc-p_2}{p_2c}\right)}{y-\frac{p_2}{c}}=1-\frac{y-\frac{p_2}{c}}{y-\frac{p_2}{c}}=0.$$

The property is satisfied.

Cross-Effect Symmetry or Integrability Condition

$$s_{12}=s_{21}\rightarrow\frac{\partial h_1}{\partial p_2}=\frac{\partial h_2}{\partial p_1}.$$

Through the Slutsky equation:

$$\left.\begin{aligned}\frac{\partial h_2}{\partial p_1}&=\frac{\partial x_2}{\partial p_1}+x_1\frac{\partial x_2}{\partial y}=0+\left(\frac{p_2}{c\,p_1}\right)\frac{1}{p_2}=\frac{1}{c\,p_1}\\ \frac{\partial h_1}{\partial p_2}&=\frac{\partial x_1}{\partial p_2}+x_2\frac{\partial x_1}{\partial y}=\frac{1}{c\,p_1}+x_2\,0=\frac{1}{c\,p_1}\end{aligned}\right\};$$

the property is satisfied.

Negativity Condition

The matrix of the substitution terms must be negative semidefinite (concavity).

$$s_{11}=\frac{\partial h_1}{\partial p_1}=\frac{\partial x_1}{\partial p_1}+x_1\frac{\partial x_1}{\partial y}=\frac{-p_2}{c\,p_1{}^2}$$

$$s_{22} = \frac{\partial h_2}{\partial p_2} = \frac{\partial x_2}{\partial p_2} + x_2 \frac{\partial x_2}{\partial y} = \frac{-y}{p_2^2} + \frac{yc - p_2}{c p_2}\frac{1}{p_2} = \frac{-y}{p_2^2} + \frac{y - \frac{p_2}{c}}{p_2^2} = \frac{-1}{p_2 c}$$

then,

$$S = \begin{bmatrix} s_{11} & s_{12} \\ s_{21} & s_{22} \end{bmatrix} = \begin{vmatrix} \frac{-p_2}{c p_1^2} & \frac{1}{c p_1} \\ \frac{1}{c p_1} & \frac{-1}{p_2 c} \end{vmatrix}$$

It is satisfied that:

$S_{11} \leq 0$

$\det [S] \geq 0$

$(-1)^n S_n \geq 0$;

the concavity is guaranteed.

Recommended Reading

Bergstrom, T.C., Varian, H.R.: Workouts in Intermediate Microeconomics, 2nd ed. USA: W. W. Norton & Company, Inc. 1990

Gravelle, H., Rees, R.: Microeconomics. 2nd ed. London: Longman Group, Ltd. 1995

Henderson, J.M., Quandt, R.E.: Microeconomic Theory. A Mathematical Approach. 3rd ed. New York: Mc Graw-Hill Book Company, Inc. 1985

Madden, P.: Concavity and Optimisation in Microeconomics. Basil Blackwell, Ltd. Oxford, U.K. 1986

Sher, N., Pinola, L.: Microeconomic Theory. Elsevier, North Holland Inc. 1980

Silberberg, E.: The Structure of Economics. A Mathematical Analysis, 2nd ed. Singapore: Mc Graw-Hill Publishing Company 1991

Varian, H.: Microeconomic Analysis. 3rd ed. USA: W. W. Norton & Company, Inc. 1992

4 Study of the Econometric Applications: Demand Functions and Systems

Consumer Marshallian demand functions are obtained by maximising the utility function (objective function) subject to a budget constraint. However, the consumer utility function is not directly observed, while its level of income and the quantities demanded are.

Therefore, it is possible to estimate empirically either the demand functions of just one good or service, or, otherwise, a demand system for more than two goods.

4.1 Demand Functions

In spite of dealing with demand functions for just one good, we actually use two goods, on the one hand, the good or service to be studied and on the other, the good or service which represents the remainder. Thus, we have the utility maximisation problem below:

$$\left.\begin{array}{ll} \max & U(x_1, x_2) \\ \\ \text{s. to} & y = p_1 x_1 + p_2 x_2 \end{array}\right\}$$

where x_1 and x_2 are the real quantities bought of good x_1 and x_2, the real quantities bought of the rest of goods p_1 and p_2, and the prices of x_1 and x_2; while variable "y" accounts for the amount of income spent by the consumer when buying x_1 and x_2.

The Marshallian demand function is as follows:

$$y_1 = y_1(p_1, p_2, y)$$

Since this demand function is homogeneous of degree zero, it can be written as

$$y = y_1\left(\frac{p_1}{p_2}, \frac{p_2}{p_2}, \frac{y}{p_2}\right)$$

where p_1 is the nominal price of the good x_1 and 'y' is the 'nominal income' so that p_1/p_2 is the relative price of x_1 and y/p_2 is the 'real income'.

There are several functional forms or expressions of demand functions, which, naturally, vary when a utility function of a specific type, such as that seen in chapter 1, is assumed. Depending on the utility function characterisation, whether it is Cobb-Douglas, Quasi-linear or CES, among others, we have Marshallian demands which depend only on the income and price of the good to be studied, the prices of both goods rather than their income, as mentioned for quasi-linear function in which $f(x_1) = x_1^{1/2}$, and the income and prices of both goods or services in the event that a CES utility function is assumed.

So far, we have shown that it is possible to obtain the Marshallian demand functions, however, nothing has been mentioned about Hicksian or Compensated demand functions. Since they are not directly observed, it is possible to use an indirect method to estimate relevant parameters for the Hicksian demands, which consists of putting forward the formerly seen Slutsky equation, in elasticity terms, and replacing the observed values of the Marshallian elasticities and of the corresponding expenditure share.

Moreover, the estimations of the Marshallian demand function parameters allow us to know automatically the estimations of indirect utility function parameters, from which a wide range of predictions of all kinds can be made.

With the aim to illustrate such predictions, we provide the following research on passenger demand functions, which allows us to obtain short and long-run elasticities of all kinds (price, cross, income).

4.2 Application I for Demand Functions: Walrasian (or Marshallian) Demand Functions for Interurban Passenger Transport[1]

The initial models of passenger transport demand were the aggregate "modal split models" in which there was an attempt to determine the number of journeys between a given set of modes of transport for two towns, taking into account the passengers' characteristics. Studies on modal split, such as Quandt and Baumol (1966), Boyer (1977), and Levin (1978), were criticised by Oum (1979) and Winston (1985), among others, for the few variables representing the motivation in the consumer behaviour, and for using very simple linear patterns in their estimations.

Several models of aggregate passenger transport demand based on the consumer behaviour, were carried out in order to improve the previous ones. The user's utility is optimised in these models, in line with the classic theory of the consumer behaviour and demand. The work by Oum and Guillen (1979) is a typical example in which the passenger demand in Canada is analysed.

Some disaggregate research has also been done on passenger transport demand, taking into account the consumer behaviour, the most significant one being McFadden (1973, 1974). In his works, the user takes a discrete choice of some of

[1] This research has been done with the collaboration of J. Baños-Pino and V. Inglada. A much wider and more detailed version of this work entitled "Marshallian Demands of Intercity Passenger Transport in Spain: 1980-1992. An Economic Analysis", has been published in Transportation Research: Part E: Logistics and Transportation Review 33-2, 79-96 (1997). © Elsevier Science Ltd.

the different modes of transport (railway, air, road transport, etc.) and it is assumed that the mode chosen optimises the utility for the user.
Spanish intercity passenger transport was first studied in Coto-Millán et al. (1994), and Coto-Millán et al. (1997). In the works by Coto-Millán et al. (1994), uniequational models were carried out in order to estimate income elasticities, using the Industrial Production Index (IPI) and Electric Power Consumption (CENER) for the 1980.01-1988.12 period, and monthly data was used in the estimations. In these works, the series were also modelled by the Box-Jenkins methodology.

An original model is offered in this paper in order to estimate price income and cross elasticities for the 1980.I-1992.IV period, by applying cointegration techniques and using monthly data. Such techniques allow us the estimation of short term elasticities, which add immediate responses to price and income changes, and long term elasticities which show the effects of price and/or income changes taking place later on.

This research will offer a model according to the second proposal above, following a microeconomic analysis and which can be considered as classic. Its structure is very simple. In the first section we present a theoretical model for the Spanish passenger transport demand. In the second section we describe the data used. The third point presents the estimations based on the different demands and finally, the main conclusions are offered in the fourth section.

4.2.1 Model

Assume a typical user whose preferences of goods verify the weak separability condition. Thus, modelling of passenger transport service demand constitutes the second stage in a two-stage budget process. That is to say, firstly, the user's income falls into two big spending categories: passenger transport services and the rest of the goods and services; secondly, the user's income is assigned to the goods and services contained in each of these two categories. That is to say, the utility function of the representative user is

$$U = U(X_1, X_2, \ldots X_k; X_k+1, \ldots, X_n)$$

where vector $X_i = (X_1, X_2, \ldots X_k)$; with i= 1, 2,..., k represents passenger transport services; vector $X_j = (X_{k+1}, \ldots, X_n)$; j= k+1,...n represents the goods and services except for those corresponding to passenger transport; and U represents a utility function which is continuous and differentiable, monotonic, increasing, and strictly quasi-concave.

The consumer equilibrium will be reduced to:

$$\max U(X_i; X_j)$$

$$\text{s. to: } P_i \cdot X_i + P_j \cdot X_j = Y$$

where the prices $P_i = (P_1, P_2, \ldots, P_k)$ and $P_j = (P_{k+1}, \ldots, P_n)$, and where Y represents the user's level of income.

First-order conditions allow us to obtain the following typical consumer Marshallian demands:

$$Xi = Xi(Pi, Pj, Y)$$

$$Xj = Xj\,(Pi, Pj, Y) \tag{4.1}$$

Of these individual demand functions, we find function (4.1) particularly interesting since it corresponds to passenger transport service.

Equation (4.1) still presents some problems. Firstly, functions such as this one should be valid for any income distribution among the different economic agents. If this were not the case, function (4.1) would provide as many values as income Y distributions among the users were possible and, therefore, such a function would not exist. Another assumption would be that income is distributed under a specific rule. Once this rule has been established, integrability conditions are verified and the existence of the aggregate Marshallian demand functions is guaranteed; Varian (1992). However, there is not data to go along these lines. In order to solve this problem we can assume in this study that all the users have the same level of income.

Function (4.1) is general enough to analyse passenger air and road transport service demands identifying the different subindexes for the amounts demanded in each service.

From 1980.I to 1992.IV, passenger transport service in Spain has been provided under different regulation conditions. The government company Iberia have the monopoly of air national transport in Spain respectively, and road transport is provided by private companies which have exclusive routes under a system called "right of testing". Liner regular road passenger transport is the most used and is regulated, while free road passenger transport (non-liner regular) is less demanded by users in Spain and is not regulated. However, given the impossibility to obtain quarterly statistical data on passenger road transport, and with the aim of approximating the interregional transport on the user's own vehicles, the premium petrol consumption variable has been used. Consumption of premium petrol has also been regulated by the government during the period of this study. Under such regulation conditions and with the aim of avoiding any problems arising from supply-demand simultaneity, we assume that the supply is exogenous in relation with prices and income and is determined by the government's decisions.

4.2.2 Data

The data on the series of passenger departures and arrivals in Spanish airports (AERV), has been obtained from the series provided by the Reports on the State of the Ministry of Transport, Tourism and Communication. No data on road transport passengers is available and the premium petrol consumption "proxy" has been used in order to approach the transport on the user's own vehicles. The QGAS variable has been obtained from the Ministry of Industry and Energy. The gas oil consumption variable (QGLEO) has also been used with the aim to approach the behaviour of regular (and trump) passenger transport in public services. However, the results obtained are significantly anomalous, and the reason for this may be that this variable shows the behaviour of road transport of goods (much more important in terms of consumption) rather than of passengers.

The data on the series of air transport tariffs (PA), has been obtained from the monthly series worked out from the tariffs of the Official State Reports, evaluated within the period in which each tariff is in force.

The data on the prices of premium petrol (PGAS) has been provided by the General Management of the Finance Ministry Forecast and State, as monthly data, also evaluated within the period in which each tariff is in force.

The data on the prices of gas oil (PGLEO) has been obtained from CAMPSA, until 1992. From then onwards, the data from the Hydrocarbon Logistic Company have been recorded for further studies.

The data on the income variable has been obtained considering the Spanish quarterly GDP as "proxy".

4.2.3 Walrasian (or Marshallian) Demands for Interurban Passenger Transport: Air and Road Transport

Equations have been estimated from the specifications of model (4.1) adjusting the variables to each mode of transport. All variables headed by letter L are in natural logs and those headed by letter D are in differences, except for the dummy variables D89.I, DS90.I, D81.I, and D89.II, which will be properly defined later on in this research. The statistical “t” is presented within brackets under each coefficient.

A cointegration approach, which has provided the most successful results of the several approaches previously attempted, Coto-Millán et al. (1994)), has been applied to obtain the estimations. For more information about this subject, see Engel and Granger (1987), Johansen and Juselius (1990), and Osterwald-Lenum (1992).

4.2.3.1 *Air Transport Demand*

Long-run

The estimated long-run equation of equilibrium cointegration gives the following results:

$$LAERV_t = \underset{(2.1620)}{2.8299} - \underset{(7.9687)}{1.2658}\, LPA_t + \underset{(19.5161)}{1.3265}\, LGDP_t.$$

R^2 adjusted = 0.93;
S.E. = 0.05;
DW = 1.07;
DF* = -3.83;
DW** = 2.08.
* Indicate statistical significance at the 10% level.
** Is the Durbin-Watson from the equation used to compute DF statistic.

In addition, if the Johansen methodology is applied to a VAR along with three lags and restricted constant, it is also concluded that there is only one cointegration vector.

After normalisation, the following cointegration relationship is obtained:

$$LAERV_t = 9.32 - 1.95\, LPA_t + 1.04\, LGDP_y.$$

In both estimated equations, the long-run elasticity of air transport demand with respect to the GDP is close to the unit or somewhat higher, with values 1.16 and

1.47, as it would correspond to normal goods and particularly to luxury goods. The estimated long-run elasticity of the own price of the good is negative with values ranging from 1.38 to 1.40, which reflects a significant response of demand to price changes.

Short-run

Short-run non-lineal and joint equation presents the following results:

$$DLAERV_t = -\underset{(5.0968)}{0.5661}\,(LAERV_{t-1} + \underset{(3.92)}{5.41} + \underset{(5.4592)}{1.5237}\,LPA_{t-1} - \underset{(11.2494)}{1.3138}\,LGDP_{t-1}) - \underset{(2.1681)}{0.423}\,DLPA_t + \underset{(2.3997)}{0.4621}\,DLPGAS_t - \underset{(3.1249)}{0.1123}\,D91.I.$$

R^2 adjusted = 0.97;
S.E. = 0.033;
F = 315.10;
DW = 1.85;
N(2) = 3.4969
ARCH (4) = 2.3194
LM(1) = 0.5013
Q(1)= 0.2218
LM(4) = 4.2837
Q(4) = 2.7744
Q(8) = 9.8620

D91.I is a dummy variable which accounts for the effects of a worker's strike in Iberia during the first term of 1991 with value 1 in this period, and 0 during the rest of the year.

The long-run elasticities obtained for this and the previous model do not differ from each other significantly. Then, long-run income elasticity is now 0.80, in comparison with the former values 1.16 and 1.47, as it corresponds to normal goods or services with an average elasticity of 1.143 close to the unit. Air transport is getting a normal good of unitary elasticity rather that a luxury good, as it was stated in Coto-Millán et al. (1994), with an estimated income-elasticity value of 1.61, from 1980.01 to 1988.12.

The negative value of the own price elasticity of the good is 0.775, in comparison with the former 1.38 and 1.40 values. The variation here is more significant although the average elasticity is 1.185.

Short and long-run elasticities are again slightly different. Short-run elasticities clearly present the inelastic feature of the demand and a substitution effect of road transport, which has never revealed before, is captured. These estimations yield again gross and net substitution relationships between air and road transport.

4.2.3.2 Road Transport Demand

Long-run

In intercity passenger road transport demand equation, the dependent variable LQGAS is the amount of premium petrol, in logs:

$$LQGAS_t = \underset{(1.4118)}{-2.3263} \ \underset{(2.2964)}{-0.1643\ LPGAS_t} \ \underset{(7.0102)}{+1.0334\ LGDP_t}.$$

R^2 adjusted = 0.94;
S.E. = 0.03;
DW = 1.72;
DF* = -6.15;
DW** = 1.96.
* Indicate statistical significance at the 1% level.
** Is the Durbin-Watson from the equation used to compute DF statistic.

Applying the Johansen methodology to a VAR with a lag and a restricted constant, it is also concluded that there is only one cointegration vector.

After normalisation, the following cointegration relationship is obtained:

$$LQGAS_t = -1.03 \quad -0.33\ LPGAS_t \quad +0.74\ LGDP_t.$$

The results obtained from the long-run estimations provide elasticities of 0.361 and 1.11 with respect to the GDP, relationships which characterise these services as basic goods rather than as luxury goods, always within the context of normal goods. The own price elasticities of the good get the negative values of 0.13 and 0.47, again referring to basic goods with inelastic demand and slight demand variations as a response to price changes (if we consider these changes as proportional to the prices changes premium petrol).

The gasoil demand equation QGLEO presents very similar values between its price and the GDP variable.

Short-run

The non lineal estimation in only one stage of road demand, provided the following results:

$$DLQGAS_t = \underset{(5.0382)}{-0.7662}\,(LQGAS_{t-1} \ \underset{(0.4007)}{+0.8814} \ \underset{(2.5316)}{+0.2387}\ LPGAS_{t-1}$$

$$\underset{(4.7223)}{-0.9099}\ DLGDP_{t-1}) \ \underset{(2.2555)}{-0.5346}\ DLPGAS_t \ \underset{(2.2053)}{+0.4199}\ DLPA_t.$$

R^2 adjusted = 0.95;
S.E. = 0.037;
F = 192.43;
DW = 2.03;
N(2) = 2.7456;
ARCH (4) = 0.2611;
LM(1) = 0.4633;
Q(1)= 0.0545;
LM(4) = 4.3756;
Q(4) = 3.7064;
Q(8) = 9.4150.

The value of GDP long-run demand elasticity now obtained of 0.765, confirms the inelasticity of the income "proxy", regarding services as basic. The same happens with QGLEO demand, which considers the regular line intercity passenger transport demand as "proxy". The negative value of long-run elasticities of the own price of the good in this model is 0.10, while the former values were 0.13 and 0.47.

The short-run elasticities estimated provide the own price of the good with the negative value 0.36 and a cross elasticity of 0.34 with respect to the price of air transport. At short-run, it is possible to speak about gross substitution relationships between road and air transport. However, we cannot meet any conclusion with respect to net substitution or complementary relationships of these transport services without any further assumption.

4.2.4 Results of the Empirical Research

A theoretical model of air passenger transport demand has been presented in this paper. With quarterly aggregated Spanish monthly data, equations of intercity air and road passenger transport demand have been specified for 1980.I and 1992.IV.

Different demand function estimations have been carried out using cointegration techniques, and have been widely evaluated, which allows us to check the adequacy of this method with respect to others used in previous works by Coto-Millán et al. (1994).

Each specific demand may require more detailed studies, especially road transport. However, having made the estimations, the following conclusions are met for income, the own price of the good and cross price elasticities:

- Long-run income elasticities are all positive and all the services are normal goods. Income elasticities are very close to the unit for air transport, and slightly below the unit for road transport.
- The own price elasticities of the good increase parallel to the quality of the service, since they increase with tariffs, and present values close to the unit for air transport. They are clearly inelastic for road transport.
- All cross elasticities present positive values below the unit. Gross and net long-run substitution relationships between air and road transport and gross substitution relationships between road and air transport can be guaranteed, but net substitution relationships between the latter pair cannot.

These estimations can be useful for the analysis and predictions of the effects of price changes, as well as for traffic and short and long-run income predictions.

4.3 Complete Demand Systems

As it has already been mentioned, it is possible to estimate a demand function system for more than two goods. In this case, it is most appropriate to consider firstly a functional form for demand equations and then, try to integrate them to obtain a utility function. However, the most common procedure used, allowing a less complex empirical treatment, consists of either specifying firstly, a functional form of utility or of the indirect utility function, and then posing the problem of maximisation, or differentiating it to obtain the Marshallian demand functions.

Following on, we present the most empirically used systems: The Linear Expenditure System (LES) and the Almost Ideal System (AIDS), the Diewert Model and the Translog Model.

4.3.1 Linear Expenditure System (LES)

The LES is the most frequently estimated demand model since its formulation by Klein and Rubin (1948) and Stone (1954). Moreover, many versions of this model allow to include time trends in the values γ_i.

Given a utility function $U(\mathbf{x})$ with a functional form

$$U(\mathbf{x}) = \alpha_i \left[\sum_{i=1}^{k} \ln(x_i - \gamma_i) \right]$$

where $x_i > \gamma_i$, where x_i represents the quantity of each good, and $\gamma_i \geq 0$ is the subsistence consumption of the good x_i and is always a positive parameter.

The problem of utility maximisation subject to budget constraint is:

$$\max \; L(x_i, \lambda) = \alpha_i \sum_{i=1}^{k} \ln(x_i - \gamma_i) - \lambda \left(\sum_{i=1}^{k} p_i x_i - y \right)$$

$$\left.\begin{array}{l}
\dfrac{\partial L}{\partial x_1} = 0 = \alpha_1 \dfrac{1}{x_1 - \gamma_1} - \lambda p_1 \\[2ex]
\dfrac{\partial L}{\partial x_2} = 0 = \alpha_2 \dfrac{1}{x_2 - \gamma_2} - \lambda p_2 \\[2ex]
\ldots\ldots \\[2ex]
\dfrac{\partial L}{\partial x_k} = 0 = \alpha_k \dfrac{1}{x_k - \gamma_k} - \lambda p_k \\[2ex]
\dfrac{\partial L}{\partial \lambda} = 0 = y - \sum_{i=1}^{k} p_i \, x_i = 0
\end{array}\right\}$$

where x_1, x_2... are the Marshallian demands similar to the derivates of the utility functions.

Focusing on two goods, the budget constraint is:

$$p_1 x_1 + p_2 x_2 = y$$

The auxiliar Lagrangian is:

$$L(x_1, x_2, \lambda) = \alpha_1 \text{Ln} \quad (x_1 - \gamma_1) + x_2 \text{ Ln}(x_2 - \gamma_2) - \lambda [p_1 x_1 + p_2 x_2 - y]$$

$$\left.\begin{aligned} \frac{\partial L}{\partial x_1} &= \frac{\alpha_1}{x_1 - \gamma_1} - \lambda p_1 = 0 \\ \frac{\partial L}{\partial x_2} &= \frac{\alpha_2}{x_2 - \gamma_2} - \lambda p_2 = 0 \\ \frac{\partial L}{\partial \lambda} &= -(p_1 x_1 + p_2 x_2) + y = 0 \end{aligned}\right\}$$

$$\lambda = \frac{\alpha_1}{p_1 x_1 - p_1 \gamma_1} = \frac{\alpha_2}{p_2 x_2 - p_2 \gamma_2};$$

from which $\alpha_1 + \alpha_2 = 1$,

$$\lambda = \frac{1}{y - (p_1 \gamma_1 - p_2 \gamma_2)}$$

by substituting λ in the first-order conditions we obtain

$$\begin{aligned} p_1 x_1 &= p_1 \gamma_1 + \alpha_1 (y - (p_1 \gamma_1 + p_2 \gamma_2)) \\ p_2 x_2 &= p_2 \gamma_2 + \alpha_2 (y - (p_1 \gamma_1 + p_2 \gamma_2)) \end{aligned}$$

from which

$$x_1 = x_1 (p_1, p_2, y) = \gamma_1 + \frac{\alpha_1 (y - (p_1 \gamma_1 + p_2 \gamma_2))}{p_1}$$

$$x_2 = x_2 (p_1, p_2, y) = \gamma_2 + \frac{\alpha_2 (y - (p_1 \gamma_1 + p_2 \gamma_2))}{p_2}$$

4.3.2 Almost Ideal Demand System

The Almost Ideal Demand System is derived from an expenditure function such as:

$$G(\mathbf{p}, u) = a(\mathbf{p})\, b(\mathbf{p})^u$$

taking logs in the expression above

$$\log G(\mathbf{p}, u) = \log a(\mathbf{p}) + u \log b(\mathbf{p})$$

where

$$\log a(\mathbf{p}) = \alpha_0 + \sum_i \alpha_i \log p_i + \frac{1}{2} \sum_i \sum_j \gamma_{ij}^{*} \log p_i \log p_m$$

$$\log b(\mathbf{p}) = \beta_0 \prod_i p_i^{\beta_i}$$

Since G (**p**, u) must be homogeneous in **p** and a (**p**), b (**p**) are positive, degree-zero linear-homogeneous and concave functions in **p**, the following conditions must be met:

$$\sum_{i=1}^{k} \alpha_i = 1$$

$$\sum_{i=1}^{k} \gamma_{ij}^{*} = \sum_{j=1}^{k} \gamma_{ji}^{*} = \sum_{i=1}^{k} \beta_i = 0$$

Note that, when u=0 , a (**p**) is the consumer subsistence expenditure.

If log G (**p**, u) is replaced by the expressions relative to log a (**p**) and log b (**p**) we have:

$$\log G(\mathbf{p}, u) = \alpha_0 + \sum_i \alpha_i \log p_i + \frac{1}{2} \sum_i \sum_j \gamma_{ij}^{*} \log p_i \log p_m + u\beta_0 \prod_i p_i^{\beta_i}$$

Applying Hotelling's Theorem it is possible to obtain the Hicksian or Compensated demand functions, that is to say

$$\frac{\partial \log G(\mathbf{p}, u)}{\partial \log p_i} = \frac{h_i(\mathbf{p}, u)\, p_i}{G\,(p, u)} = S_i.$$

Since the Hicksian demand functions are not directly observed, for an empirical treatment, it is usual to estimate a system of expenditure rates such as:

$$S_i = \alpha_i + \sum_{j=i}^{k} \gamma_{ij} \log p_i + \beta_i \log\left(\frac{y}{P}\right)$$

where P is the price index given by

$$\log P = \alpha_0 + \sum_{i=1}^{k} \alpha_i \log p_i + \frac{1}{2} \sum_{i=1}^{k} \sum_{j=1}^{k} \gamma_{ij} \log p_i p_j.$$

This system is almost linear with the only exception of term P, which represents the price index.

4.3.3 Diewert Demand Model

Dierwert (1971), proposes the use of the Leontief indirect utility function V (**L**), where

$$\mathbf{L} = \frac{\mathbf{p}}{y} = \left(\frac{p_1}{y}, \frac{p_2}{y}, \ldots, \frac{p_n}{y}\right) = (L_1, L_2, \ldots, L_n)$$

and where V (**L**) can be specified as

$$V(\mathbf{L}) = \sum_{i=1}^{n} \sum_{j=1}^{m} b_{ij} L_i^{\frac{1}{2}} L_j^{\frac{1}{2}} + 2 \sum_{j=1}^{m} b_{0j} L_j^{\frac{1}{2}} + b_{00}$$

where

$$b_{ij} = b_{ji}; b_{ij} \geq 0$$

so that, by applying Roy's identity, it is possible to obtain the Marshallian demand functions:

$$x_i = x_i(L_1,...,L_n) = x_i\left(\frac{p_1}{y_1},...,\frac{p_n}{y_n}\right)$$

that is to say

$$x_i = \frac{\left[\sum_{j=1}^{n} b_{ij} p_i^{-1/2} p_j^{-1/2}\right] y}{\sum_{k=1}^{n}\sum_{m=1}^{n} b_{km} p_k^{1/2} p_m^{1/2}}$$

4.3.4 Translog Demand Model

By this we refer to the demand function systems obtained from a logarithmic transcendental indirect utility function such as:

$$\log V(\mathbf{L}) = \alpha_0 + \sum_{i=1}^{n} \alpha_i \log L_i + \frac{1}{2}\sum_{i=1}^{n}\sum_{j=1}^{n} \beta_{ij} \log L_j$$

where L is the quotient of price vector **p** and the level of income y. Then, it must be satisfied that

$$\beta_{ij} = \beta_{ji};\ \sum_{i=1}^{n} \alpha_i = 1\ ;\ \sum_{j=1}^{n} \beta_{ij} = 0$$

so that such a function is homogeneous of degree one in prices **p**.

The following is a demand equation system obtained from the former function and restrictions-n:

$$x_i = x_i(\mathbf{L}) = x_i(\mathbf{p}, y) = \frac{L_i^{-1}\left(\alpha_i + \sum_{j=1}^{n} \beta_{ij} \log L_j\right)}{\sum_{k=1}^{n} \alpha_k + \sum_{k=1}^{n}\sum_{m=1}^{n} \beta_{km} \log L_m}$$

$$\forall i = 1,2,...,n$$

4.4 Application II for Demand Systems : Estimation of an Almost Ideal Demand System (AIDS): Particular Disaggregation for the Main Transport Services[2]

The main purpose of this study is to analyse transport demand using a complete demand system approach. There are other approaches to analyse transport service demand such as those provided by uniequational models, Probit and Logit - but the information they provide is different - and they are usually disaggregated for a particular transport route or line. In the present approach, the information refers to several expenditure groups on which consumers spend their income. Such an exposure allows us to estimate richer and more accurate economic information for goods and services and budget restriction than that provided by other approaches.

From the early fifties, equations systems of goods and service demand began to be estimated for two main purposes: firstly, for obtaining the most characteristic features of the markets of these goods and services; and secondly, for making predictions about consumers' behaviour. These objectives have also led to the formulation of different specifications for the demand systems in an attempt to account for more effects and less restrictions and which, in short, tried to provide increasingly perfected demand systems. The complete demand systems which have been most widely used are: The Linear Expenditure System (LES, Stone (1954)), Rotterdam Model (RM, Theil, (1965)) and the Almost Ideal Demand System (AIDS, Deaton and Muellbauer (1980a)). These models have been generally made for big groups of goods and services of the type: food, clothes and footwear, rental property, energy, etc., in which transport constitutes a broad and heterogeneous group of services. On the whole, transport is grouped along with energy and communications of every kind such as posting, telephone, telex, etc.. Literature has focused mainly on the study of the behaviour of the demand for these big groups of goods and services, some of them specific such as food. However, there are virtually no studies with reference to transport except for the work by Rolle (1996). The main surveys in transport demand literature are: Waters II (1984), Waters II (1989), Oum, Waters II and Yong (1990), Goodwin, Oum, Waters II and Yong (1991), but no studies using the present approach appear in them.

The present study carried out for Spain can be freely applied to other countries. Undoubtedly, the study carried out for other countries will allow international comparisons of the main results.

4.4.1 Model: Almost Ideal Demand System

As can be seen in Coto-Millán et al (1997), the modeling of transport service demand constitutes the second stage of an intertemporal two-stage budget decision process. If we assume weakly separable preferences among the various big groups of goods and services, there will be a first stage in which individuals allocate their

---

[2] This research has been done with the collaboration of U. Carrascal.

income optimally among the big groups of goods and services, and a second stage in which individuals decide within each group of goods and services how much is going to be spent on each particular goods or service. AIDS is the demand system chosen to model the second stage of this optimisation process. There are plenty of empirical works in the economic literature, on AIDS models for food and general goods and services. The main references for general goods and services are Deaton and Muellbauer (1980) Deaton and Muellbauer (1993). These authors formulated the AIDS system as follows. An initial function G (**p**,u) is first formulated, obtaining from it a compensated demand function system by applying Hotelling's theorem. By the indirect function it is later possible to express utility depending on prices and nominal income (**p**, y), thus obtaining the non-compensated demand functions. The Almost Ideal Demand System is derived from an expenditure function such as:

$$G(\mathbf{p}, u) = a(\mathbf{p})\, b(\mathbf{p})^{u}$$

taking logs in the expression above

$$\log G(\mathbf{p}, u) = \log a(\mathbf{p}) + u \log b(\mathbf{p})$$

where

$$\log a(\mathbf{p}) = \alpha_0 + \sum_i \alpha_i \log p_i + \frac{1}{2}\sum_i \sum_j \gamma_{ij}^{*} \log p_i \log p_m$$

$$\log b(\mathbf{p}) = \beta_0 \prod_i p_i^{\beta_i}$$

By substituting in the expression above the terms log a(**p**) and log b(**p**) for their values and operating in the function we get an almost ideal demand system formed by the following equations:

$$\log G(\mathbf{p}, u) = \alpha_0 + \sum_i \alpha_i \log p_i + \frac{1}{2}\sum_i \sum_j \gamma_{ij}^{*} \log p_i \log p_m + u\beta_0 \prod_i p_i^{\beta_i}.$$

Applying Hotelling's Theorem it is possible to obtain the Hicksian or Compensated demand functions, that is to say

$$\frac{\partial \log G(\mathbf{p}, u)}{\partial \log p_i} = \frac{h_i(\mathbf{p}, u)\, p_i}{G(p, u)} = S_i.$$

Since the Hicksian demand functions are not directly observed, for an empirical treatment, it is usual to estimate a system of expenditure rates such as:

$$S_i = \alpha_i + \sum_{j=i}^{k} \gamma_{ij} \log p_j + \beta_i \log\left(\frac{y}{P}\right)$$

where P is the price index given by

$$\log P = \alpha_0 + \sum_{i=1}^{k} \alpha_i \log p_i + \frac{1}{2}\sum_{i=1}^{k} \sum_{j=1}^{k} \gamma_{ij} \log p_i p_j.$$

This system is almost linear with the only exception of term P, which represents the price index.

4.4.2 Data

In the present work we disaggregate the total expenditure of consumers into the following seven categories:

group 1: food, drinks and tobacco, clothes and footwear, rental property (real or reported) of houses and other housing expenses;
group 2: large home furnishing, transport goods, medical service and health expenses, entertainment, education, culture, driving lessons, car renting, others;
group 3: tires, spare parts, repairing and maintenance, fuel, lubricants, garage, parking, tolls;
group 4: individual and collective urban local transport and underground transport;
group 5: road and railway transport;
group 6: posting and communications;
group 7: telephone and telegraph.

These series have been obtained from the Family Expenditure Survey 1990-1991, which shows the consumption, income and demographic data on Spanish families. The sample accounts for 20,679 Spanish families. For a more detailed analysis of these data, see Carrascal (1997).

4.4.3 Estimation of the Model

The stochastic version of AIDS model is given by the following expression:

$$S_i = \alpha_i + \sum_{j=i}^{k} \gamma_{ij} \log p_j + \beta_i \log\left(\frac{y}{P}\right)$$

where, as usual, we substitute the original price index into price index P (Stone, 1954), which allows us to express the model in terms of linear equations in the parameters

$$\log P = \alpha_0 + \sum_{i=l}^{k} \alpha_i \log p_i + \frac{1}{2} \sum_{i=l}^{k} \sum_{j=l}^{k} \gamma_{ij} \log p_i p_j .$$

The following conditions must be met in the above demand system:

Aggregation Condition (Engel and Cournot):

$$\sum_i \alpha_i = 1 \text{ and } \sum_i \beta_i = \sum_i \gamma_{ij} = 0;$$

Homogeneity:

$$\sum_{i=1}^{n} \gamma_{ij} = 0;$$

Symmetry (or Integrability):

$$\gamma_{ij} = \gamma_{ji} \qquad (i, j, \ldots, n);$$

Negativity:

(s_{ij}) negative semidefinite of degree (n-1).

Subsequently, the restrictions imposed must be subject to a hypothesis testing. The aggregation, homogeneity and symmetry (or integrability) hypotheses are usually tested by a corrected version of the likelihood ratio test with the aim of approximating its asymptotic distribution to a finite distribution. The negativity hypothesis is tested when we observe that the elements of the main diagonal of the cross substitution effect matrix, that is, the Hicksian own price elasticities, are all negative.

Estimating Seemingly Unrelated Regression Equations (SURE) of the type of Zellner (1962) we obtain the following elasticities:

Table 4.1. Estimated elasticities

ε_{11}	-0.88	ε_{21}	-0.10	ε_{31}	-0.13	ε_{41}	-0.14	ε_{51}	-0.07	ε_{61}	-0.34	ε_{71}	-0.03
ε_{12}	-0.17	ε_{22}	-0.78	ε_{32}	-0.07	ε_{42}	-0.03	ε_{52}	0.02	ε_{62}	0.09	ε_{72}	-0.07
ε_{13}	-0.01	ε_{23}	0.00	ε_{33}	-0.88	ε_{43}	-0.03	ε_{53}	-0.00	ε_{63}	0.00	ε_{73}	-0.02
ε_{14}	-0.00	ε_{24}	-0.00	ε_{34}	-0.01	ε_{44}	-0.71	ε_{54}	-0.03	ε_{64}	-0.03	ε_{74}	-0.00
ε_{15}	-0.00	ε_{25}	0.00	ε_{35}	-0.00	ε_{45}	-0.02	ε_{55}	-0.78	ε_{65}	-0.04	ε_{75}	0.00
ε_{16}	-0.00	ε_{26}	-0.00	ε_{36}	-0.00	ε_{46}	0.00	ε_{56}	-0.00	ε_{66}	-0.28	ε_{76}	0.00
ε_{17}	-0.00	ε_{27}	-0.00	ε_{37}	-0.00	ε_{47}	0.00	ε_{57}	0.01	ε_{67}	0.01	ε_{77}	-0.81
ε_{1y}	1.08	ε_{2y}	0.89	ε_{3y}	1.11	ε_{4y}	0.94	ε_{5y}	0.87	ε_{6y}	0.58	ε_{7y}	0.94
df	0.00	df	0.00	df	0.00	df	0.00	df	0.00	df	0.00	df	0.00

* For the estimation of these elasticities the average values of the prices paid by each family have been considered. As happens in the above case, many families (in many cases more than 50%) do not declare these expenses in the surveys, which does not allow us the non-linear estimation.

In table 4.1 we can observe at the bottom line (DIF) that the difference between the sums in each column and the income elasticity for each goods is approximately zero (- 2.5E-06; 3.04E-06; 8.59E-06; -4.8E-05; 5.5E-05; 0.00028 and -1.7E-05), a result that agrees with the conventional consumer theory. Interpreting the estimation results of the elasticities above we can observe that the own price elasticities ε_{11}, ε_{22},... ε_{77} all have a negative sign and are lower than the unit, which is the expected behaviour for inelastic demands. On the other hand, the cross elasticities with a negative sign are predominant, except for ε_{23}, ε_{25}, ε_{52}, ε_{57}, ε_{62}, ε_{63}, ε_{67}, ε_{75}, and ε_{76}. The reason for this behaviour is that the complementary relationships prevail in consumption, as against substitution relationships. Such a result is usual in complete demand systems.

To interpret the substitution relationships, we assume that the effects of the expenditure on goods and services not directly related with transport cancel each other. The substitution relationship between Group 2 and Group 3, that is, the positive sign of ε_{23}, stands out. We assume, as said before, that the effects of expenses other than the purchase of transport goods (vehicles) neutralise each other, then the substitution relationship means that the individuals who spend more on transport goods (in Group 2), spend less on tires, repairing and maintenance, garage, etc.. This is reasonable from the point of view of economic theory. On the other hand, the opposite of the former proposition presents a complementary relationship. Therefore, consumers who spend more on tires, repairing and maintenance, garage, etc. also spend more on the purchase of transport goods (vehicles). Again, the substitution relationship between Group 2 and 5 is interesting. Therefore, consumers who use their own vehicle more, (buy more transport goods, *ceteris paribus*) demand less road and railway transport. The opposite of the former proposition is also true as can be observed in the sign of ε_{52}. The substitution relationships remaining, although they may be of interest for other studies, do not require further commentary for the purpose of this study.

From the estimations above, we observe that only two income elasticities are over the unit: ε_{1y} and ε_{3y}, while the remaining ones are lower than the unit. This is natural if we consider that transport services are essential services. What explains income elasticity ε_{1y} may be that this group includes the rest of the *domestic expenses* and these expenses involve the purchase of houses. It can also be explained by drinks and footwear, which deviate Group 1 slightly towards luxury goods. In ε_{3y} the deviation may spring from the expenses of repairing and maintenance, garage, parking and tolls, which again deviate Group 3 towards luxury goods. However, ε_{2y} , ε_{4y} and ε_{5y} are income elasticities which are clearly lower than the unit, all the results being apparently suitable.

4.4.4 Conclusions

In this study, we have used a complete demand system of AIDS type in order to analyse Spanish transport service demand. The application of a model of these characteristics allows us to obtain information about the expenses by a family in various big groups of goods and services, particularly those corresponding to transport services. The functional form AIDS is flexible and does not impose too many restrictions when the estimation is being carried out. The homogeneity restriction of degree one in prices is verified giving information about the lack of money illusion in the families' behaviour. Symmetry and aggregation restrictions are also verified. The model exposed presents suitable econometric results and provides reasonable own-price, cross and income elasticity estimations, from the point of view of economic theory.

An important conclusion derived from this study, in view of the empirical results, is that the response of transport services demand before price changes is always inelastic. Such inelastic behaviour is higher in urban individual and collective local transport and underground transport than in road and railway transport as well as in one's own vehicle.

Another interesting conclusion is that income elasticities are low (lower than the unit) for transport services. These are just slightly higher than the unit for the goods and services in Group 2, which correspond to tires, spare parts, repairing and maintenance, fuel and lubricants, garage, parking and tolls.

These estimations can be useful as a base for the analysis of political measures regarding tariff changing, as well as for making predictions about traffic and income in the medium term.

Basic References

Afriat, S.: The construction of utility functions from expenditure data. International Economic Review 8, 67-77 (1967)

Barten, A.P.: Estimating demand equations. Econometrica 36, 2, 213-51 (1968)

Deaton, J., Muellbauer, J.: Economics and Consumer Behaviour. 1st re-printed copy of 1980 version. Cambridge, U:K: Cambridge University Press 1993

Deaton, J., Muellbauer, J.: An Almost Ideal Demand System. American Economic Review 70, 3, 312-326 (1980)

Deaton, J., Muellbauer, J.: Functional forms for labour supply and commodity demands with and without quantity restrictions. Econometrica 49, 6, 1521-32 (1981)

Diewert, W.E.: A note on the elasticity of derived demand in the n-factor case. Economica, 192-8 (1971)

Diewert, W.E.: Duality approaches to microeconomic theory. In: Arrow, K. and M. Intriligator Handbook of Mathematical Economics Vol. 2. Amsterdam: North –Holland 1982

Freixas, X., Mas-Collel, A.: Engel curves leading to the weak axiom in the aggregate, Econometrica 55-3, 515-531 (1987)

Hildenbrand, W.: Market Demand: Theory and Empirical Evidence. Princeton: Princeton University Press 1994

Mas-Collel, A., Whinston, M. D., Green, J. R.: Microeconomic theory. New York: Oxford University Press 1995

Muellbauer, J.: Household composition. Engel curves and welfare comparisons between households. European Economic Review 5, 103-122 (1974)

Muellbauer, J.: Identification and consumer unit scales. Econometrica 43-4,807-809 (1975)

Pollak, R., Wales, T. J.: Estimation of Complete Demand Systems from Household Budget Data: The Linear and Quadratic Expenditure Systems. American Economic Review 69, 216-221 (1978)

Stone, J.E.: Linear expenditure system and demand analysis: An application to the pattern of British demand. Economic Journal 64, 511-527 (1954)

Varian, H.: Microeconomic Analysis, 3rd ed. Norton & Company 1992

Zellner, A.: An Efficient Method of Estimating Seemingly Unrelated Regressions and Test for Aggregation Bias. Journal of the American Statistical Association 57, 348-368 (1962)

References and Further Reading

Boyer, K.D.: Minimum Rate Regulations, Modal Split Sensitives, and the Railroad Problem. Journal of Political Economy 85-3, 493-512 (1977)

Coto-Millán, P.: Recent History of OPEC: An Analysis through the functions of demand. Working Paper. University of Oviedo, Department of Economics 1989

Coto-Millán, P.: Determinants of Private Demand for Sea transport in Relation to the International Market: An Empirical Approach. Working Paper. University of Oviedo, Department of Economics 1990

Coto-Millán, P.: The sea transport of coal and iron ore: recent evolution and perspective (I) and (II). Newsletter of EIMS 15 and 16, 32-36 and 39-43 (1991)

Coto-Millán, P.:The sea transport of cement: recent evolution and perspective. Newsletter of EIMS 18, 33-37 (1992)

Coto-Millán, P.: Internal and External Trade according to transportation Means in Spain (1974-1986), (I), (II) and (III). Newsletter of EIMS 21, 22 and 23, 17-23, 17-23 and 17-22 (1993)

Coto-Millán, P.: National Air and road Passenger Transport Competition in Spain. Working Paper.University of Cantabria, Department of Economics 1994

Coto-Millán, P.: Scale of Economies, Elasticities of Substitution and Behavior of the Railway Transport. Working Paper 94.01. University of Cantabria, Department of Economics 1994

Coto-Millán, P.: The conditioned demands of Spanish sea Transport 1975-1990. International Journal of Transport Economics XXII-3, 325-346 1995

Coto-Millán, P.: Intermodal Competition on Inter-Urban Rail: Theoretical and Empirical Microfoundations. International Journal of Transport Economics XXIII-3, 379-382 (1996)

Coto-Millán, P.: Maritime Transport Policy in Spain (1974-1995). Transport Policy. Unit of Transport Studies 3, 37-41. Oxford University 1996

Coto-Millán, P. et al.: Intercity Public Transport in Spain 1980-1988: Elasticities, Prices, Income and Time series. Working Paper. University of Cantabria, Department of Economics 1994

Coto-Millán, P., Baños-Pino, J.: Derived Demands for General Cargo shipping in Spain, 1975-1992, an Economic Approach. Applied Economics Letters 3, 175-178 (1996)

Coto-Millán, P., Carrascal, U.: An Almost Ideal Demand System for Transport Consumer Behaviour. Working Paper. University of Cantabria, Department of Economics 1997

Coto-Millán, P., Carrascal, U.: Estimating Engel Curves for Transport expenditures: evidence from UK household budget data. International Journal of Transport Economics 25-3, 379-80 (1998)

Coto-Millán, P., Baños-Pino, J., Inglada, V.: Marshallian Demands of Intercity Passenger Transport in Spain: 1980-1992. An Economic Analysis. Transportation Research: Part E: Logistics and Transportation Review 33-2, 79-96 (1997)

Goodwin, P. B., Oum, T. H., Waters II, W. G., Yong, J. S.: An Annoted Bibliography on Demand Elasticities. Working Paper 682. Transport Studies Unit, University of Oxford 1991

Goodwin, P.B.: A Review of New Demand Elasticities with Special Reference to Short and Long-Run Effects of price Changes. Journal of Transport Economics and Policy, May, 155-169 (1992)

Johansen, S., Juselius, K.: Maximum likelihood estimation and inference on cointegration with applications to the demand for money. Oxford Bulletin of Economics and Statistics 52, 169-210 (1990)

Levin, R.C.: Allocation in Surface Freight Transportation: Does Rate Regulation Matter?. Bell Journal of Economics 9-1, 18-45 (1978)

McFadden, D.: Conditional Logit Analysis of Qualitative Choice Behavior. In: Zaremka, P. Frontiers in econometrics. NY & London: Academic Press 1973

McFadden, D.: The Measurement of Urban Travel Demand. Journal of Public Economics 3, 303-28 (1974)

Osterwald-Lenum, M.: A Note with Fractiles of the Asymptotic Distribution of the Maximun Likelihood Cointegration Rank Test Statistics: Four Cases. Oxford Bulletin of Economic and Statistics 54, 461-472 (1992)

Oum, T. H.: A warning on the Use Linear of Logits Models in Transport Mode Choice Studies. Bell Journal of Economics 10-1, 374-387 (1979)

Oum, T. H., Guillen, D.: The Structure of intercity Travel Demands in Canada: Theory, Tests and empirical Results. Working Paper 79-18. Queen's University 1979

Oum, T. H., Waters II, W. G., Yong, J. S.: A survey of recent Estimates of Price Elasticities of Demand for Transport. World Bank Working Paper 359. Washington D.C 1990

Quandt, R., Baumol, W.: The demand for Abstract Transport Modes: Theory and Measurement. Journal of Regional Science 6-2, 13-26 (1966)

Rolle, J.D.: Estimation of Swiss railway demand with computation of elasticities. Transportation Research: Part E: Logistics and Transportation Review 33-2, 117-27 (1997)

Stone, R.: The Measurement of Consumer's Expenditure and behaviour in the United Kingdom, 1920-1938 .Vol. I, Cambridge 1954

Waters II, W.G.: A Bibliography of Articles Relevant to Transportation Appearing in Major Economics Journals: 1960-1981. Centre for Transportation Studies, University of British Columbia 1984

Waters II, W.G.: A Bibliography of Articles Relevant to Transportation Appearing in Major Economics Journals: 1982-1987. Centre for Transportation Studies, University of British Columbia 1989

Winston, C.: The Demand for Freight Transportation: Models and Applications. Transportation Research 17, 419-27 (1983)

Winston, C.:Conceptual Developments in the Economics of Transportation: An interpretative survey. Journal of Economic Literature XXIII, 57-94 (1986)

PART II: PRODUCTION AND FIRM SUPPLY ANALYSIS

5 Theory of Production, Cost and Behaviour of the Firm: A Comprehensive Reformulation

Once we have analysed the consumer equilibrium, we shall put forward the points concerning production, for which a similar method to that employed in chapter 1 will be used. In the first section, a brief introduction to the firm's conventional theory will be presented. In the second section, we shall study the production possibility set and the existence of production function. In the next section, we shall present the properties of the production function. Then, we shall pose firstly the most genuine profit maximisation problem subject to a technological restriction, to follow with the same problem fixing the costs, that is, the income maximisation problem subject to a level of cost. A particular case of this problem is obtaining a specific level of production, which makes possible the output maximisation subject to a budget constraint on the acquisition of the inputs so that the firm changes only the suitable level of output. We shall pose the loss minimisation problem which is similar to as the profit maximisation problem and which will be presented next fixing the income, that is, the cost minimisation problem subject to a level of income. Finally, we shall study an especially interesting case of this problem, which is that of cost minimisation subject to a level of output; in this case, the firm will change only the level of cost. In the six cases a perfect competition in the input and output markets is assumed, which means that output prices and demand depend on output market conditions, while input prices -rather than the amount- depend on input market conditions.

The joint production shall also be dealt with in this chapter. On the whole, the firms produce two or more outputs at the same time, a practice which is called joint production. Here we will deal with the most simple case of joint production - that in which there are two outputs and only one input- and include a figure showing the path towards i-input and j-output generalisation. In this case, the firm maximises the profit and minimises the loss for a particular technological restriction for which the levels of output and input costs will be modified. It is possible that the firm wishes either to maximise the level of income for a given level of output, or to minimise the amount of inputs for a level of income. These two alternatives correspond with particular cases of the two initial possibilities of joint production in its most simple case.

In all the above-mentioned sections of this chapter, the firm can modify all the levels of input and therefore, we shall consider this study essentially a long-run analysis. Subsequently, it seems appropriate to include in this chapter a special section for the study of the firm's short-run equilibrium with regard to short-run single production although it will also offer a figure showing the path towards joint production generalisation. Finally, we shall present the elasticity of substitution.

5.1 Theory of the Firm

The conventional theory of the firm, i.e.; that which is reflected in Microeconomics handbooks, assumes that the firm behaves so as to maximise its profits. The profit maximisation problem faces a technological restriction, which appears in the book of science and techniques, and gives information about the feasibility of the different production plans. It is assumed that in the firm the manager takes into account the common request of owners and shareholders for profit maximisation. Moreover, firms contract all the inputs and services necessary for the productive process so that all costs, without exception, are pre-estimated by them. Therefore, we would say that the extra profits in free competition companies are zero. Therefore, in a fully specified model of competitive general equilibrium, there cannot possibly be an economy with increasing or decreasing returns to scale technologies, otherwise, the firm's technology must present constant returns to scale. Again, in this case, the extra profits are always zero. There is only one way to run a firm efficiently. In fact, society is rather like a firm.

There are other restrictions such as those effected by the markets, i.e.; those which refer to the effects of other agents, either consumers or producers, on the firm. Such restrictions disappear when complete markets are considered. This means that the firm signs contracts in every market (suppliers, consumers), in which any contingency is covered, and no unexpected event or incident not foreseen at the outset is likely to take place. Once the firm has signed these contracts, it executes an optimisation program in which shadow prices, which are exactly those at the market, are fixed. All this means that market universality does not fail, no matter how asymmetrical information or transaction costs may be. A broader firm's theory would make this universality fail leading to incomplete markets and introducing asymmetrical information and/or transaction costs.

A very common asymmetry of information in the firm is that arising between its manager and its owners or shareholders. The former may have individual interests, which do not coincide with those of the latter. In addition, the consequences of their behaviour cannot be directly observed. Such asymmetrical information is known as the Principal-Agent Problem or the Agency Problem, and accounts for the opposition between the managers' interests, who may be interested in maximising sales and income, for example, and the interests of owners or shareholders, who may want profit maximisation. If, in addition, the second group is numerous (the Principal), the control of the manager (the Agent) becomes a public good for them, and some of them can have a free-rider behaviour.

As far as transaction costs, introduced by Coase (1937), are concerned, there are possible further contingencies in every transaction or contract, which cannot be covered, with the subsequent extra costs or benefits not reflected in the initial contract. On the whole, we could say that the theory of contracts assumes that it is not useful to extend the length of the contract. Although there is an attempt to specify all the possible contingencies, there can always be further extra costs and benefits not reflected in the initial contract; we can never foresee all the unexpected events, which may happen. The universe of all the possible states is neither a closed or limited set. We cannot determine all that may happen. Firms are no longer black boxes in which it is very difficult to make out what happens inside and outside, once the optimal program has been executed. However, firms will not accept passively the virtual Walrasian tâtonnement fixing the prices of the inputs and outputs, but will establish contracts in the market, which are always incomplete. From these incomplete contracts a role for capital (property) emerges, so that the results of the firm are controlled. In complete markets, capital (property) was not a source of income -everything was contracted- but in incomplete markets, it is. By adding the idea of incomplete markets through the above-mentioned examples, a broader theory of the firm may be developed to obtain more accurate conclusions on questions such as the optimal size of the firm, its optimal structure -as regards who must own the inputs be they complementary or substitutive-, the optimal investment in innovations, etc. See Holmström and Milgrom (1987), Milgrom (1981), Hart (1995) and Williamson (1981) on these issues.

The approach followed on this issue is the development of the theories of production, cost and firm's behaviour within a general Walras-Arrow-Debreu (W-A-D-type competitive equilibrium. On this view, the concept of a free-competition firm assumes that:

1 firms behave parametrically with respect to prices;
2 firms' technology is of decreasing returns to scale;
3 number of firms is fixed;
4 the Walrasian tâtonnement determines the prices of the inputs and outputs statically and automatically. This is what the free-competition dynamics of firms means.

The result of this approach is compatible with that obtained from the point of view of a free-competition firm for isolated markets, that is, with a partially competitive Marshallian equilibrium in which the concept of a free-competition firm assumes that:

1 firms behave parametrically or strategically as regards prices depending on the number of firms existing with respect to the size of the market;
2 the firm's technology presents first increasing and subsequently decreasing returns to scale;
3 the number of firms is variable;
4 the dynamics of competition allows a re-structuring depending on the changing conditions of demand and/or technology and a determining of competitive equilibrium.

Although the above-mentioned approaches may seem substantially different in their assumptions, there are many ways to make them compatible as regards the main result of economic efficiency, although they do not provide the same prescriptions on other issues. However, this result is the most desirable property of a competitive equilibrium, whether general or partial. This means that there is an anonymous and informationally universal and decentralised mechanism -the competitive market-, which allocates resources and allows the various economic agents to optimise and achieve their optimal state.

5.2 Production Possibility Set and Existence of Production Function

The theory of the firm is worked out from the definition of 'technology'. By this term we mean a production process, a way of combining inputs to produce outputs.

Assume $X_i \subset R^n$ is a production possibility set which is a set of feasible production plans, and 'n' the number of possible inputs and outputs introduced in the productive process:

$$x = \{y \in R^n / y \text{ is a feasible production plan}\}.$$

We will formulate the following series of assumptions about the technical production relationships of the firm, which will allow us to represent the technology of a company with a production function.

1 **Closed.** Production possibility set, X_i, is closed, that is to say, the frontier of technologically feasible input-output vectors is also feasible.
2 **Possibility of inaction.** Production possibility set, X_i, inaction is possible, $0 \in X_i$, that is to say, a complete shutdown of business is possible. Therefore, X_i is non-empty.
3 **Free disposal.** That is to say, $X_i \supset (-R_+^n)$, the firm can absorb any amount of inputs and outputs without any additional cost.
4 **No free lunch.** $X_i \cap -R_+^n = \{0\}$, production is not free; there is no output without input consumption.
5 **Irreversibility of production.** $X_i \cap (-X_i) = \{0\}$, it is impossible to reverse a productive technology to transform an amount of output into the same amount of input that was used to generate with the output.
6 **Convexity.** The set X_i is convex, that is to say, if $X_1, X_2, \in X_i$, the techniques $\{\lambda X_1 + (1-\lambda) X_2\} \in X$ for all $0<\lambda<1$. Moreover, strict convexity will be required, that is to say $\{\lambda X_1 + (1-\lambda) X_2\} \in$ interior of X, for all $0<\lambda<1$.
7 **Divisibility.** The set X_i is divisible if all the production activities are divisible. That is to say, for all $X_1 \in X_i$, y $k \in [0, 1]$, then $kX_1 \in X_i$.
8 **Additivity (or free entry).** If two vectors (X_1, X_2) are technologically possible this implies that their addition is possible too, $X_1 + X_2 \in X_i$.

Proposition 1: a production possibilities set satisfying the assumptions of closed, possibility of inaction, free disposal, no free lunch, irreversibility of production, convexity, divisibility and additivity, guarantees the existence of a production functions x such as:

$$\mathbf{X}: R_+^n \rightarrow R_+$$

where **x** is the production function which represents technology providing as great a level of output as possible for each input-output vector. A real valued function x (**y**) is called a production function if:

$$x(\mathbf{y}) = \max\{x > 0 / \mathbf{y} \in V(x)\}$$

where V (x) is the input requirement set:

$$V(x) = \{y / y \in R_+^n;\ x \in R_+;\ (x, -y) \in X\}.$$

For example, for a company with only one output x and two inputs (y_1, y_2), it is possible to represent its technology by introducing an input-output vector which is only a list with one positive entry and two negative ones such as

$$\begin{bmatrix} -y_1 \\ -y_2 \\ x \end{bmatrix}.$$

The input-output vector, sometimes called a netput vector, can be more particularly expressed such as

$$\begin{bmatrix} -3 \\ -2 \\ 5 \end{bmatrix}.$$

This is a production plan, which uses 3 input units of y_1 and 2 of y_2 to obtain 5 units of the output x.

Graphically, and assuming only one input y_1 and one output x, the production possibility set can be observed in Fig. 5.1:

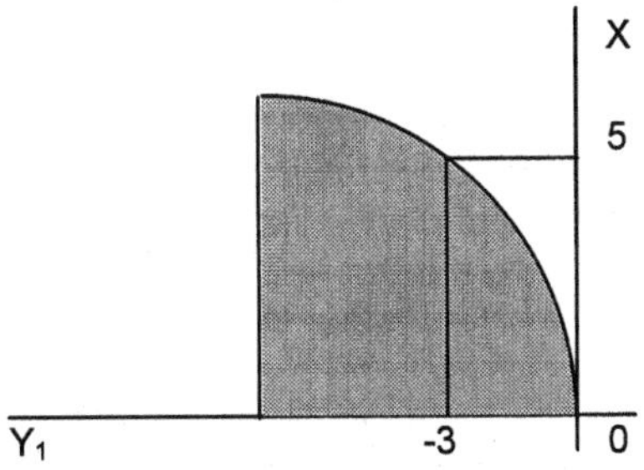

Fig. 5.1. Production possibility set

5.3 Properties of Production Function

As well as proving the existence of a production function, these assumptions guarantee the following properties:

5.3.1 Efficiency

Efficiency is satisfied when a production vector generates the optimum output and there is no other feasible production vector that generates more output without using more input.

5.3.2 Differentiability and Continuity

The production function satisfies differentiability and continuity.

5.3.3 Strict Quasi-concavity

The production function satisfies strict quasi-concavity when the production possibility set is strictly convex.

5.4 The Firm´s Equilibrium: Classic Demand, Profit and Direct Supply Functions

In this section, we will study the individual firm's equilibrium, that is to say, the profit maximisation problem, obtaining the classic demand, profit and supply functions after solving this problem. We will also study the most important properties of this function as well as the meaning of the Lagrange multiplier.

5.4.1 Profit Maximisation

The problem now is

$$\max \Pi = I - C = p\,x\,(y_1, y_2, y_3) - w_1 y_1 - w_2 y_2 - w_3 y_3$$

$$\text{s. to } x\,(y) \geq x$$

$$y \geq 0 \tag{5.1}$$

where x (y) is the production function for some input regular, convex and monotonic technology.

That is to say:

$$\max \Pi = p\,x\,(y_1, y_2, y_3) - (w_1 y_1 + w_2 y_2 + w_3 y_3)$$

$$\text{s. to } x\,(y) \geq x$$

$$y \geq 0.$$

The solutions to this problem give us predictions of the firm's market behaviour.

Therefore, the first-order conditions for maximisation are:

$$\partial \Pi / \partial y_1 = p\,x'\,(y_1) - w_1 = 0$$

$$\partial \Pi / \partial y_2 = p\,x'\,(y_2) - w_2 = 0$$

$$\partial \Pi / \partial y_3 = p\,x'\,(y_3) - w_3 = 0$$

that is, the first-order conditions require that the marginal value product, or more generally, the marginal revenue product of factor i is equal to its price:

$$p\ MP\ (y_1) = w_1$$

$$p\ MP\ (y_2) = w_2$$

$$p\ MP\ (y_3) = w_3$$

therefore,

$$p\ x'(y_1) / w_1 = p\ x'\ (y_2) / w_2 = p\ x'(y_3) / w_3$$

$$MP(y_1) / w_1 = MP(y_2) / w_2 = MP(y_3) / w_3$$

$$MP(y_1) / MP(y_2) = w_1 / w_2 = MRTS_{1,2}$$

$$MP(y_2) / MP(y_3) = w_2 / w_3 = MRTS_{2,3}$$

$$MP(y_1) / MP(y_3) = w_1 / w_3 = MRTS_{1,3} \tag{5.2}$$

which shows that the maximisation of profit (5.1) will take place when the price of the input is similar to its marginal productivity (MP). It is directly analogous to the SMR of consumer theory. This means that there is a similarity between the MRTS of the factors and the quotient of the input prices (5.2). The pondered marginal productivities must be verified in the equilibrium.

The second-order conditions require that the marginal productivities are non-decreasing at the optimum, or that the determinant on the bordered Hessian matrix alternates its sign.

$$\left|\overline{H_2^u}\right| = \left|H_3^L\right| = \begin{vmatrix} \Pi_{11} & \Pi_{12} & -w_1 \\ \Pi_{21} & \Pi_{22} & -w_2 \\ -w_1 & -w_2 & 0 \end{vmatrix} = \begin{vmatrix} 0 & -w_1 & -w_2 \\ -w_1 & \Pi_{11} & \Pi_{12} \\ -w_2 & \Pi_{12} & \Pi_{22} \end{vmatrix} > 0,$$

$$\left|\overline{H_3^u}\right| = \left|H_4^L\right| = \begin{vmatrix} \Pi_{11} & \Pi_{12} & \Pi_{13} & -w_1 \\ \Pi_{21} & \Pi_{22} & \Pi_{23} & -w_2 \\ \Pi_{31} & \Pi_{32} & \Pi_{33} & -w_3 \\ -w_1 & -w_2 & -w_3 & 0 \end{vmatrix} = \begin{vmatrix} 0 & -w_1 & -w_2 & -w_3 \\ -w_1 & \Pi_{11} & \Pi_{12} & \Pi_{13} \\ -w_2 & \Pi_{21} & \Pi_{22} & \Pi_{23} \\ -w_3 & \Pi_{31} & \Pi_{32} & \Pi_{33} \end{vmatrix} < 0.$$

The second-order conditions require that the production function is strictly concave. The results only correspond to the regions where the outputs and inputs have non-negative values and the production function is strictly concave. This requirement ensures the quasi-concavity of the production function at least where the combination of factors produces the maximum output.

5.4.2 Properties of Input Classic Demand and Output Direct Supply Functions

This firm's equilibrium yields a series of properties:

5.4.2.1 *Decreasing*

$y_i = y\ (w_1, w_2, w_3, p)$ is decreasing in w.

5.4.2.2 *Existence*

From the first-order conditions for the problem of profit maximisation we can solve functions of the type

$y_i = y\ (w_1, w_2, w_3, p)$ for all i = 1,2,3,

which represent the input classical demand functions of the producer. These functions obtained from applying the primal method are similar to the ordinary demand functions studied in the consumer equilibrium.

Then, as we have started above from the expression

$x = x\ (y_1, y_2, y_3)$

from the last two functions -input classic demand and production function-, we can obtain a output supply function of the kind establishing the different combinations of inputs for which profit maximisation is satisfied, that is to say:

$x = s\ (w_1, w_2, w_3, p)$

which is increasing in p.

5.4.2.3 *Homogeneity*

Input demand and direct supply functions are homogeneous of degree zero in (w_1, w_2, w_3, p), since they only depend on the relative prices.

5.4.2.4 *Symmetry*

The cross-substitution effect is symmetrical:

$$\frac{\partial y_i(w,p)}{\partial w_j} = \frac{\partial y_j(w,p)}{\partial w_i}$$

5.4.2.5 *Negativity*

The own-substitution effect, $\partial y_i\ (w, p) / \partial w_i$ is negative for all i.

5.4.2.6 *Negative Semi-definite*

$D^2y(p, w)$ is a negative semi-definite matrix.

5.4.3 Profit Function

We have seen in the previous section that through the solution of the primal we obtained a maximisation of income subject to restrictions of the cost of the inputs.

This solution eases the inputs demand functions expressing the quantities of the inputs required to produce the maximum of one output subject to cost restrictions. However, if we substitute the values of the input classic demand, which maximise the profit (i.e.; $y_i = y\ (w_1, w_2, w_3, p)$in the following profit function:

$$\Pi = p\ x\ (y_1, y_2, y_3) - [(w_1\ y_1) + (\ w_2\ y_2) + (\ w_3\ y_3)]$$

$$\text{s. to } x\ (y) \geq y$$

$$y \geq 0$$

we shall obtain a profit function expressed in terms of the prices of inputs and outputs. That is to say, we start from $x = x\ (y_1, y_2, y_3)$ to $\Pi\ (y_1, y_2, y_3)$,

$$\Pi = \Pi\ (y_1, y_2, y_3) = x\ [y_1\ (w_1, w_2, w_3, p), y_2\ (w_1, w_2, w_3, p), y_3\ (w_1, w_2, w_3, p)] =$$

$$= \max\ \{\ x\ (y_i) \ /\ C = w_i\ y_i\}$$

5.4.4 Properties of the Profit Function: Hotelling´s Theorem

5.4.4.1 Non-decreasing

The profit function, Π, will be non-increasing with respect to the prices of the inputs (w_1, w_2, w_3) and non-decreasing with respect to the price of the outputs generated. If $(w'_1, w'_2, w'_3) > (w_1, w_2, w_3)$ and $p' < p$, then:

$$\Pi(\ w'_1, w'_2, w'_3, p') < \Pi\ (w_1, w_2, w_3, p).$$

5.4.4.2 Homogeneity

The profit function is homogeneous of degree one in p and ω:

$$\Pi\ (k\ w_1, k\ w_2, k\ w_3, k\ p) = k\ \Pi\ (w_1, w_2, w_3, p).$$

5.4.4.3 Convexity

The profit function is convex in p and w.

5.4.4.4 Continuity

The profit function is a continuous function in p and w.

5.4.4.5 Hotelling´s Theorem

Again, as in the procedure used in consumer theory in which we started from the expenditure function to obtain the ordinary or Hicksian demand functions through Hotelling's Theorem, we can obtain the input classic demand function from the profit function applying Hotelling's Theorem, which states that the input classic demand is identical to the derivative of the profit function with respect to the input prices:

$$y_i = y\ (w_1, w_2, w_3, p) = \partial\ \Pi\ (w_1, w_2, w_3, p)\ /\ \partial\ w_i \text{ for all } i = 1,2,3$$

and

$$x = s(w_1, w_2, w_3, p) = \partial \Pi (w_1, w_2, w_3, p) / \partial p \text{ for all } i = 1,2,3$$

Proof:
Establish a function $\psi (w_1, w_2, w_3, p)$ such as:

$$\psi (w_1, w_2, w_3, p) = \Pi (w_1^0, w_2^0, w_3^0, p^0) - (px^0 - w_1y_1^0 - w_2y_2^0 - w_3y_3^0)$$

where y_1^0 and y_2^0 are quantities of the inputs which maximise the profit given a price p^0 and where $\Pi (w_1^0, w_2^0, w_3^0, p^0)$ specifies the combination of input prices which maximise the profit. Naturally, the expression $(px^0 - w_1y_1^0 - w_2y_2^0 - w_3y_3^0)$ of the function ψ is always inferior or equal to $\Pi (w_1^0, w_2^0, w_3^0, p^0)$ since it is the profit optimiser. The combination of prices for which both expressions are nearer is produced when:

$$\partial \psi (w_1, w_2, w_3, p) / \partial w_i = 0; i = 1,2,3.$$

At this point, the function will reach a minimum and it will be satisfied that

$$\partial \psi (w_1, w_2, w_3, p)/\partial \omega_i = [\partial \Pi (w_1^0, w_2^0, w_3^0, p^0)/\partial w_i] - \psi (w_1^0, w_2^0, w_3^0, p^0) = 0$$

then

$$\partial \Pi (w_1^0, w_2^0, w_3^0, p^0)/\partial w_i = y (w_1, w_2, w_3, p)$$

with which the theorem is demonstrated. □

5.5 The Firm's Equilibrium (Primal A)

In this section, we pose the income maximisation problem subject to a particular cost, which will be called Primal A. This problem is shown as an intermediate step between the generic profit maximisation problem and the particular output maximisation problem subject to a particular level of cost (which will be presented in the following section).

$$\max I = p\, x (y_1, y_2, y_3)$$

$$\text{s. to } C = w_1y_1 + w_2y_2 + w_3y_3. \tag{5.3}$$

The problem we present here (5.3) is very similar to that studied in the above section. From the economic point of view, the relevant functions generated in this problem are identical to those generated in the profit maximisation problem (previous section) so that they will not be repeated.

5.6 The Firm's Equilibrium (Primal B): Marshallian Demand and Indirect Supply Functions

In this section we shall study the particular case for the producer equilibrium of output maximisation, a problem from which the Marshallian and indirect supply demand functions are derived. We will also study the main properties of these functions and the economic meaning of the Lagrange multiplier.

5.6.1 Output Maximisation

At this point we must highlight a variant of the general case so far explained. The primal of producer equilibrium can be established for the particular output maximisation subject to the level of cost.

In such a case, the function to maximise will be that of output rather than income, that is to say:

$$x = x\,(y_1, y_2, y_3)$$

at the same time the restriction will be the cost of the factors expressed as

$$C = w_1y_1 + w_2y_2 + w_3y_3$$

then the solution of its maximisation through the Lagrange multiplier

$$\max x = x\,(y_1, y_2, y_3)$$

$$\text{s. to } C = w_1y_1 + w_2y_2 + w_3y_3 \qquad (5.4)$$

that is to say, the Lagrangian intermediate function of (5.4) is:

$$\max R\,(y_1, y_2, y_3, \lambda) = x\,(y_1, y_2, y_3) - \lambda\,(w_1y_1 + w_2y_2 + w_3y_3 - C)$$

then we obtain the first-order conditions for maximisation

$$\partial R / \partial y_1 = x'\,(y_1) - \lambda\, w_1 = 0$$

$$\partial R / \partial y_2 = x'\,(y_2) - \lambda\, w_2 = 0$$

$$\partial R / \partial y_3 = x'\,(y_3) - \lambda\, w_3 = 0$$

$$\partial R / \partial \lambda = C - w_1y_1 - w_2y_2 - w_3y_3 = 0$$

from the first two we have that

$$x'\,(y_1) / w_1 = x'\,(y_2) / w_2 = x'\,(y_3) / w_3$$

from maximisation in this particular case of the objective function, in which prices are equal to 1, we can solve one of the function types

$$y_i = \varepsilon\,(w_1, w_2, w_3, C) \text{ for all } i = 1, 2, 3$$

called input ordinary (or Marshallian) demands.

The second-order (sufficient) conditions for maximisation require that the determinant on the bordered Hessian matrix alternates its sign:

$$\left|\overline{R_2^u}\right| = \left|R_3^L\right| = \begin{vmatrix} R_{11} & R_{12} & -w_1 \\ R_{21} & R_{22} & -w_2 \\ -w_1 & -w_2 & 0 \end{vmatrix} = \begin{vmatrix} 0 & -w_1 & -w_2 \\ -w_1 & R_{11} & R_{12} \\ -w_2 & R_{12} & R_{22} \end{vmatrix} > 0,$$

$$\left|\overline{R_3^u}\right| = \left|R_4^L\right| = \begin{vmatrix} R_{11} & R_{12} & R_{13} & -w_1 \\ R_{21} & R_{22} & R_{23} & -w_2 \\ R_{31} & R_{32} & R_{33} & -w_3 \\ -w_1 & -w_2 & -w_3 & 0 \end{vmatrix} = \begin{vmatrix} 0 & -w_1 & -w_2 & -w_3 \\ -w_1 & R_{11} & R_{12} & R_{13} \\ -w_2 & R_{21} & R_{22} & R_{23} \\ -w_3 & R_{31} & R_{32} & R_{33} \end{vmatrix} < 0.$$

5.6.2 Properties of the Input Marshallian Demand and Indirect Supply Functions

These functions satisfy the same properties as the classical demand functions put forward above.

Given that

$$x = x\,(y_1, y_2, y_3)$$

as in the general case, we obtain the indirect good supply function, which establishes the different combinations of, inputs for which maximisation is satisfied, that is to say:

$$x = \varepsilon\,(w_1, w_2, w_3, C).$$

5.6.2.1 *Decreasing*

The function $y_i = \phi\,(x, C)$ is decreasing in w.

5.6.2.2 *Existence*

The Input Marshallian Demand (or Input Indirect Demand) exists and is of the type:

$$y_i = \phi\,(w_1, w_2, w_3, C)$$

which is decreasing in w.

Also, the Indirect Good Supply Function exists and is of the type:

$$x = \varepsilon\,(w_1, w_2, w_3, C)$$

which is increasing in C.

5.6.2.3 *The Lagrange Coefficient (λ)*

$dx/dC = \lambda$ represents the inverse of marginal cost[1].

---

[1] $dC = w_1\,dy_1 + w_2\,dy_2 + w_3\,dy_3$

5.6.2.4 *Homogeneity*

The Marshallian or Input Indirect Demand and the Indirect Supply are homogeneous of degree zero in (w_1, w_2, w_3).

5.6.2.5 *Negativity*

The own-substitution effect $\partial y_i (w, C) / \partial w_i$ is negative for all i.

5.6.2.6 *Symmetry*

The cross-substitution effect is symmetrical:

$$\frac{\partial y_i(w,C)}{\partial w_j} = \frac{\partial y_j(w,C)}{\partial w_i}.$$

5.6.2.7 *Negative Semi-definite*

$D^2 y$ (C, **w**) is a negative semi-definite matrix.

5.6.2.8 *Roy's Identity*

The Marshallian Demands can be obtained by applying Roy's Identity. Given the indirect supply function ε (**w**, C) and the cost constraint, the Marshallian Input Demand can be obtained as follows:

$$y_i = \phi(\mathbf{w}, C) = -\left[\frac{\frac{\partial\varepsilon(w, C)}{\partial w_i}}{\frac{\partial\varepsilon(w, C)}{\partial C}}\right]; (i = 1, 2, 3).$$

5.7 The Firm´s Equilibrium: Input Classic Demand and Output Direct Supply Functions

In this section, we provide the Dual A - corresponding to the Primal A- with the same functions as those in section 5.3, as expected. The reason for this is a more

---

$w_1 = \partial x / \lambda \partial y_1$; $w_2 = \partial x / \lambda \partial y_2$; $w_3 = \partial x / \lambda \partial y_3$;
with
$dx = (\partial x / \partial y_1)\, dy_1 + (\partial x / \partial y_2)\, dy_2 + (\partial x / \partial y_3)\, dy_3$
given that,
$dC/dx = 1/\lambda$

didactic (more symmetrical) exposure of the whole subject. However, from an economic point of view, it is of little interest.

5.7.1 Loss Minimisation

As mentioned at the beginning of this chapter, a dual methodology will be applied to obtain a producer equilibrium through profit maximisation, loss minimisation, or minimisation of the production cost for a level of income fixed beforehand. That is to say,

$$\min L = -w_1 y_1 - w_2 y_2 - w_3 y_3 + p\, x\,(y_1, y_2, y_3) \tag{5.5}$$

The necessary first-order conditions resulting from minimisation of (5.5) are:

$$\partial L / \partial y_1 = w_1 - px'(y_1) = 0;$$

$$\partial L / \partial y_2 = w_2 - px'(y_2) = 0;$$

$$\partial L / \partial y_3 = w_3 - px'(y_3) = 0;$$

from which

$$w_1 / px'(y_1) = w_2 / px'(y_2) = w_3 / px'(y_3).$$

As in the case of the primal, dual first-order conditions imply that the condition of the firm's equilibrium must be produced.

That is to say, the variation of the profit resulting from an increase of the income available for getting the inputs, must be naturally similar to the increase of the capital required for getting more profit so as to reach that level.

For the dual problem, the second-order condition means that the determinant on the bordered Hessian matrix is negative:

$$\left|H_3^S\right| = \begin{vmatrix} 0 & -L_1 & -L_2 \\ -L_1 & -L_{11} & -L_{12} \\ -L_2 & -L_{21} & -L_{22} \end{vmatrix} < 0, \left|H_4^S\right| = \begin{vmatrix} 0 & -L_1 & -L_2 & -L_3 \\ -L_1 & -L_{11} & -L_{12} & -L_{13} \\ -L_2 & -L_{21} & -L_{22} & -L_{23} \\ -L_3 & -L_{31} & -L_{32} & -L_{33} \end{vmatrix} < 0.$$

5.7.2 Properties of Input Classic Demand and Output Direct Supply Functions

From the equilibrium reached, and solving, we obtain

$$w_1 / px'(y_1) = w_2 / px'(y_2) = w_3 / px'(y_3).$$

The same as in the previous section, these functions are homogeneous of degree zero in (ω_1, ω_2, ω_3, p), and the Lagrange coefficient (λ^0) represents the marginal loss obtained as a result of the change in the income available for getting inputs.

$$y\,(tw_1, tw_2, tw_3, tp) = ty\,(w_1, w_2, w_3, p).$$

5.7.3 Loss and Input Classic Demand Functions: Hotelling's Theorem

The loss function has the same properties as the profit function mentioned in 5.4.2, that is to say: increase, homogeneity of degree one and continuous, and we can obtain input classic demand functions from the loss function applying Hotelling's Theorem.

5.8 The Firm's Equilibrium (Dual A)

Here we will pose the cost minimisation problem subject to a particular level of income, which will be called Dual A. This problem is shown as an intermediate step between the general loss minimisation problem (or profit maximisation) above and the cost minimisation problem subject to a level of output (in the next section).

$$\min C = w_1 y_1 + w_2 y_2 + w_3 y_3$$

$$\text{s. to } I = px(y_1, y_2, y_3). \tag{5.6}$$

As can be seen in (5.6), the problem above is very similar to (but not the same as) that posed in the previous section. However, all the relevant functions derived from this problem are identical to those generated in the previous section, and therefore they will not be repeated.

5.9 The Firm's Equilibrium (Dual B): Input Conditioned Demand and Cost Functions

In this section, we shall show Dual B -corresponding to Primal B- of the firm's equilibrium, as previously seen in section 5.6, however, it must be said that, from an economic point of view, the present section is much more interesting than that. Besides, it provides new, economically relevant functions. Here we have the new input conditioned demands and cost functions. We shall also study the properties of these functions as well as the meaning of the Lagrange multiplier.

Moreover, the problem of cost minimisation posed here is 'part' of the problem of profit maximisation, posed as Primal A, as seen in section 5.5, since, provided a producer maximising profits produces an amount of output x*, at a price p, from the inputs (y_1, y_2, y_3) to the costs (w_1, w_2, w_3), the amounts of inputs (y_1, y_2, y_3) constitute the combination of minimum cost that produce the amount of output x*, given the prices of the inputs (w_1, w_2, w_3). Otherwise, the producer would not be maximising its profits. Therefore, economists usually employ the expression 'cost minimisation is the dual problem of profit maximisation' and although this is not completely true -the accurate definition of the dual is: 'the dual of the dual is the primal', or else, primal =1/dual, nevertheless the term 'duality' in economics is more liberally used referring to Shephard's Lemma, Roy's Identity, Hotelling's Theorem, etc., and a great deal of the material treated in this book.

5.9.1 Cost Minimisation

As mentioned at the beginning of this study, a dual methodology will be applied to obtain the firm equilibrium. Now, we shall estimate the minimum production cost for a production volume fixed beforehand.

$$\min C = w_1 y_1 + w_2 y_2 + w_3 y_3$$

$$\text{s. to } x = x(y_1, y_2, y_3). \tag{5.7}$$

The Lagrangian of expression (5.7) is

$$\min C(y_1, y_2, y_3, \mu) = w_1 y_1 + w_2 y_2 + w_3 y_3 - \mu(x(y_1, y_2, y_3) - x).$$

The necessary first-order conditions resulting from minimisation are:

$$\partial C / \partial y_1 = w_1 - \mu \xi'(y_1) = 0, \ \mu = w_1 / \xi'(y_1)$$

$$\partial C / \partial y_2 = w_2 - \mu \xi'(y_2) = 0, \ \mu = w_2 / \xi'(y_2)$$

$$\partial C / \partial y_3 = w_3 - \mu \xi'(y_3) = 0, \ \mu = w_3 / \xi'(y_3)$$

$$\partial C / \partial \mu = \xi(y_1, y_2, y_3) - x = 0$$

from which

$$w_1 / \xi'(y_1) = w_2 / \xi'(y_2) = w_3 / \xi'(y_3)$$

As in the case of the primal, dual first-order conditions imply that the condition of firm's equilibrium must be produced. Although as a consequence of maximising an output against a cost minimisation we can observe that:

$$\lambda \text{ (Primal)} = 1/\mu \text{ (Dual)}.$$

For the dual problem, the second-order condition means that the determinant on the bordered Hessian matrix is negative:

$$|H_3^S| = \begin{vmatrix} 0 & -C_1 & -C_2 \\ -C_1 & -\mu C_{11} & -\mu C_{12} \\ -C_2 & -\mu C_{21} & -\mu C_{22} \end{vmatrix} < 0, \quad |H_4^S| = \begin{vmatrix} 0 & -C_1 & -C_2 & -C_3 \\ -C_1 & -\mu C_{11} & -\mu C_{12} & -\mu C_{13} \\ -C_2 & -\mu C_{21} & -\mu C_{22} & -\mu C_{23} \\ -C_3 & -\mu C_{31} & -\mu C_{32} & -\mu C_{33} \end{vmatrix} < 0.$$

Since the multiplier μ is the reciprocal of λ, the second-order conditions are the same as those for the output maximisation for a level of cost.

5.9.2 Properties of the Input Conditioned Demand

5.9.2.1 Non-decreasing

$y_i = \xi(w_1, w_2, w_3, x)$ is non-decreasing in x.

5.9.2.2 Existence

From the first-order conditions of the dual we would infer the existence of

$y_i = \xi\,(w_1, w_2, w_3, x)$,

decreasing in ω;

$C = \xi\,(w_1, w_2, w_3, x)$,

which implies, as stated above, that

$$C\,(w_1, w_2, w_3, x) = w_1\, y_1 + w_2\, y_2 + w_3\, y_3 = w_1\, \xi\,(w_1, w_2, w_3, x) +$$
$$+\, w_2\, \xi\,(w_1, w_2, w_3, x) + w_3\, \xi\,(w_1, w_2, w_3, x).$$

5.9.2.3 Homogeneity

The input conditioned demand is homogeneous of degree zero in (w_1, w_2, w_3).

5.9.2.4 The Lagrange Coefficient (μ)

$\mu = dC/dx = LMC$ represents the marginal cost obtained as a result of the change in the output.

5.9.2.5 Negativity

The own-substitution effect $\partial\, \xi_i\,(w, x)\,/\,\partial\, w_i$ is negative for all i.

5.9.2.6 Symmetry

The cross-substitution effect is symmetrical so that:

$$\frac{\partial \xi_i(w,x)}{\partial w_j} = \frac{\partial \xi_j(w,x)}{\partial w_i}$$

5.9.2.7 Negative Semi-definite

$D^2\xi\,(w, x) \le 0.$

5.9.3 Properties of Cost Function: Shephard's Lemma

5.9.3.1 Increase

This property seems to be quite clear since, if the output restriction increases the costs of the factors required for getting that output will automatically increase (increasing with respect to the output). On the other hand, if we maintain a level of output and there is an increase of the prices of the factor, an increase in the costs will also take place (non-decreasing with respect to the price of the factors).

5.9.3.2 Homogeneity

Since the input conditioned demand functions $y_i = \xi (w_1, w_2, w_3, x)$ are homogeneous of degree zero and the cost functions are established as $c = w \xi (w_1, w_2, w_3, x)$, it will be inferred that these are homogeneous of degree one in (w_1, w_2, w_3).

5.9.3.3 Concavity

The cost function is a concave function.

5.9.3.4 Continuity

The cost function is a continuous function.

5.9.3.5 Shephard's Lemma

Equally as in the case of consumer equilibrium, we could obtain the compensated or Hicksian demand function from the cost function (Hotelling's Theorem). In the problem of producer equilibrium we can obtain the input conditioned demand function by simple differentiation with respect to factor prices. This property results from Shephard's Lemma.

For this

$$y_i = \xi (w_1, w_2, w_3, x) = \partial C (w_1, w_2, w_3, x) / \partial w_i; (i = 1, 2, 3)$$

That is to say, solving with respect to the variables of the productive input prices of the cost function, we obtain the expressions of the input conditioned demand function.

Proof:
This can be proved by application of the Envelope Theorem. However, other proofs are possible and we well consider one here.

Assume $y^0 = \xi^0 (w_1^0, w_2^0, w_3^0, x^0)$ a given combination of prices of inputs (w_1^0, w_2^0, w_3^0) minimised by C for a level of output of x^0 also given. If we define a function t such as

$$t (w_1, w_2, w_3, x^0) = C (w_1, w_2, w_3, x) - (p_1x_1 + p_2x_2 + p_3x_3)$$

its derivative is

$$\partial t (w_1, w_2, w_3, x^0) / \partial w_i = [\partial C (w_1, w_2, w_3, x) / \partial w_i] - \xi^0 (w_1^0, w_2^0, w_3^0, x^0)$$

$C (w_1, w_2, w_3, x)$ is a minimiser of the production cost and will reach a minimum when $t (w_1, w_2, w_3, x) = 0$ so that $\partial t (w_1, w_2, w_3, x^0) / \partial w_i = 0$, then:

$$\partial C (w_1, w_2, w_3, x) / \partial w_i = \xi^0 (w_1^0, w_2^0, w_3^0, x^0),$$

which demonstrates Shephard's Lemma. □

5.10 Diagrammatic Representation of the Main Relationships

In figure 5.2, we present a summary of the analysis carried out so far. Note that this figure has many similarities with respect to figure 1.2 and figures 5.3 to 5.5, which will be presented later. Figures in economic theory are similar to the polyhedral structures used by chemists to represent organic molecules. There are rectangles which represent the atoms (coloured balls) and lemmas and theorems which represent the molecular links. Therefore, optimisation figures attempt to recreate the models. We offer the different functions in order, as they are obtained from the optimisation hypotheses developed. The most valuable and suggestive problems and the relevant functions generated are the profit maximisation and cost minimisation problems (Dual B). The former enables us to obtain the classic factor demand functions, the profit and supply functions from the first-order conditions, and also provides an exercise for comparative statics, that is, it reports the signs of the variations of each one of the variables explained for these functions before changes in their explained variables as a result of the second-order conditions. The cost minimisation problem enables us to obtain the input conditioned demand and cost functions also from the first-order conditions. Again, the second-order conditions provide an exercise for comparative statics.

Note that, from an economic view, the cost minimisation problem subject to a level of income (Dual A) is scarcely relevant; however, it provides symmetry and therefore adds an attractive or at least non-trivial didactic approach. On the other hand, the first-order conditions of the output maximisation problem subject to a certain level of cost (Primal B), provide indirect demand functions for a level of cost, and conditioned supply functions also for a level of cost. These functions are less interesting from an economic point of view since they assume that the firm has previously estimated a fixed cost. The problem is only interesting when this cost (in Primal B) coincides with the cost minimised for a level of output (in Dual B), or when the output maximised in Primal B coincides with the output fixed in Dual B. However, symmetry is again added to the general exposure of duality and an interesting didactic exercise is provided. The second-order conditions of this maximisation problem will provide again the expected signs for the variables explained of the input indirect demand functions (subject to a level of cost), or input conditioned demand functions, and supply functions subject to a level of cost or the output indirect supply, before changes in their respective explicative variables.

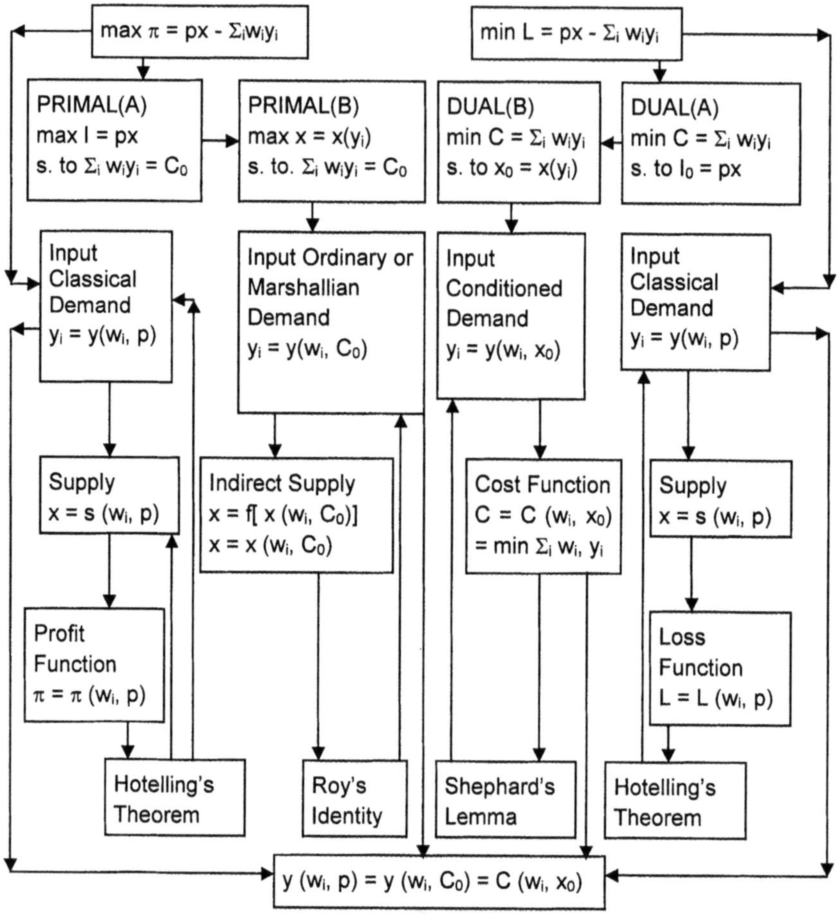

Fig. 5.2. Long-run and single production (the relationships between functions)

Figure 5.2 has some similarities with respect to figure 1.2 -from chapter 1 of this book- in relation with the consumer's optimisation problems. There is a more general similarity as regards a maximisation problem and a minimisation problem with the same results in figure 5.2 in income and costs and in utility and expenditure in figure 1.2. There is a more formal similarity in the output maximisation problem subject to a level of cost and in the cost minimisation with respect to a level of output. In fact, the theorems are maintained. That is, Hotelling's Theorem (or Shephard's Lemma for consumption) is similar to Shephard's Lemma for production in that both are supported by the derivative property. In addition, Roy's identity for consumption is similar to Roy's identity for production.

The generic profit maximisation problem enables us to generate input demand, product supply and profit functions from the first-order conditions, so the following problem:

$$\max \Pi = px - wy$$

enables us to obtain from the first-order conditions functions of the type

$$y = y\,(p, w)$$

$$x = s\,(p, w)$$

$$\Pi = \Pi\,(p, w).$$

The problem equivalent to this will be:

$$\min L = wy - px$$

or else

$$\min\,(-\,(px - wy))$$

In the output maximisation subject to a level of cost (Primal B) the functions are well defined in comparison with the profit function in the profit maximisation problem which, as seen, requires only the existence of return and quasi-concavity or the production function rather than concavity. This means that the input conditioned demand functions subject to a level of cost of the type $y = y\,(w, C)$ (indirect demands) and the conditioned supply functions subject to a level of cost (indirect supply) of the type $x = e\,(w, C)$ are in turn well defined. What is the use of these functions for economists?. The functions generated from this problem give information about the firm's behaviour when it contracts the inputs and supplies its outputs for a given level of cost. The question is: what is the amount of output chosen by the firm for the level of cost fixed?. Shephard (1953) has proved that every cost function -originated in a cost minimisation problem subject to a level of output - has a corresponding particular productive technology since the cost minimisation problem subject to a level of output takes part in the profit maximisation problem. If a firm that maximises profits chooses the amount of outputs to be produced and of inputs to be used at fixed output and input prices, then the levels of input chosen will necessarily constitute the minimum cost method to produce the level of output given at certain input prices. Otherwise, the firm would not be maximising profits! Now, since the output maximisation problem subject to a level of cost is the primal (Primal B), the fundamental duality theorem for production and, therefore, the amounts of the equilibrium factor demand -obtained from the first-order conditions- will have to coincide.

$$y = \xi\,(w, C)$$

$$y = \xi\,(w, x).$$

This is natural if we remember that the first-order conditions of Primal B are obtained from pairs of the type

$$x'(y_1) / w_1 = x'(y_2) / w_2 = x'(y_3) / w_3.$$

On the other hand, the first-order conditions of Dual B are obtained from pair relationships of the type

$$w_1 / p\,\xi'(y_1) = w_2 / p\,\xi'(y_2) = w_3 / p\,\xi'(y_3).$$

As could not be otherwise, the quotients of the marginal products by the prices of the factors are equal in both problems. However, the economist is more interested in the cost minimisation problem in which a new function, non-generated in the profit maximisation problem, is developed. On the other hand, in the output maximisation problem subject to a level of cost, some functions are generated for explained variables already obtained in the profit maximisation problem, such as the input demand and output supply functions. However, the explained variables are now different. The new specifications about input conditioned demand and supply subject to a level of cost are only interesting when the input combination chosen by the firm is the optimal one. Nevertheless, this combination will always be optimal if the theorem of production duality is verified. But again, the functions generated in the output maximisation problem cannot be generalised for more outputs, that is, for multiple production. And yet, the cost functions obtained from the cost minimisation process are still well defined. This is the case in the cost minimisation problem of the firm subject to different levels of output such as:

$$\min C = y_1 w_1 + y_2 w_2 + y_3 w_3$$

$$\text{s. to } F(x_1, x_2, x_3, y_1, y_2, y_3) = 0. \quad (5.8)$$

The corresponding Lagrangian of (5.8) is

$$V = \Sigma\, w_i\, y_i + \rho\, g(x_1, x_2, x_3, y_1, y_2, y_3),$$

the first-order conditions are

$$\partial V / \partial y_1 = w_1 + \rho\, g'(y_1) = 0$$

$$\partial V / \partial y_2 = w_2 + \rho\, g'(y_2) = 0$$

$$\partial V / \partial y_3 = w_3 + \rho\, g'(y_3) = 0$$

$$\partial V / \partial \rho = g(x_1, x_2, x_3, y_1, y_2, y_3) = 0$$

from which the following relationship is obtained:

$$g'(y_1) / w_1 = g'(y_2) / w_2 = g'(y_3) / w_3$$

$$MP(y_1) / w_1 = MP(y_2) / w_2 = MP(y_3) / w_3$$

$$MP(y_1) / MP(y_2) = w_1 / w_2 = MRTS_{1,2}.$$

This is the marginal rate of technical substitution between two pairs of factors. In other words, the condition necessary for the cost minimisation of many products is identical to that of only one product. The Langrange multiplier ρ has now a somewhat different meaning since it measures the rate at which the minimum production cost is reduced if the restriction on the production function is slightly reduced, that is, if it is possible to have the levels of production given with a smaller number of factors.

5.11 Joint Production

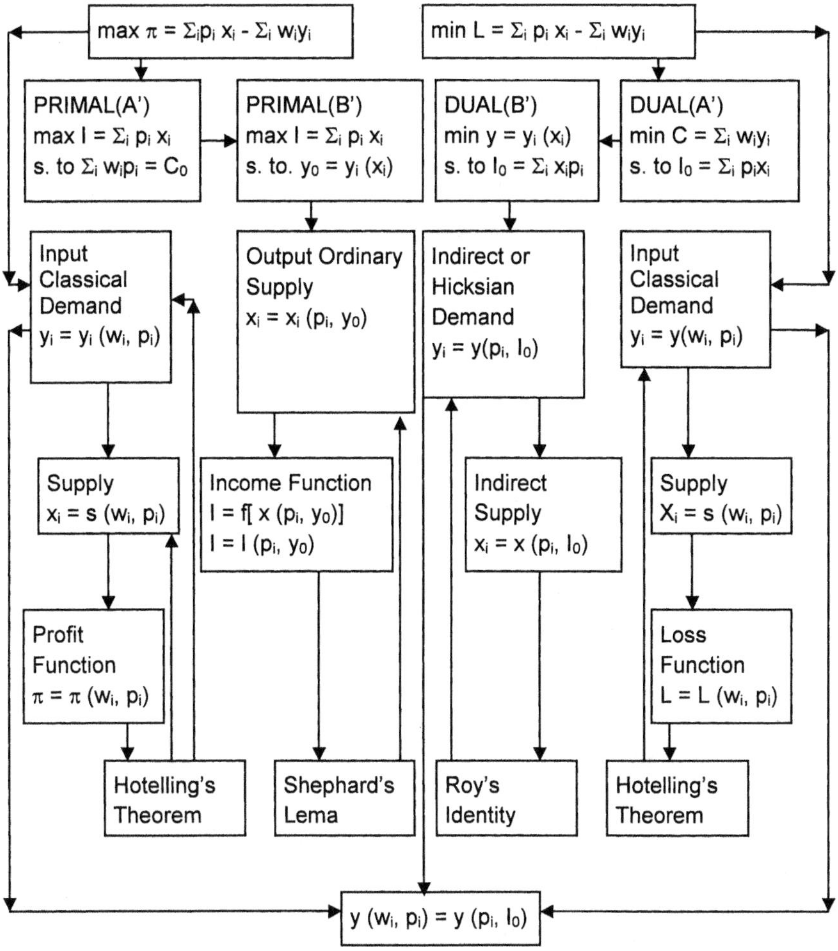

Fig. 5.3. Long-run and joint production (the relationships between functions)

In figure 5.3 we present joint production. The general case of joint production generates functions very similar to those seen in figure 5.2. The main functions generated are of the type:

$$y = y\,(\mathbf{p}, \mathbf{w})$$

$$x = x\,(\mathbf{p}, \mathbf{w})$$

$$\Pi = \Pi\,(\mathbf{p}, \mathbf{w})$$

A simple case of joint production is that in which, from only two inputs (y_1, y_2), we can obtain two outputs (x_1, x_2). The production function can be expressed in an implicit form as

$$\psi\,(x_1, x_2, y_1, y_2) = 0.$$

From here, we can now define the problem of profit maximisation:

$$\max P = p_1x_1 + p_2x_2 - w_1y_1 - w_2y_2$$

$$\text{s. to } y\,(x_1, x_2, y_1, y_2) = 0. \qquad (5.9)$$

The auxiliary Lagrange function of (5.9) is:

$$L\,(x_1, x_2, y_1, y_2, \sigma) = p_1\,x_1 + p_2\,x_2 - w_1\,y_1 - w_2\,y_2 - \sigma\,\psi\,(x_1, x_2, y_1, y_2)$$

with the following first-order conditions:

$$\left.\begin{aligned} p_1 - \sigma\frac{\partial\psi}{\partial x_1} &= 0 \\ p_2 - \sigma\frac{\partial\psi}{\partial x_2} &= 0 \\ -\omega_1 - \sigma\frac{\partial\psi}{\partial y_1} &= 0 \end{aligned}\right\} -\omega_2 - \sigma\frac{\partial\psi}{\partial y_1} = 0$$

from the previous conditions it is possible to write:

$$\left.\begin{aligned} \frac{\partial\psi/\partial x_1}{\partial\psi/\partial x_2} &= -\frac{dx_1}{dx_2} = \frac{p_1}{p_2} = MRT_{12} \\ \frac{\partial\psi/\partial y_1}{\partial\psi/\partial y_2} &= -\frac{dy_1}{dy_2} = \frac{w_1}{w_2} = MRTS_{12} \\ \frac{\partial\psi/\partial y_1}{\partial\psi/\partial x_2} &= -\frac{dy_1}{dx_2} = \frac{w_1}{p_2} = MRS_1^1 \end{aligned}\right\}$$

where MRT_{12} represents the marginal rate of transformation of the output x_1 with respect to x_2; $MRTS_{12}$ is the marginal rate of technical substitution of the input x_1 into the input x_2; and $MRS_1^{\,1}$ is the marginal rate of substitution of the output x_1 into the input y_1, where it is possible to define MRT_{21}, $MRTS_{21}$, $MRS_1^{\,2}$, and $MRS_2^{\,2}$ as other marginal rates of transformation such as output-output, marginal rate of technical substitution such as input-input; marginal rate of substitution such as output-input and input-output; all of them being determined by the productive technology.

The second-order conditions require that the determinant on the bordered Hessian matrix for the maximisation problem, designated as F, is

$$F\,(-1) > 0.$$

Moreover, analogously to the case of simple production, it is possible to assert that there are classical input demand functions such as:

$$y_1 = y_1\ (p_1, p_2, w_1, w_2)$$

$$y_2 = y_2\ (p_1, p_2, w_1, w_2),$$

so, similarly, we can also state that there are direct supply functions of the type

$$x_1 = x_1\ (p_1, p_2, w_1, w_2)$$

$$x_2 = x_2\ (p_1, p_2, w_1, w_2).$$

Finally, we can define profit functions for joint production substituting the previous supplies:

$$\Pi_1 = \Pi_1\ (p_1, p_2, w_1, w_2)$$

$$\Pi_2 = \Pi_2\ (p_1, p_2, w_1, w_2).$$

We can again apply Hotelling's Theorem to these functions in order to get the classical input demand:

$$\frac{\partial \Pi_1(p_1, p_2, w_1, w_2)}{\partial w_1} = y_1(p_1, p_2, w_1, w_2).$$

We can also state that the profit function satisfies the same properties as in the single production.
We have posed profit maximisation (or loss minimisation) and cost minimisation (Dual B), but we cannot pose here (joint production) the problems of the profit maximisation for two outputs (Primal B). On the contrary, in the cost minimisation problem, it is possible to obtain cost functions of the type:

$$C_1 = C_1\ (w_1, w_2, x_1, x_2)$$

$$C_2 = C_2\ (w_1, w_2, x_1, x_2).$$

Another particular problem can be considered now, which is that of maximising the output returns subject to a level of input. We shall call this problem Primal B'. We assume the simplification of only one input and two outputs so that it is possible to generate functions such as

$$\mathbf{x} = \xi\ (\mathbf{p}, \mathbf{y})$$

$$I = I\ (\mathbf{p}, \mathbf{y}).$$

Therefore, these are output conditioned supply and income functions for the input -for a level of input -. Here we have found an interesting new function: the income conditioned function for a level of input. However, the output supply function found was already known in a more general version such as

$$\mathbf{x} = x\ (\mathbf{p}, \mathbf{w}).$$

On the other hand, the problem here posed allows us to modify the outputs, given their prices, for a given level of input. Although we only consider one input and its amount is fixed, we continue to consider that the firm is still in the long-run, given that it can modify the combination of the outputs produced at certain fixed prices for the outputs and inputs and also a fixed amount of input.

The Dual B' problem can be posed as an input minimisation problem for a fixed level of income and generates the following functions:

$$\mathbf{x} = \phi\ (\mathbf{p}, \mathrm{I})$$

$$\mathbf{y} = \mathrm{y}\ (\mathbf{p}, \mathrm{I});$$

therefore, these are output conditioned supply functions for a level of income and input conditioned demand functions for a level of income. We shall see these two cases in more detail in sections 5.11.1 and 5.11.2.

5.11.1 Income Maximisation

The firm produces and sells its outputs at fixed prices (prices at the free output market) and purchases the inputs at fixed prices also (prices at the free input market). When we assume that the firm modifies amounts of outputs in order to maximise income, and that the output prices are fixed and that there is only one input y_0 at a fixed amount, then we have

$$\left.\begin{array}{l} \max \mathrm{I} = p_1 x_1 + p_2 x_2 \\ \text{s.to } y^0 = y\,(x_1, x_2) \end{array}\right\}$$

$$L = (p_1 x_1 + p_2 x_2) + \lambda\,(-y\,(x_1, x_2) + y)$$

$$\left.\begin{array}{l} \dfrac{\partial L}{\partial x_1} = p_1 \text{ - } \lambda\, y'(x_1) = 0 \\ \dfrac{\partial L}{\partial x_2} = P_2 - \lambda\, y'(x_2) = 0 \\ \dfrac{\partial L}{\partial \lambda} = -y\,(x_1, x_2) + y = 0 \end{array}\right\}$$

$$p_1 = \lambda\, y'(x_1) \Rightarrow p_1\, \mathrm{MP}\,(x_1) = \lambda$$

$$p_2 = \lambda\, y'(x_2) \Rightarrow p_2\, \mathrm{MP}\,(x_2) = \lambda$$

$$\frac{p_1}{p_2} \frac{\mathrm{MP}\,(x_1)}{\mathrm{MP}\,(x_2)} = 1$$

MRT= Marginal Rate of Transformation: $p_1 / p_2 = \mathrm{MP}\ (x_2) / \mathrm{MP}\ (x_1)$

where MRT is the marginal rate of transformation and the Lagrange multiplier is the marginal product value.

From here it is possible to obtain other output supply functions such as the output conditioned supply functions:

$$x_1 = \gamma\,(p_1, p_2, y^0)$$
$$x_2 = \gamma\,(p_1, p_2, y^0).$$

The second-order condition requires that the determinant on the bordered Hessian matrix is positive for which the marginal rate of transformation must be increasing.

In the following income relationship,

$$I = p_1\, x_1 + p_2\, x_2$$

the amounts of the outputs x_1 and x_2 can be substituted into the above output conditioned supply in order to obtain the following income function:

$$I = p_1{}^{\gamma}\,(p_1, p_2, y^0) + p_2{}^{\gamma}\,(p_1, p_2, y^0);$$

that is

$$I = I\,(p_1, p_2, y^0).$$

This is the firm's income function for a fixed level of input y^0.

To this income function, we can apply the following derivative property or Shephard's Lemma:

$$\frac{\partial I}{\partial p_i} = \frac{\partial I(p_1, p_2, y^0)}{\partial p_i}$$

We have obtained, again, the output conditioned supply for a fixed level of input.

5.11.2 Input Minimisation

Assume now that the firm wishes to minimise the amount of input necessary to obtain a fixed income. In such a case, the firm will decide only upon the amount of input and will assume that both the prices and the amounts of outputs are fixed. Thus, once an isoincome line has been given, we will have to find the minimum curve of product transformation.

$$\left.\begin{array}{l} \max y = y\,(x_1, x_2) \\ \text{s.to } I^0 = p_1x_1 + p_2x_2 \end{array}\right\}$$

$$y = y(x_1, x_2) + \mu\,(I^0 - p_1x_1 - p_2x_2)$$

$$\left.\begin{array}{l} \dfrac{\partial y}{\partial x_1} = y'(x_1) - \mu p_1 = 0 \\[2ex] \dfrac{\partial y}{\partial x_2} = y'(x_2) - \mu p_2 = 0 \\[2ex] \dfrac{\partial y}{\partial \mu} = I^0 - p_1x_1 - p_2x_2 = 0 \end{array}\right\}$$

$$y'(x_1) = \frac{1}{MP(x_1)} = p_1 \Rightarrow \frac{1}{\mu} = p_1 MP(x_1)$$

$$y'(x_2) = \frac{1}{MP(x_2)} = p_2 \Rightarrow \frac{1}{\mu} = p_2 MP(x_2)$$

$$\frac{p_1}{p_2} \frac{MP(x_2)}{MP(x_1)} \Leftrightarrow 1 = \frac{p_1 MP(x_1)}{p_2 MP(x_2)}$$

where μ is the inverse of the marginal rate of the income-product of each output x_1, x_2 and, therefore, it will be verified that

$$\lambda = 1/\mu .$$

From here, it is possible to obtain the following supply functions:

$$x_2 = x_2 (I^0, p_1, p_2)$$

$$x_1 = x_1 (I^0, p_1, p_2).$$

These are output indirect supplies for a fixed level of income.

It is now possible to substitute in the objective function $y = y (x_1, x_2)$ the output indirect supplies above in order to obtain the following function:

$$y = y (I^0, p_1, p_2)$$

This function is input indirect demand for fixed income and levels of output. Roy's identity can be applied to this input indirect demand and the output indirect supply will again be obtained. This process is described in figure 5.3.

5.12 Short-Run

So far, we have made a long-run analysis in which the whole range of inputs can be combined by the firm. However, it is easy to assume situations in which some quantities of inputs are considered fixed. This is the case in the short-run analysis. Figure 5.4 represents short-run simple production while figure 5.5 shows joint and short-run production.

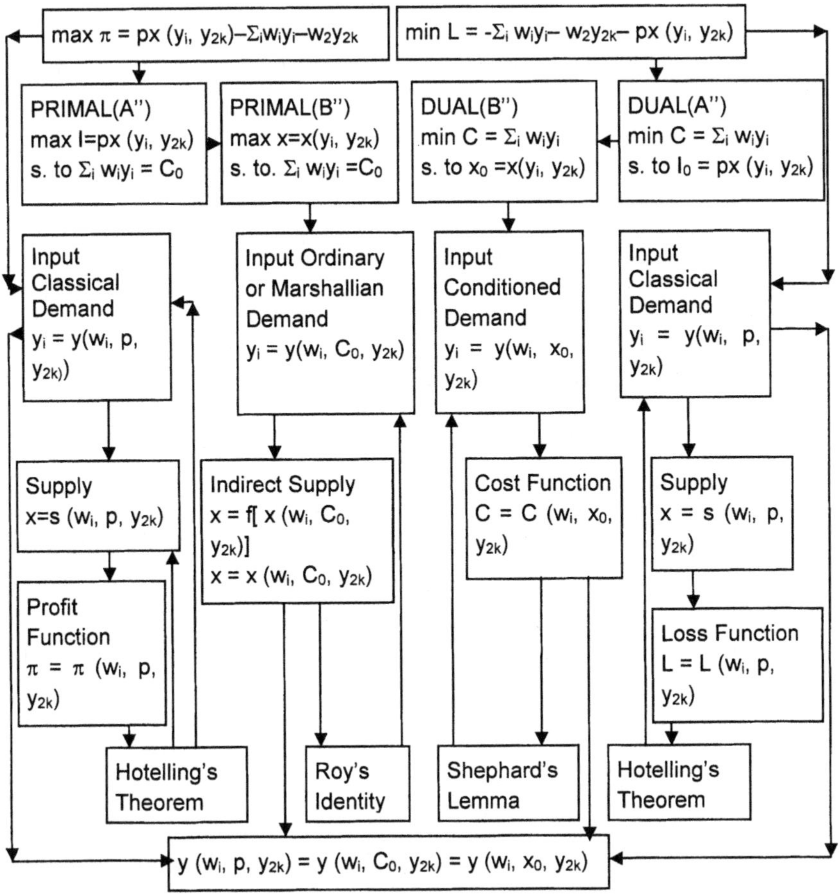

Fig. 5.4. Short-run and single production (the relationships between functions)

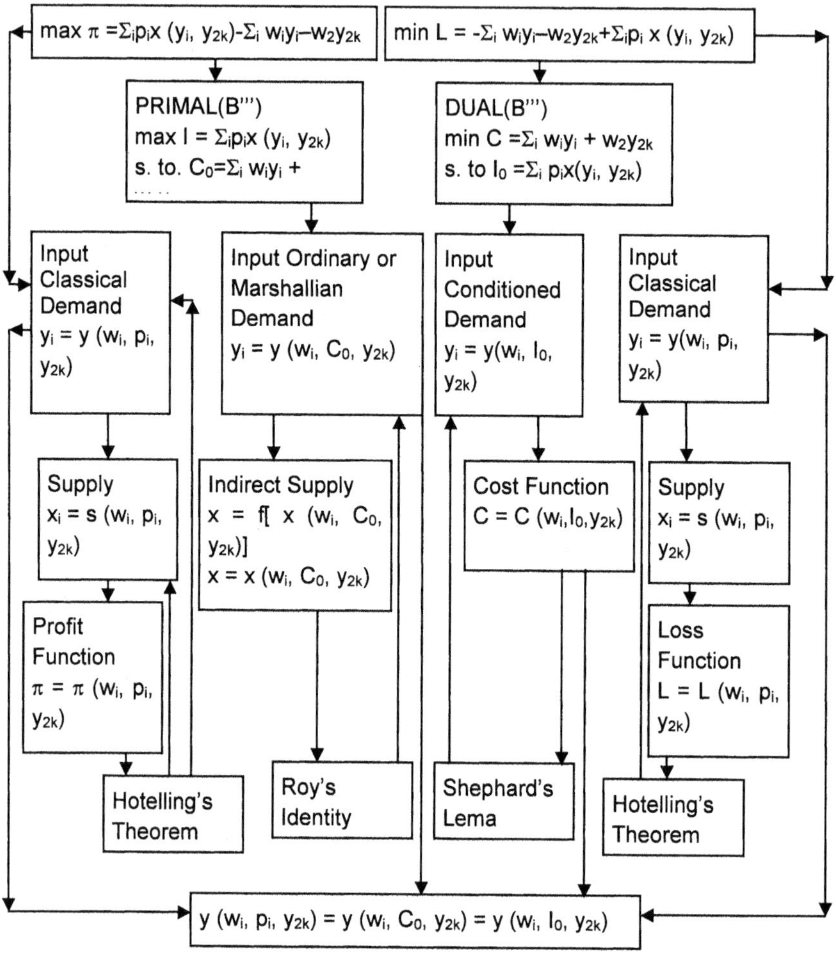

Fig. 5.5. Short-run and joint production (the relationships between functions)

5.12.1 Short-Run and Single Production

The problem is posed for a quantity of output x with a price p, and two inputs y_1, as a variable input, y_{2k}, as a fixed input with prices w_1, w_2, as follows:

$$\max \prod = p\,x - w_1\,y_1 - w_2\,y_{2k}$$

The first-order conditions are

$$G\,(x_1, y_1, y_{2k}) = p\,x\,(y_1, y_{2k}) - (w_1\,y_1 + w_2\,y_{2k})$$

$$\frac{\partial G}{\partial y_1} = p\, x'(y_1) - w_1 = C$$

$$\frac{\partial G}{\partial y_{2k}} = 0$$

from which the following demand functions can be obtained:

$$y_1 = y_1\,(p, w_1, y_{2k})$$

or otherwise these supply functions:

$$x = x\,(p, w_1, w_2, y_{2k})$$

or finally, the following profit functions:

$$\Pi = \Pi\,(p, w_1, w_2, y_{2k}).$$

We can also pose the problem as (Dual B")

$$\left.\begin{array}{l} \min C = w_1\, y_1 + w_2\, y_{2k} \\ \text{s.to } x = x\,(y_1, y_{2k}) \end{array}\right\}$$

in which the auxiliary Lagrange function is

$$F\,(x, y_1, y_{2k}, y) = w_1\, y_1 + w_2\, y_{2k} - \lambda\,(x, y_1, y_{2k}) - x)$$

$$\left.\begin{array}{l} \dfrac{\partial F}{\partial y_1} = w_1 - y\ \ x'(y_1) = 0 \\ \dfrac{\partial F}{\partial y_2} = 0 \\ \dfrac{\partial F}{\partial \lambda} = x\,(y_1, y_{2k}) - x = 0 \end{array}\right\}$$

from which we can obtain

$$y_1 = y_1\,(x, w_1, w_2, y_{2k})$$

and also

$$C = C\,(x, w_1, w_2, y_{2k})$$

where

$$C = C\,(x, w_1, w_2, y_{2k})$$

which can be expressed as

$$C = y_1\, w_1 + y_{2k}\, w_2.$$

This means that the short-run cost function has as a particular characteristic the existence of a constant term (y_2, w_2) which is independent from the volume of production and represents the short-run fixed costs as follows:

$$C\ (x, y_{2k}) = VC\ (x, y_{2k}) + FC\ (y_{2k}).$$

Analogously, we can obtain short-run input demand, profit and supply functions. Samuelson (1954) formulates the Principle of Le Chatelier for the supply functions: the competitive firm's short-run supply functions such as $x = x\ (p, w_1, w_2, y_{2k})$ are more inelastic than the long-run functions such as $x = x\ (p, w_1, w_2)$. Moreover, the higher the number of inputs considered as fixed, the more inelastic these functions are.

Primal B" and the functions generated in it are similar to Primal B and therefore, do not need further explanation.

5.12.2 Short-Run and Joint Production

As far as the joint and short-run production are concerned we would have cost function of the type

$$C = C\ (x_1, x_2, w_1, w_2, y_{2k})$$

or otherwise

$$C\ (x_1, x_2, y_{2k}) = VC\ (x_1, x_2, y_{2k}) + FC\ (y_{2k}).$$

If y_{2k} coincides with the quantity of optimum long-run demand for fixed short-run inputs at given prices, then

$$C\ (x_1, x_2, y_{2k}) = C\ (x_1, x_2)$$

when

$$y_{2k} = y\ (x_1, x_2).$$

Thus, each short-run function of the type $C\ (x_1, x_2, y_{2k})$ coincides in one of its points with the long-run cost function $C\ (x_1, x_2)$. This means that the latter function involves the great deal of short-run cost functions obtained changing the different values of y_{2k}, which means that

$$\frac{\partial C\ (x_1, x_2, y_{2k})}{\partial y_{2k}} = 0,$$

which yields y_{2k} depending on (x_1, x_2), and, substituting in $C\ (x_1, x_2, y_{2k})$, provides the long-run function $C\ (x_1, x_2)$.

In figure 5.5 we show a particular case which can be modelised. It is the income maximisation (Primal B''') subject to a level of cost, and the cost minimisation (Dual B''') subject to a level of income. The results in terms of the functions generated are naturally similar to those provided by the problems of profit maximisation and loss minimisation. However, the functions in B''' are well-defined, since they are problems delimited beforehand. It is not necessary, therefore, to restrict technology in these functions under the additional assumption of decreasing returns to scale, and the assumption of quasi-concave production function is enough to guarantee the existence of an optimal solution.

5.13 Reflections on the Main Relationships Designed

As a prior condition to obtain the maximum profit the firm must maximise production at a given cost, maximise income at a given level of input, minimise the levels of input for a level of income, maximise income for a level of cost,... etc. This means that the new functions characterise productive technologies in the same way as the cost function, after Shephard (1953), characterises the production function. These functions are generated when the optimisation problems previous to profit maximisation are solved. So, certain functions are generated when the cost minimisation problem is solved. The next step is posing duality. That is to say, given any of these new functions can we find the remaining relevant functions? Are those relevant production functions, profit functions, etc. the original functions? Or, do they, at least, have the same properties as the original functions? Here we explain procedures which allow us to answer the first question. In the next chapter, we offer exercises for particular functions which illustrate the second and third questions. However, a general theory to deal properly with the last two questions would exceed the aims of this book.

Having exposed all the above, we have generated the following new functions in figure 5.2:

* Input Marshallian demand functions for a level of cost (for a particular level of cost);
* Output indirect supply function for a level of cost (for a particular level of cost).

Both functions have been generated when the output condition maximisation problem for the cost has been solved, that is, in simple production and in the long-run. Why aren't these functions usually presented in handbooks? Probably because the output maximisation problem for a level of cost is not well-defined in joint production.

Other functions in figure 5.3 are the following:

* Output conditioned supply function for a level of input (for a particular level of input);
* Income function for a level of input (for a particular level of input);
* Output indirect supply function for income (for a particular level of income);
* Input indirect demand function for income (for a particular level of income).

From the four functions above, the first two have been generated from the income maximisation problem subject to a level of input while the next two have been generated from an input minimisation problem subject to the level of income. These functions are long-run and refer to joint production. Why don't these functions usually appear in the handbooks? The reason is that we are concerned with a particular case in which there is only one input and the functions are not well-defined for two or more inputs.

Other functions in figure 5.4 are the following:

* Input Marshallian demand function for a level of cost with a fixed input (or several fixed inputs), that is, input Marshallian demand function for a short-run level of cost;
* Output indirect supply function for the level of cost with a fixed input (or several fixed inputs), that is, output indirect supply function for a short-run level of cost.

The two functions above have been generated from the output maximisation problem in the short-run and in simple production. Why don't these functions usually appear in the handbooks? Again, the problem of considering more than one output is not well defined.

Other functions are:

* Long-run cost function with joint production;
* Short-run cost function with joint production.

The two functions above have been generated from a cost minimisation problem subject to a production level of several outputs, with an efficient technique both in the short- and long-run.

On the whole, we have six new functions: two in simple production and four in joint production, all of them at long-run. Moreover, we have obtained four new more functions: two for long-run simple production and two for joint production (in the long-run and in the short-run respectively).

What are the advantages of the ten new functions put forward here? The new functions allow us to model the particular situations and to do empirical research when the statistics available are limited. This statistical information significantly affects the evolution of empirical research in Microeconomics and Industrial Organisation. When only historic aggregated series was available, the possibilities of empirical analysis were minimal and only some papers on demand measurement, technical change, estimations of demand elasticities and elasticities of substitution -which subject will be presented in next section- could be considered empirical studies on Applied Microeconomics or Industrial Organisation. With so few statistics, the firm was studied in particular cases, as for example the case of RENFE presented in Chapter 6. Later, the availability of big cross-sectional samples -such as the cross-section of the shipping industry presented in chapter 6, data panels, etc., have recently allowed us to observe the behaviour of the firm through time in a disaggregated way, which has allowed a significant advance in empirical research.

5.14 The Elasticity of Substitution

The elasticity of substitution captures the relationship between the input ratio and the curvature of the isoquants.

Assuming $x = x(y_1, y_2)$ as the production function, the input direct elasticity of substitution (DES) will be defined as

$$\sigma = -\frac{dL\,(y_2/y_1)}{dL\,(x_2/x_1)} = \frac{dL\,(y_2/y_1)}{dL\,(x_1/x_2)}$$

where (x_1, x_2) are the partial derivative of x (y_1, y_2) with respect to (y_1, y_2). The direct elasticity of substitution is always positive, $\sigma = 1$ and σ = constant for the CES, even $\sigma = \infty$, when the inputs can substitute one another perfectly and the isoquants are linear.

In the case of a function x = x (y_1, y_2....y_n), the direct elasticity of substitution (DES) between the inputs i, j, is defined as

$$\sigma_{ij} = \frac{x_i\, x_j\, (y_i\, x_i + y_j\, x_j)}{y_i\, y_j\, (x_{ij}\, x_j^2 - 2\, x_{ij}\, x_i\, x_j + x_{jj}\, x_i^2)}$$

where(x_i, x_j) represent the first partial derivatives of x = x (y_1, y_2....y_n) with respect to (i, j) and analogously, are defined as (x_{ii}, x_{jj}, x_{ij}, x_j^2, x_i^2).

σ_{ij} can be also expressed, for the inputs K and L, such as:

$$\sigma_{KL} = \frac{d(K/L)/(K/L)}{d(MRTS)/(MRTS)} = \frac{d(K/L)/(K/L)}{d(w/r/(w/r)}$$

since

$$MRTS_{LK} = \frac{MPL}{MPK} = \frac{w\omega}{r} = -\frac{dK}{dL}.$$

Allen and, later, Uzawa (1962) start from the cost function instead of the production function, thus,

$$C = C\,(x, w_1, w_2) = x\,C\,(1, w_1, w_2)$$

is the cost function corresponding to the production function:

$$x = x\,(y_1, y_2)$$

with the Allen-Uzawa elasticity of substitution σA, such as:

$$\sigma A_{12} = \frac{C\left(\dfrac{\partial^2 C}{\partial w_1 \partial w_2}\right)}{\left(\dfrac{\partial C}{\partial w_1}\dfrac{\partial C}{\partial w_2}\right)}.$$

For the use of a generic production function, the Allen-Uzawa elasticity of substitution between the inputs i and j, σA_{ij} is defined as

$$\sigma A_{ij} = \frac{C\left(\dfrac{\partial^2 C}{\partial w_i \partial w_j}\right)}{\left(\dfrac{\partial C}{\partial w_i}\dfrac{\partial C}{\partial w_j}\right)}$$

Note that $\sigma A_{ij} = \sigma A_{ji}$, that is to say, the symmetry is verified, Morishima (Blackorby and Russell, 1989) exposes a non-symmetrical Allen-Uzawa elasticity of substitution defined as

$$\sigma M = \frac{\partial L_n\left(\dfrac{C_1}{C_2}\right)}{\partial L_n\left(\dfrac{w_1}{w_2}\right)}$$

for two inputs (y_1, y_2) and a product x. Note that C_1 is the production cost x with the input y_1, and C_2 the firm's cost x with the input y_2. On the other hand, (w_1, w_2) are the prices of the inputs.

For a generic function, Morishima's elasticity of substitution between the inputs i, j, σM_{ij}, is defined as:

$$\sigma M_{ij} = \frac{\partial L_n\left(\dfrac{C_i}{C_j}\right)}{\partial L_n\left(\dfrac{w_i}{w_j}\right)}$$

Note that $\sigma M_{ij} \neq \sigma M_{ji}$ is asymmetrical and can be interpreted as follows: the various relative prices of the inputs provide different elasticities of substitution depending on the price (i^{th} or j^{th}) of the modified input.

Basic References

Chambers, K.G.: Applied Production Analysis. Cambridge University Press 1980

Gravelle, H., Rees, R.: Microeconomics, 3rd ed. Longman Group UK Limited 1994

Nadiri, M.I.: Producers Theory. In: Arrow, K. J. and Intriligator: Handbook of Mathematical Economics. Amsterdam: North Holland 1982

Mas-Collel, A., Whinston, M. D., Green, J. R.: Microeconomic theory. New York: Oxford University Press 1995

Varian, H.: Microeconomic Analysis. 3rd ed. W.W. Norton & Company 1992

References and Further Reading

Blackorby, C., Primont, D., Russell, R.: Duality, Separability and Functional Structure Theory and Economic Application. Amsterdam: North-Holland 1979

Blackorby, C., Russel, R.: Will the real elasticity of substitution please stand up? (A comparison of the Allen/Uzawa and Morishima Elasticities). American Economic Review 79, 882-888 (1989)

Coase, R.: The Nature of the Firm. Economica 4, 386-405 (1987)

Chung, J. W.: Utility and Production Functions. Theory and Applications. Blackwell, Oxford 1994

Debreu, G.: Theory of Value. New York: Wiley 1959

Diewert, W. E.: Duality Approaches in Microeconomic Theory. Handbook of Mathematical Economics, vol. II. New York: North-Holland 1982

Diewert, W.: Frontiers in Quantitative Economics. Vol. I and II. North-Holland, Intriligator M.D. 1972

Hart, O.: Firm's contracts and financial structure. Oxford University Press 1995

Holmström, B., Milgrom, P.: Aggregation and linearity in the provision of intertemporal incentives. Econometrica SS, 303-328 (1987)

Koopmans, T.: Three Essays on the State of Economic Science, Essay, I. New York: McGraw-Hill 1957

McFadden, D.: Cost, Revenue and Profit Functions. In: Fuss, M. and D. McFadden: Production Economics: A dual approach to theory and applications. Amsterdam: North-Holland 1978

Milgrom P.: Good news and bad news: Representation theorems and applications. Bell Journal of Economics 13, 380-391 (1981)

Milgrom, P., Roberts, J.: Limit pricing and entry under incomplete information: an equilibrium analysis. Econometrica 50, 443-459 (1982)

Nikaido, H.: Convex Structures and Economic Theory. Academic Press 1968

Shephard, R.: Cost and Production Functions. Princeton: Princeton University Press 1953

Shephard, R.: Theory of Cost and Production Functions. Princeton: Princeton University Press 1970

Silberberg, E.: The Structure of Economics. A Mathematical Analysis, 2nd ed. Singapore: Mc Graw-Hill Publishing Company 1991

Williamson, O.: The Modern Corporation: Origins, Evolution, Attributes. Journal of Economic Literature 19, 1537-1568 (1981)

6 Alternative Theories on Companies

There are theoretical models of the company other than the neo-classical profit maximiser. Such alternative models are a response to the emergence of companies with more complex aims, the separation between ownership and control and conflict between different interest groups within the company, such as shareholders, management and workers.

6.1 Baumol's Sales Income Maximisation Model

We owe the most classic theory to Baumol[1]: it posits a model in which companies maximise sales income, I, subject to the constraint of minimum profits π_0. Hence the utility function changes; Baumol justifies this in a number of ways. The main reason for it is that directors' remuneration and prestige correlate positively with companies' sales income rather than profits.

In a way, Baumol is saying that sales income provides an image of the company's market share, its size, and directors' interests rather than owners' or shareholders' interests, as to some extent the latter are content with a particular profit minimum.

The model is formalised as follows:

$$\left.\begin{array}{l} \text{Max } I = I\,(x;\,G) \\ \text{subject to} \quad \text{(i)}\ \pi \geq \pi_0 \\ \qquad\qquad\quad \text{(ii)}\ \pi = I\,(x;\,G) - C\,(x) - G \end{array}\right\}$$

The income function is non-linear, with a defined finite maximum, G, advertising and sales promotion expenses, and finally π, profits, the minimum level being π_0.

Lagrange's intermediate function:

$$\text{Max } L\,(x;\,G;\,\lambda) = I\,(x;\,G) - \lambda\,[\,I\,(x;\,G) - C\,(x) - G - \pi_0]$$

The first-order conditions of which are:

[1] Baumol, W. J.: *Business Behaviour, Value and Growth*. Macmillan, ed. rev. Harcourt, Brace and World 1967.

$$\left.\begin{aligned}
&\frac{\partial L}{\partial G} = \frac{\partial I}{\partial G} - \lambda \frac{\partial I}{\partial G} + \lambda = 0 \\
&\frac{\partial L}{\partial x} = \frac{\partial I}{\partial x} - \lambda \left[\frac{\partial I}{\partial x} - MC(x) \right] = 0 \\
&\frac{\partial L}{\partial \lambda} = I(x;G) - C(x) - G - \pi_0 = 0
\end{aligned}\right\}$$

From which we obtain:

$$\frac{\partial I}{\partial G} = \lambda \frac{\partial I}{\partial G} - \lambda \Rightarrow \frac{\partial I}{\partial G}(1-\lambda) = -\lambda$$

$$\frac{\partial I}{\partial G} = \frac{\lambda}{\lambda - 1}$$

$$\frac{\partial I}{\partial x} = -\lambda MC(x) + \lambda \frac{\partial I}{\partial x} \Rightarrow \frac{\partial I}{\partial x}(1-\lambda) = -\lambda MC(x)$$

$$\frac{\partial I}{\partial x} = \frac{\lambda}{\lambda - 1} MC(x)$$

We now see that $\frac{\partial I}{\partial x}$ is marginal income, MI(x), while $\frac{\partial C}{\partial x}$ is marginal cost, MC(x). If we were looking at a neo-classical company, the first-order condition would give us the following result:

$$MI\ (x) = MC\ (x)$$

However, on the Baumol model, the result is:

$$\frac{\partial I}{\partial x} = MI(x) = \frac{\lambda}{\lambda - 1} MC(x)$$

This equilibrium condition differs from the equilibrium condition of a neo-classical company in the term:

$$\frac{\lambda}{\lambda - 1}$$

Only when:

$$\frac{\lambda}{\lambda - 1} = 1$$

are a neo-classical company's results and those of a Baumol company the same. Only when:

$\lambda = -\infty$ (zero cost to increase profits)

does such equivalence arise.

Further, this quotient is defined as follows:

$$0 < \frac{\lambda}{\lambda - 1} < 1$$

Or, as another way of seeing it, $\lambda < 0$, since advertising and sales promotion expenses are positive and marginal income is also positive.

This means that MC(x) > MI(x), i.e., the marginal cost exceeds marginal income, thus a Baumol company offers greater output than a neo-classical company. Therefore, a Baumol company loses some of its potential profits for the sake of gaining greater market share.

Moreover, $\frac{\partial I(x)}{\partial G} < 1$ means that a Baumol company spends more on advertising and sales promotion than a neo-classical company.

Figure 6.1 shows in graphical form how the production level of neo-classical company x_N is smaller than that of Baumol company x_B.

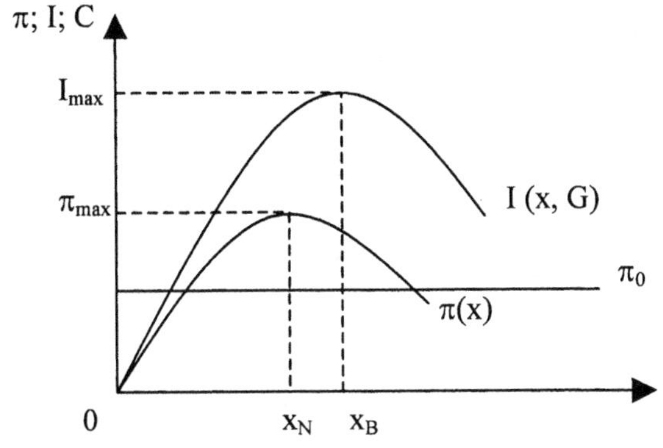

Fig. 6.1

A Baumol company's behaviour has its own internal logic, too. Thus, if we increase overheads or place a tax on profits, such changes alter output and the advertising and sales promotion spent. These disturbances would not apply to a neo-classical company.

Hence a tax on profits would move the profit curve π (x) downward, while not altering the equilibrium output, as seen from figure 6.2:

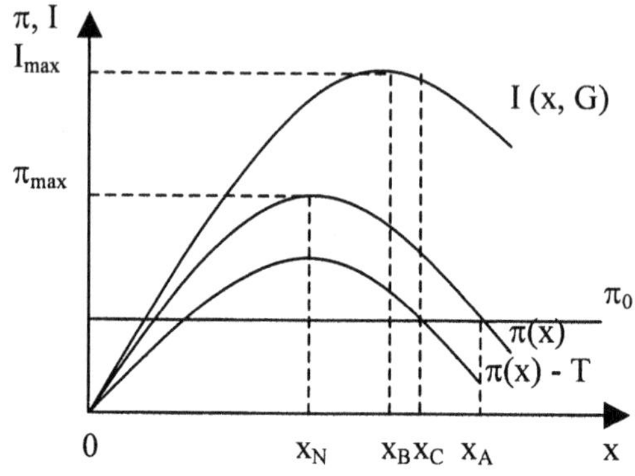

Fig. 6.2

In other words, the maximum-profit output is still the same, but the maximum income with $\pi = \pi_0$ decreases from x_A to x_C. Therefore a drop in production is the company's response to increased tax pressure.

6.2 Marris's Production Volume Maximisation Model

Marris[2] posits the company's goal to be maximisation of its balanced growth rate, a mixed utility function with two arguments: profits and production volume.

The idea is to maximise[3] a directors' utility function such as:

$$U = U(x, \pi)$$

where, as before, x and π represent the company's production level and profits, while U represents the utility of the directors. Let us also assume that

$$U(x, \pi) = \beta x + (1 - \beta)\pi$$

i.e., utility can be expressed as a linear function of x and π.

The problem now is:

$$\text{Max } U(x, \pi) = \beta x + (1 - \beta)px - (1 - \beta)C(x)$$

where the first-order condition is:

$$\beta + (1 - \beta)p - (1 - \beta)MC(x) = 0$$

i.e.:

---

[2] Marris, R.: A Model of the Managerial Enterprise. *Quarterly Journal of Economics* (1963); Marris, R.: *Theory of Managerial Capitalism*. Macmillan 1964.

[3] This approach is owed to Ames, E.: Soviet Economic Processes. London 1965. In: Archibald, G. C. *Theory of the Firm*. Penguin 1971.

$$MC(x) - p = \frac{\beta}{1-\beta}$$

thus:

If $\beta = 0$, then $p = MC(x)$; whereas, if $\beta = 1$, we have pure production volume maximisation, leaving the relation $MC(x) - p = \frac{\beta}{1-\beta}$ indeterminate, unless a restriction is placed on maximum allowed losses. Finally, if β is positive and less than 1, the marginal cost will always exceed the price as an indicator that a production-oriented company will outstrip the maximum-profit output.

Note that if $\beta = 1$, the requirement of not making a loss is necessary to fulfil the second-order conditions of maximum $U(x, \pi)$, as they imply the following:

$$-(1-\beta)\frac{\partial MC(x)}{\partial x} < 0$$

i.e.,

$$-\frac{\partial MC(x)}{\partial x} - \beta\frac{\partial MC(x)}{\partial x} < 0$$

hence

$$-\frac{\partial MC(x)}{\partial x} < \beta\frac{\partial MC(x)}{\partial x}$$

meaning simply that

$$0 \leq \beta$$

Graphically, output x_M represents the maximum-profit output, output x_Z represents the maximum loss-covering production level, and output x_A represents output for a company whose goal function is the utility function:

$$U(x, \pi) = \beta x + (1 - \beta)\pi;\ \beta \in (0, 1)$$

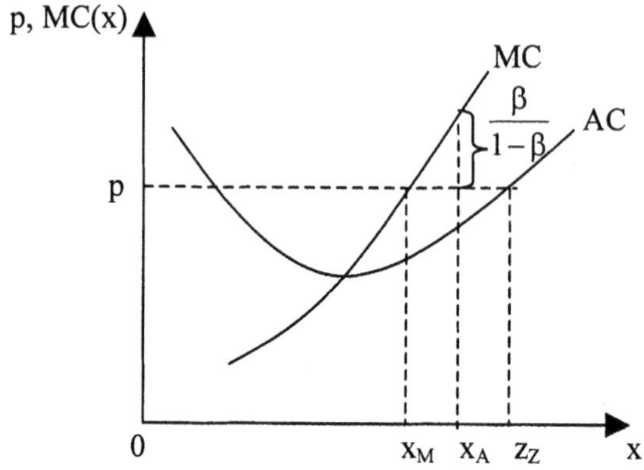

Fig. 6.3

The result of this model is inefficient allocation in the sense that the company produces more than what it would produce as a neo-classical company and also remunerates the factors at above competitive prices. Formally,

$$\text{Max } U(x, \pi) = \beta x(y_1; y_2) + (1 - \beta)[px(y_1; y_2) - \sum_i x_i y_i]$$

subject to: $x = x(y_1; y_2)$

The first-order conditions are:

$$\beta x(y_1; y_2) + (1 - \beta)[px(y_1; y_2) - w_i] = 0; \ (i = 1, ..., r)$$

giving rise to:

$$w_i = px(y_1; y_2) + \frac{\beta}{1-\beta} x(y_1; y_2) = \left(p + \frac{\beta}{1-\beta}\right) x(y_1; y_2)$$

This last expression shows that the factors are remunerated at above their physical marginal products, since $\frac{\beta}{1-\beta}$ is positive. However, the quotient of the marginal products is equal to the quotient of the factor prices, i.e.:

$$\frac{w_i}{w_j} = \frac{x_i(y)}{x_j(y)} \quad (i, j = 1, ..., r)$$

Which means that the overpayment is proportional for all factors.

6.3 Cooperative Company Model

This model represents a company that does not maximise profit but the excess of workers. Let us assume that only the output x is produced on the basis of input y, which represents the labor variable. The company is price-accepting with respect to the final product.

The company's profits will be:

$$\left.\begin{aligned} &\pi(x) = px - w\psi(x) - L \\ &\text{or} \\ &\pi(y) = px(- wy - L) \end{aligned}\right\}$$

where L is workers' remuneration, which we assume is fixed, $\psi = x^{-1}(y)$, is the inverse function of demand. The worker's excess, if we assume the fixed debt taken on by the cooperative company is L, will be[4]:

$$E(x) = \frac{px - L}{\Psi(x)}$$

$$E(y) = \frac{px(y) - L}{y}$$

Free maximisation of E(y) leads to:

$$E'(y) = \frac{px'(y)y - [px(y) - L]}{y^2} = \frac{px'(y) - E(y)}{y} = 0$$

Therefore, the price-accepting cooperative company will have an excess per capita in equilibrium:

$$E(y) = px'(y)$$

In other words, its excess will be equal to its physical marginal product of labor for the price, i.e., the value of the physical marginal productivity of labor.

The sufficient conditions for the existence of the maximum are:

$$E''(y) = \frac{1}{y^2}[px''(y)y - E'(y)y - px'(y) + E(y)]$$

Substituting for the values of E(y) and E'(y) we have:

$$E''(y) = \frac{px''(y)}{y} < 0$$

---

[4] The excess per worker, as profits are:

$$\pi(x) = px - w\psi(x) - L$$

and the excess will be:

$$E(x) = \frac{px - L}{\Psi(x)} - w$$

i.e., income over and above wages.

which will be fulfilled provided that x''(y) < 0, i.e., the marginal productivity of labor must be decreasing.
What is the difference between the equilibrium attained with this cooperative company and the equilibrium achieved by a neo-classical company?

If fixed debt, i.e., expenses for remuneration of fixed factors, is equal in the cooperative company and the neo-classical company, the equilibrium coincides. But modifications of the relevant variables will give rise to different predictions. Thus, if debt L for fixed expenses is reduced, the neo-classical company will not change its equilibrium output. However, when debt L decreases in the cooperative company the quantity of work contracted decreases and hence equilibrium output goes down.

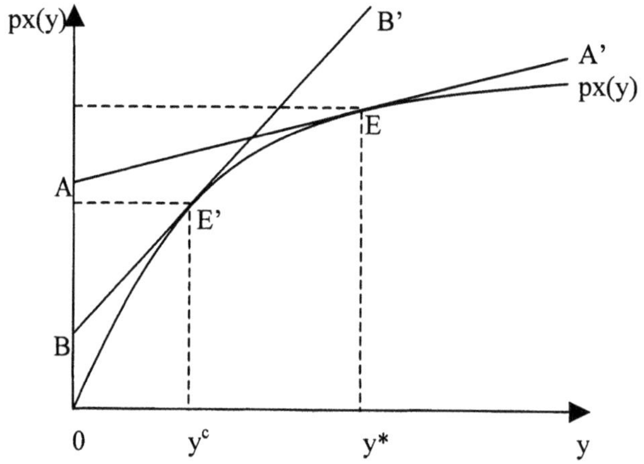

Fig. 6.4

Figure 6.4 shows graphically that the total income curve, px(y), is concave with respect to the X axis through decrease of the marginal productivity of labor. If the equilibrium is at E, which is the equilibrium of the profit-maximising company and of the cooperative company in the initial situation, with a debt reduction L the equilibrium will become E'. That is to say, from contracting y^* there is a decrease to contracting y^c. The reason for this is that on reducing fixed debt, L, of the cooperative company from, for instance, OA to OB, the equilibrium is altered, as the straight line BB' will meet E' on the income curve, and the work contracting figure will be lower, since:

$$y^c < y^*$$

Formally, this is shown on differentiation of the first-order equilibrium conditions of the cooperative company:

$$\frac{\partial^2 E}{\partial y^2} dy + \frac{\partial^2 E}{\partial y \partial L} = 0$$

hence:

$$\frac{\partial y}{\partial L} = \frac{\partial^2 E / \partial y \partial L}{\partial^2 E / \partial y^2} = -\frac{1}{E''(y)y^2} > 0$$

On the other hand, the cooperative company also responds in a way contrary to that of a competitive firm if the product sale-price changes. Thus, in a neo-classical company, a rise in the price causes an increase in the output produced and the contracted quantity of the labor factor. Figure 6.5 shows this fact in graphical form.

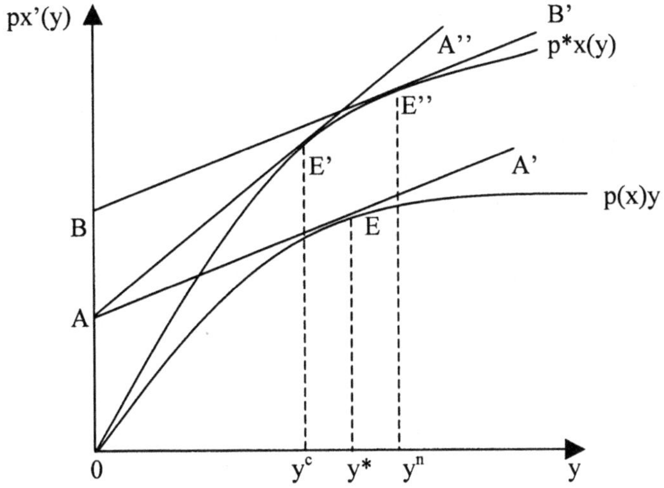

Fig. 6.5

The initial equilibrium is given by point E, with contracting level y^*, for both the neo-classical and the cooperative company. If the price p is increased to p^*, the income curve moves upwards in parallel, from AA'(px(y)) to BB'($p^*x(y)$). The no-classical (profit-maximising) company is now placed at E'', with a contracting level y^n of the labor variable factor greater than y^*, i.e., $y^n > y^*$. The cooperative company, whose debt has not varied, will maximise the AA'' inclination and move to E', decreasing the quantity of labor contracting to y^c and thus reducing output, while the worker's excess rises.

Formally, we can arrive at this result by differentiating with respect to the price:

$$x'(y)dp + px''(y)\frac{dy}{dp}dp - \frac{1}{y^2}\left[yx(y)dp + ypx'(y)\frac{dy}{dp}(px(y) - L)dp\right] = 0$$

Through operations, we arrive at:

$$\frac{dy}{dp}dp = \frac{x(y) - yx'(y)}{xpx''(y)} < 0$$

That is to say that the cooperative firm tends to reduce its output when conditions improve, i.e., if sale prices rise or remuneration of fixed expenses decreases, which is just the opposite of what happens with a neo-classical company, which takes advantage of these improvements. In fact, the cooperative company takes advantage of the improved conditions by increasing the excess of each worker, while reducing the contracting of work and hiring of workers. The result of the cooperative company is thus an inefficient allocation of resources.

6.4 Behavioural Models of the Company

A company can be viewed as an entity with a range of different and idiosyncratic components and, in particular, in dynamic contexts a company has routine components. Therefore the behaviour of a company and its management when facing uncertainty, according to Nelson and Winter (1982), is to look at the company's production history and adopt production 'routines'. There are costs associated with changing 'routines' and with organisation members adapting to such changes. For instance, how should labor and capital be combined? Facing such a decision, one may adopt a routine solution or else invest in order to try to adopt a 'better routine' over the long term.

This means that production functions are not certain, as in the neo-classical context, but involve uncertainties and vary over time. Note that there is a 'common component' in such uncertainty, alongside an 'idiosyncratic component'. Nelson and Winter hold that it is unlikely that a company will know what the distribution of the 'common' and the 'idiosyncratic component' is in the production function. What the company's managers know is the pattern of production activities performed in the past, i.e., the company's 'routine'. The owners provide physical resources and must constantly resolve conflicts between employees, suppliers and other economic agents; they must find a 'truce' in which the agents of the conflicting parties 'agree' or become 'reconciled' and thus produce.

In sum, the company is like a battlefield in which the opposing interests of managers, workers, capitalists, customers and other agents clash and are settled in one way or another.

6.5 Company Models Based on Transaction Cost Economy

A company is an entity within which there occur transactions between agents. What is the difference between a transaction made within a company and a market transaction?

Williamson's (1985) transaction cost economy theory is based on the idea that, on performing a transaction, the agents involved incur a number of costs. There are 'ex ante' and 'ex post' costs depending on whether they are incurred before making a contract or afterwards. The key issue is that such 'transaction costs' are not as clearly perceived as 'explicit costs'. Whenever an individual enters a contract, he faces a very wide range of contingencies; in fact, when the contingencies appear, a new negotiation may have to be engaged in.

Moreover, individuals try to maximise their own interests. There is an 'agency problem' or a problem of delegation by a principal to an agent.

Individuals can be classified in line with Williamson (1985) and Kreps (1995) on a three-by-three table, where the first dimension is the individual's degree of rationality and the second is his orientation in seeking his own interests.

On this model there are three categories for the degree of rationality: complete rationality, limited rationality and a behavioural individual. The completely rational individual can assess and select from among the different options at no cost and instantaneously. The limited-rationality individual cannot assess the different options, incurs costs and must prepare for ex ante and ex post contingencies. The behavioural individual follows a pattern of behaviour that does not maximise a utility function.

The second dimension is individuals' orientation in seeking his own interests. In this case, individuals can be classified into three categories: the utopian individual, who besides maximising his own interests pursues 'the common good'; the honest individual, who maximises his own interest while complying with 'honor' or 'ethics'; and the opportunist, who pursues his own interests and fails to meet some of his obligations.

Figure 6.6 represents the classification outlined above:

<table>
<tr><th></th><th>Utopian</th><th>Honest</th><th>Opportunistic</th></tr>
<tr><td>Behavioural</td><td colspan="3">Evolutionary theory</td></tr>
<tr><td>Limited R.</td><td rowspan="2">Team theory</td><td>Temporary equilibrium</td><td>Transaction Cost Economy</td></tr>
<tr><td>Complete R.</td><td>General equilibrium</td><td>Information Economy</td></tr>
</table>

Fig. 6.6

So if an individual is behavioural, his orientation in seeking his own interests is irrelevant, as he does not act in his own interest. Evolutionary theories such as Nelson and Winter's (1985), applied to decisions by consumers and companies, are best suited to explain that situation.

With limited or complete rationality and in the case of utopian individuals, 'team theory' would apply, in which individuals have the same utility function, something like a social welfare function. Even if all individuals do not have the same information, all act to maximise a sole criterion of global welfare.

Completely rational and honest individuals would give rise to general equilibrium. In this case, there is no private or misleading information. Completely rational and opportunistic individuals give rise to information-economy models, such as models of moral risk and incentives, adverse selection and signal transmission in the market.

Finally, limited-rationality honest individuals behave in a way explained by 'temporary equilibrium', while limited-rationality opportunistic individuals are explained precisely the transaction cost economy model.

Furthermore, Williamson classifies transactions themselves into three types: transaction with specific assets, transactions with a degree of uncertainty and transactions with frequency.

A transaction with specific assets is defined as an exchange relationship in which one party becomes linked to another. For instance, a tyre-rubber manufacturer located near a car factory.

A transaction with uncertainty is where the complexity of the transaction gives rise to limited rationality.

A transaction frequently repeated can generate rules that, though costly, can be amortised through spreading them out over many other transactions. However, this cannot happen if the transaction is not repeated.

Transactions can also be classified by the modes or rules that govern them. Thus, we have complete and incomplete contracts. The first type details all contingencies while the second does not. We can also have an explicit, rigid contract, such as the rules of a game, or an implicit contract whose rules arise from custom and daily practice, such as rights of way between land properties. Contracts can also be long term or short term, and re-negotiable or not re-negotiable. The former does not contemplate constraints of liquidity, wealth, etc., while the latter contemplates such constraints ex ante.

A classic contract is one in which all issues are specified. A neo-classical three-party contract, on the other hand, adds a third party who will determine damages between the parties in the event of any contingency. A bilateral relationship is one lacking a formal agreement in which each party trusts in its own ability to solve the range of contingencies. A particular case is a hierarchical relationship, in which the party higher up in the hierarchy determines how the contract is to be performed.

Finally, when one party to the transaction controls the assets of the counterparty, we find a unified governing structure. Here, ownership is coupled to control.

Figure 6.7 shows transactions according to their degree of frequency, specificity of assets and governing structure.

	Non-specific	Intermediate specificity	Highly specific
Occasional	Classical	Trilateral	Trilateral or unified
Frequent	Classical	Bilateral (hierarchical)	Unified

Fig. 6.7

Figure 6.7 is owed to Williamson and means that, for instance, if the assets are non-specific, whether the relationship is frequent or occasional a classic contract is more usual. When the assets are intermediately specific, contracts are either trilateral (if occasional) or bilateral, including hierarchical if they are more frequent. When assets are very specific, contact costs are very high and the governing structure must be unified, i.e., one party acquires the other achieving total control.

By way of conclusion, a company fits in with a unified governing structure. Thus, a company is an entity that holds assets and in behalf of which goods are consumed in the various transactions between agents, be they individuals or other companies. We are not concerned here with whether the company is a public limited company, a sole trader, etc. Our concern is to relate a company thus conceived with the market. The relationship is clear, companies act in markets playing the same role as individual consumers; in the end, consumers offer productive services and demand consumer goods through a range of transactions of all kinds. Such transactions are framed under contracts that must always be incomplete, as individuals are limited-rationality opportunists. Thus production models are configured in which problems arise of moral risk, adverse selection, signaling and incentives. Therefore, transaction cost theory is an eclectic theory between the neo-classical view, where the physical aspects of production are key (the company is a black box) and a personalistic perspective encompassing such concepts as power, culture, dependency, etc., making for a psycho-social approach over and above physical and natural resources.

References

Ames, E.: Soviet Economic Processes. London 1965. In: Archibald, G. C. *Theory of the Firm*. Penguin 1971

Baumol, W. J.: *Business Behaviour, Value and Growth*. Macmillan, ed. rev. Harcourt, Brace and World 1967

Kreps, D. M.: *A Course in Microeconomic Theory*. McGraw-Hill 1995

Marris, R.: A Model of the Managerial Enterprise. *Quarterly Journal of Economics* (1963)

Marris, R.: *Theory of Managerial Capitalism*. Macmillan 1964

Nelson, R., Winter, S.: *An Evolutionary Theory of Economic Change*. Cambridge, Mass., Belknap/Harvard University Press 1982

Vanek, J.: *The General Theory of Labor-Managed Market Economies*. N. York 1970

Williamson, O.: *The Economic Institutions of Capitalism*. New York, Free Press 1985

Segura, J.: *Análisis Microeconómico*. Alianza Universidad Textos 1988

7 Main Forms of Production and Cost Functions

As in chapter 2, we present in this chapter the main functional forms in a basically instrumental manner, describing, in two main sections, the Cobb-Douglas and CES functional forms. For such functional forms, the input classic demand, profit and supply functions are obtained from the first and second-order conditions of the profit maximisation problem, as well as the input conditioned demand and cost functions. Moreover, the Hotelling and Shephard theorems are proved and the long-run average and marginal cost curves are obtained. In both functional forms, we perform a duality application at the end.

Finally, at the end of the chapter, some reading is also recommended here and more practical exercises are provided.

7.1 The Cobb-Douglas Production Function

7.1.1 Characterisation

The production possibility set is:

$$X_i = \{(x, -y_1, -y_2) \text{ in} R^3_+ : x \leq \gamma\, y_1^{\alpha_1} y_2^{\alpha_2}\}.$$

The input requirement set is:

$$V(x) = \{(y_1, y_2) \text{ in} R^2_+ : x \leq \gamma y_1^{\alpha_1} y_2^{\alpha_2}\}.$$

The isoquants are:

$$Q(x) = \{(y_1, y_2) \text{ in} R^2_+ : x = \gamma y_1^{\alpha_1} y_2^{\alpha_2}\}.$$

Finally, the Cobb-Douglas Production Function is:

$$f(y_1, y_2) = x = \gamma y_1^{\alpha_1} y_2^{\alpha_2}$$

7.1.2 The Marginal Rate of Technical Substitution (MRTS)

$$\mathrm{MRTS} = \frac{-dy_2}{dy_1} = \frac{\dfrac{\partial f}{\partial y_1}}{\dfrac{\partial f}{\partial y_2}} = \frac{f_1}{f_2}$$

$$f_1 = \frac{\partial f(y_1, y_2)}{\partial y_1} = \alpha_1 \gamma \frac{y_1^{\alpha_1}}{y_1} y_2^{\alpha_2} = \alpha_1 \frac{x}{y_1}$$

$$f_2 = \frac{\partial f(y_1, y_2)}{\partial y_2} = \alpha_2 \gamma\, y_1^{\alpha_1} \frac{y_2^{\alpha_2}}{y_2} = \alpha_2 \frac{x}{y_2}$$

Then

$$\mathrm{MRTS} = \frac{\alpha_1 \dfrac{x}{y_1}}{\alpha_2 \dfrac{x}{y_2}} = \frac{\alpha_1}{\alpha_2} \frac{y_2}{y_1}$$

depends only on the relative shares of the inputs and/or the absolute quantities.

7.1.3 The Elasticity of Substitution

$$\sigma = \frac{d \ln\left(\dfrac{y_2}{y_1}\right)}{d \ln \mathrm{MRTS}} = \frac{\dfrac{d\left(\dfrac{y_2}{y_1}\right)}{\left(\dfrac{y_2}{y_1}\right)}}{\dfrac{d\mathrm{MRTS}}{\mathrm{MRTS}}} = \frac{d\left(\dfrac{y_2}{y_1}\right)}{d\mathrm{MRTS}} \frac{\mathrm{MRTS}}{\dfrac{y_2}{y_1}}$$

$$\mathrm{MRTS} = \frac{\alpha_1}{\alpha_2} \frac{y_2}{y_1} \Rightarrow \frac{y_2}{y_1} = \frac{\alpha_2}{\alpha_1} \mathrm{MRTS}$$

then we have that

$$\frac{d\left(\dfrac{y_2}{y_1}\right)}{d\mathrm{MRTS}} = \frac{\alpha_2}{\alpha_1}$$

and therefore:

$$\sigma = \frac{\alpha_2}{\alpha_1}\left(\frac{\frac{\alpha_1}{\alpha_2}\frac{y_2}{y_1}}{\frac{y_2}{y_1}}\right) = 1.$$

7.1.4 Returns to Scale

The Cobb-Douglas Function is homogeneous of degree $(\alpha_1 + \alpha_2)$. Then if we have

$E = \alpha_1 + \alpha_2 > 1 \Rightarrow$ increasing returns to scale.

$E = \alpha_1 + \alpha_2 = 1 \Rightarrow$ constant returns to scale.

$E = \alpha_1 + \alpha_2 < 1 \Rightarrow$ decreasing returns to scale.

7.1.5 The Profit Function and Input Demand Functions

The maximising behaviour of the profits of a competitive firm can be expressed as follows:

$$\max P\, f(\mathbf{y}) - \mathbf{w}(\mathbf{y})$$

w and **y** being vectors.

That is to say,

$$\max \Pi^0 = \max P\left[\gamma\, y_1^{\alpha_1} y_2^{\alpha_2}\right] - w_1 y_1 - w_2 y_2$$

The first-order conditions are

$$\left.\begin{aligned} \frac{\partial \Pi^0}{\partial y_1} &= P\alpha_1 \frac{x}{y_1} - w_1 = 0 \\ \frac{\partial \Pi^0}{\partial y_2} &= P\alpha_2 \frac{x}{y_2} - w_2 = 0 \end{aligned}\right\} \rightarrow \frac{\alpha_1}{\alpha_2}\frac{y_2}{y_1} = \frac{w_1}{w_2}.$$

From the first derivate we have that

$$P\alpha_1 \gamma\, y_1^{\alpha_1 - 1} y_2^{\alpha_2} - w_1 = 0$$

solving y_2

$$y_2^{\alpha_2} = \frac{w_1}{P\alpha_1 \gamma\, y_1^{\alpha_1 - 1}} \rightarrow y_2 = \frac{w_1^{\frac{1}{\alpha_2}}}{\left(P\alpha_1 \gamma\, y_1^{\alpha_1 - 1}\right)^{\frac{1}{\alpha_2}}}$$

from the second derivate we have

$$y_2^{\alpha_2 - 1} P \alpha_2 \gamma\, y_1^{\alpha_1} - w_2 = 0,$$

on the other hand

$$y_2^{\alpha_2 - 1} = \frac{w_1^{\frac{\alpha_2 - 1}{\alpha_2}}}{\left(P \alpha_1 \gamma\, y_1^{\alpha_1 - 1}\right)^{\frac{\alpha_2 - 1}{\alpha_2}}}$$

then

$$P \alpha_2 \gamma\, y_1^{\alpha_1} \frac{w_1^{\frac{\alpha_2 - 1}{\alpha_2}}}{\left(P \alpha_1 \gamma\, y_1^{\alpha_1 - 1}\right)^{\frac{\alpha_2 - 1}{\alpha_2}}} = w_2$$

rearranging

$$P P^{\frac{1-\alpha_2}{\alpha_2}} \alpha_2 \alpha_1^{\frac{1-\alpha_2}{\alpha_2}} \gamma \gamma^{\frac{1-\alpha_2}{\alpha_2}} y^{\alpha_1} y_1^{\frac{(1-\alpha_2)(\alpha_1 - 1)}{\alpha_2}} = w_2\, w_1^{\frac{1-\alpha_2}{\alpha_2}}$$

we have

$$(P \gamma)^{\frac{1}{\alpha_2}} y_1^{\frac{\alpha_1 + \alpha_2 - 1}{\alpha_2}} = \frac{w_2}{\alpha_2} \left(\frac{w_1}{\alpha_1}\right)^{\frac{1-\alpha_2}{\alpha_2}}$$

solving y_1 we obtain

$$y_1^{\frac{\alpha_1 + \alpha_2 - 1}{\alpha_2}} = \frac{w_2}{\alpha_2} \left(\frac{w_1}{\alpha_1}\right)^{\frac{1-\alpha_2}{\alpha_2}} (P \gamma)^{-\frac{1}{\alpha_2}}$$

$$y_1 = \left[\frac{w_2}{\alpha_2} \left(\frac{w_1}{\alpha_1}\right)^{\frac{1-\alpha_2}{\alpha_2}} (P \gamma)^{-\frac{1}{\alpha_2}}\right]^{\frac{\alpha_2}{\alpha_1 + \alpha_2 - 1}} =$$

$$= \left(\frac{w_2}{\alpha_2}\right)^{\frac{\alpha_2}{\alpha_1 + \alpha_2 - 1}} \left(\frac{w_1}{\alpha_1}\right)^{\frac{1-\alpha_2}{\alpha_1 + \alpha_2 - 1}} (P \gamma)^{\frac{-1}{\alpha_1 + \alpha_2 - 1}}$$

$$y_1 = \left[\frac{\left(\frac{w_2}{\alpha_2}\right)^{\alpha_2}\left(\frac{w_1}{\alpha_1}\right)^{1-\alpha_2}}{P\gamma}\right]^{\frac{1}{\alpha_1+\alpha_2-1}},$$

which is the demand for input y_1.

Likewise, we obtain the following demand function for input y_2:

$$y_2 = \left[\frac{\left(\frac{w_1}{\alpha_1}\right)^{\alpha_1}\left(\frac{w_2}{\alpha_2}\right)^{1-\alpha_1}}{P\gamma}\right]^{\frac{1}{\alpha_1+\alpha_2-1}}$$

Substituting y_1 (P, **w**) and y_2 (P, **w**) into the profit equation we obtain the profit function Π (P, **w**)

$$\Pi(P,\mathbf{w}) = P\gamma\left[\frac{\left(\frac{w_2}{\alpha_2}\right)^{\alpha_2}\left(\frac{w_1}{\alpha_1}\right)^{1-\alpha_2}}{P\gamma}\right]^{\frac{\alpha_1}{\alpha_1+\alpha_2-1}}\left[\frac{\left(\frac{w_1}{\alpha_1}\right)^{\alpha_1}\left(\frac{w_2}{\alpha_2}\right)^{1-\alpha_1}}{P\gamma}\right]^{\frac{\alpha_2}{\alpha_1+\alpha_2-1}} -$$

$$-w_1\left[\frac{\left(\frac{w_2}{\alpha_2}\right)^{\alpha_2}\left(\frac{w_1}{\alpha_1}\right)^{1-\alpha_2}}{P\gamma}\right]^{\frac{1}{\alpha_1+\alpha_2-1}} - w_2\left[\frac{\left(\frac{w_1}{\alpha_1}\right)^{\alpha_1}\left(\frac{w_2}{\alpha_2}\right)^{1-\alpha_1}}{P\gamma}\right]^{\frac{1}{\alpha_1+\alpha_2-1}}$$

From the first addend we have that

$$(P\gamma)^{1-\frac{\alpha_1}{\alpha_1+\alpha_2-1}-\frac{\alpha_2}{\alpha_1+\alpha_2-1}} = (P\gamma)^{\frac{\alpha_1+\alpha_2-1-\alpha_1-\alpha_2}{\alpha_1+\alpha_2-1}} = (P\gamma)^{\frac{-1}{\alpha_1+\alpha_2-1}}$$

therefore,

Π (P, **w**) =

$$(P\gamma)^{\frac{-1}{\alpha_1+\alpha_2-1}}\left[\left(\frac{w_2}{\alpha_2}\right)^{\frac{\alpha_1\alpha_2}{\alpha_1+\alpha_2-1}}\left(\frac{w_2}{\alpha_2}\right)^{\frac{(1-\alpha_1)\alpha_2}{\alpha_1+\alpha_2-1}}\left(\frac{w_1}{\alpha_1}\right)^{\frac{(1-\alpha_2)\alpha_1}{\alpha_1+\alpha_2-1}}\left(\frac{w_1}{\alpha_1}\right)^{\frac{\alpha_1\alpha_2}{\alpha_1+\alpha_2-1}}\right. \quad \square$$

$$-w_1\left(\frac{w_2}{\alpha_2}\right)^{\frac{\alpha_2}{\alpha_1+\alpha_2-1}}\left(\frac{w_1}{\alpha_1}\right)^{\frac{1-\alpha_2}{\alpha_1+\alpha_2-1}}-w_2\left(\frac{w_1}{\alpha_1}\right)^{\frac{\alpha_1}{\alpha_1+\alpha_2-1}}\left(\frac{w_2}{\alpha_2}\right)^{\frac{1-\alpha_1}{\alpha_1+\alpha_2-1}}\Bigg]=$$

$$=\left(\frac{1}{P\gamma}\right)^{\frac{1}{\alpha_1+\alpha_2-1}}\left[\left(\frac{w_2}{\alpha_2}\right)^{\frac{\alpha_1\alpha_2+\alpha_2-\alpha_1\alpha_2}{\alpha_1+\alpha_2-1}}\left(\frac{w_1}{\alpha_1}\right)^{\frac{\alpha_1-\alpha_1\alpha_2+\alpha_1\alpha_2}{\alpha_1+\alpha_2-1}}-\right.$$

$$\left.-w_1\left(\frac{w_2}{\alpha_2}\right)^{\frac{\alpha_2}{\alpha_1+\alpha_2-1}}\left(\frac{w_1}{\alpha_1}\right)^{\frac{\alpha_1}{\alpha_1+\alpha_2-1}-1}-w_2\left(\frac{w_1}{\alpha_1}\right)^{\frac{\alpha_1}{\alpha_1+\alpha_2-1}}\left(\frac{w_2}{\alpha_2}\right)^{\frac{\alpha_2}{\alpha_1+\alpha_2-1}-1}\right]$$

given $\alpha_1+\alpha_2-1=A$ and taking the common factor

$$\Pi(P,\mathbf{w})=\left(\frac{1}{P\gamma}\right)^{\frac{1}{A}}\left[\left(\frac{w_2}{\alpha_2}\right)^{\frac{\alpha_2}{A}}\left(\frac{w_1}{\alpha_1}\right)^{\frac{\alpha_1}{A}}\right]\left[1-\frac{w_1}{\frac{w_1}{\alpha_1}}-\frac{w_2}{\frac{w_2}{\alpha_2}}\right]=$$

$$=\left(\frac{1}{P\gamma}\right)^{\frac{1}{A}}\left(\frac{w_2}{\alpha_2}\right)^{\frac{\alpha_2}{A}}\left(\frac{w_1}{\alpha_1}\right)^{\frac{\alpha_1}{A}}(1-\alpha_1-\alpha_2)$$

$$\Pi(P,\mathbf{w})=-A\left(\frac{1}{P\gamma}\right)^{\frac{1}{A}}\left(\frac{w_2}{\alpha_2}\right)^{\frac{\alpha_2}{A}}\left(\frac{w_1}{\alpha_1}\right)^{\frac{\alpha_1}{A}},$$

which is the profit function.

Π (P, **w**) > 0 when $A<0 \Rightarrow \alpha_1+\alpha_2-1<0$,

then, when $\alpha_1+\alpha_2<1$ (decreasing returns to scale).

Π (P, **w**) = 0

when we have constant returns to scale, and

Π (P, **w**) > 0

then we have increasing returns to scale.

7.1.6 Hotelling's Theorem

By deriving the profit function with respect to an input price, we get the demand for the said input:

$$\frac{\partial \Pi}{\partial w_1} = -A\left(\frac{1}{P\gamma}\right)^{\frac{1}{A}}\left(\frac{w_2}{\alpha_2}\right)^{\frac{\alpha_2}{A}}\left(\frac{1}{\alpha_1}\right)^{\frac{\alpha_1}{A}}\frac{\alpha_1}{A} w_1^{\frac{\alpha_1}{A}-1} =$$

$$= \left(\frac{1}{P\gamma}\right)^{\frac{1}{A}}\left(\frac{w_2}{\alpha_2}\right)^{\frac{\alpha_2}{A}} \alpha_1^{\frac{-\alpha_1}{A}+1} w_1^{\frac{\alpha_1}{A}-1} = \left(\frac{1}{P\gamma}\right)^{\frac{1}{A}}\left(\frac{w_2}{\alpha_2}\right)^{\frac{\alpha_2}{A}}\left(\frac{w_1}{\alpha_1}\right)^{\frac{\alpha_1}{A}-1}$$

$$\frac{1}{A} = \frac{1}{\alpha_1+\alpha_2-1}$$

then we have

$$\frac{\partial \Pi}{\partial w_1} = \left[\frac{\left(\frac{w_2}{\alpha_2}\right)^{\alpha_2}\left(\frac{w_1}{\alpha_1}\right)^{1-\alpha_2}}{P\gamma}\right]^{\frac{1}{\alpha_1+\alpha_2-1}} = -y_1$$

7.1.7 The Cost Function and Input Conditioned Demand Functions

The profit-maximising behaviour can be stated as follows:

$$\left.\begin{array}{l} \min C = w_1\, y_1 + w_2\, y_2 \\ \text{s.to} \quad x = \gamma\, y_1^{\alpha_1}\, y_2^{\alpha_2} \end{array}\right\},$$

which is the dual.

The additional Lagrangian would be

$$C(y_1, y_2, \lambda) = w_1\, y_1 + w_2\, y_2 - \lambda\left[\gamma\, y_1^{\alpha_1}\, y_2^{\alpha_2} - x\right]$$

where the first-order conditions are

$$\frac{\partial C}{\partial y_1} = w_1 - \lambda\,\gamma\,\alpha_1\, y_1^{\alpha_1-1}\, y_2^{\alpha_2} = w_1 - \lambda\frac{\alpha_1\, x}{y_1} = 0$$

$$\frac{\partial C}{\partial y_2} = w_2 - \lambda\,\gamma\,\alpha_2\, y_1^{\alpha_1}\, y_2^{\alpha_2-1} = w_2 - \lambda\frac{\alpha_2\, x}{y_2} = 0$$

from which we obtain

$$\frac{w_1}{w_2} = \frac{\alpha_1\, y_2}{\alpha_2\, y_1} \rightarrow y_2 = \frac{w_1\, \alpha_2}{w_2\, \alpha_1} y_1$$

on the other hand, from the restriction we have

$$y_2 = \left(\frac{x}{\gamma \, y_1^{\alpha_1}} \right)^{\frac{1}{\alpha_2}} = x^{\frac{1}{\alpha_2}} \gamma^{-\frac{1}{\alpha_2}} y_1^{-\frac{\alpha_1}{\alpha_2}} .$$

Substituting in the first-order conditions

$$x^{\frac{1}{\alpha_2}} \gamma^{-\frac{1}{\alpha_2}} y_1^{-\frac{\alpha_1}{\alpha_2}} = \frac{w_1}{w_2} \frac{\alpha_2}{\alpha_1} y_1,$$

and solving y_1:

$$x^{\frac{1}{\alpha_2}} \gamma^{-\frac{1}{\alpha_2}} \frac{w_2}{w_1} \frac{\alpha_1}{\alpha_2} = y_1 \, y_1^{\frac{\alpha_1}{\alpha_2}} = y_1^{\frac{\alpha_1+\alpha_2}{\alpha_2}}$$

where $\alpha_1 + \alpha_2 = E$, represents the returns to scale. Then we have

$$y_1 = \left[\frac{\alpha_1}{\alpha_2} \frac{w_2}{w_1} \gamma^{-\frac{1}{\alpha_2}} x^{\frac{1}{\alpha_2}} \right]^{\frac{\alpha_2}{\alpha_1+\alpha_2}} = \left(\frac{\alpha_1}{\alpha_2} \frac{w_2}{w_1} \right)^{\frac{\alpha_2}{E}} \gamma^{-\frac{1}{E}} x^{\frac{1}{E}} = \hat{y}_1(\mathbf{w}, x).$$

Input conditioned demand for y_1.

Likewise, the input conditioned demand for y_2 is

$$y_2 = \hat{y}_2(\mathbf{w}, x) = \left(\frac{\alpha_2}{\alpha_1} \frac{w_1}{w_2} \right)^{\frac{\alpha_1}{E}} \gamma^{-\frac{1}{E}} x^{\frac{1}{E}}$$

The cost function is obtained by substituting y_1 and y_2 into the objective function

$$C(\mathbf{w}, x) = w_1 \, y_1 + w_2 \, y_2 = w_1 \left[\left(\frac{\alpha_1}{\alpha_2} \frac{w_2}{w_1} \right)^{\frac{\alpha_2}{E}} \left(\frac{x}{\gamma} \right)^{\frac{1}{E}} \right] +$$

$$+ w_2 \left[\left(\frac{\alpha_2}{\alpha_1} \frac{w_1}{w_2} \right)^{\frac{\alpha_1}{E}} \left(\frac{x}{\gamma} \right)^{\frac{1}{E}} \right] =$$

$$= \left(\frac{x}{\gamma} \right)^{\frac{1}{E}} \left[\left(\frac{\alpha_1}{\alpha_2} \right)^{\frac{\alpha_2}{E}} w_2^{\frac{\alpha_2}{E}} w_1^{-\frac{\alpha_2}{E}+1} + \left(\frac{\alpha_2}{\alpha_1} \right)^{\frac{\alpha_1}{E}} w_1^{\frac{\alpha_1}{E}} w_2^{1-\frac{\alpha_1}{E}} \right]$$

finally we have

$$C(\mathbf{w},x)=\left(\frac{x}{\gamma}\right)^{\frac{1}{E}} w_1^{\frac{\alpha_1}{E}} w_2^{\frac{\alpha_2}{E}}\left[\left(\frac{\alpha_1}{\alpha_2}\right)^{\frac{\alpha_2}{E}}+\left(\frac{\alpha_2}{\alpha_1}\right)^{\frac{\alpha_1}{E}}\right]$$

which is the long-run cost function.

7.1.8 Shephard's Lemma

It can be observed that the Shephard's Lemma is satisfied:

$$\frac{\partial C}{\partial w_i}=\hat{y}_i$$

$$\frac{\partial C}{\partial w_1}=\left(\frac{x}{\gamma}\right)^{\frac{1}{E}}\frac{\alpha_1}{E} w_1^{\frac{\alpha_1}{E}-1} w_2^{\frac{\alpha_2}{E}}\left[\left(\frac{\alpha_1}{\alpha_2}\right)^{\frac{\alpha_2}{E}}+\left(\frac{\alpha_2}{\alpha_1}\right)^{\frac{\alpha_1}{E}}\right]$$

where

$$\frac{\alpha_1}{E}\left[\left(\frac{\alpha_1}{\alpha_2}\right)^{\frac{\alpha_2}{E}}+\left(\frac{\alpha_2}{\alpha_1}\right)^{\frac{\alpha_1}{E}}\right]=\frac{\alpha_1}{E}\left[\left(\frac{\alpha_1}{\alpha_2}\right)^{\frac{\alpha_2}{E}}+\frac{\alpha_2}{\alpha_1}\left(\frac{\alpha_1}{\alpha_2}\right)^{\frac{\alpha_2}{E}}\right]=$$

$$=\frac{\alpha_1}{E}\left(\frac{\alpha_1}{\alpha_2}\right)^{\frac{\alpha_2}{E}}\left(1+\frac{\alpha_2}{\alpha_1}\right)=\frac{\alpha_1}{E}\left(\frac{\alpha_1}{\alpha_2}\right)^{\frac{\alpha_2}{E}}\frac{\alpha_1+\alpha_2}{\alpha_1}=\left(\frac{\alpha_1}{\alpha_2}\right)^{\frac{\alpha_2}{E}}$$

then

$$\frac{\partial C}{\partial w_1}=\left(\frac{x}{\gamma}\right)^{\frac{1}{E}}\left(\frac{w_2}{w_1}\right)^{\frac{\alpha_2}{E}}\left(\frac{\alpha_1}{\alpha_2}\right)^{\frac{\alpha_2}{E}}=\left(\frac{\alpha_1}{\alpha_2}\frac{w_2}{w_1}\right)^{\frac{\alpha_2}{E}}\left(\frac{x}{\gamma}\right)^{\frac{1}{E}}=\hat{y}_1(\mathbf{w},x)$$

It can be observed that if we have constant returns to scale it is satisfied that:

$$C(\mathbf{w},x)=x\,C(\mathbf{w})=x\,C(\mathbf{w},1)$$

in this case $E=\alpha_1+\alpha_2=1$, then

$$C(\mathbf{w},x)=\frac{x}{\gamma}w_1^{\alpha_1}\,w_2^{\alpha_2}\left[\left(\frac{\alpha_1}{\alpha_2}\right)^{\alpha_2}+\left(\frac{\alpha_2}{\alpha_1}\right)^{\alpha_1}\right]$$

and on the other hand we have that

$$C(\mathbf{w},1)=\frac{1}{\gamma}w_1^{\alpha_1}\,w_2^{\alpha_2}\left[\left(\frac{\alpha_1}{\alpha_2}\right)^{\alpha_2}+\left(\frac{\alpha_2}{\alpha_1}\right)^{\alpha_1}\right]$$

therefore it is satisfied that

$$C(\mathbf{w},x)=x\left\{\frac{1}{\gamma}\;w_1^{\alpha_1}w_2^{\alpha_2}\left[\left(\frac{\alpha_1}{\alpha_2}\right)^{\alpha_2}+\left(\frac{\alpha_2}{\alpha_1}\right)^{\alpha_1}\right]\right\}=x\,C(\mathbf{w},1)=x\,C(\mathbf{w}).$$

7.1.9 LRAC and LRMC Curves

The functional expression of the Long Run Average Cost Curve is the following:

$$\mathrm{LRAC}(\mathbf{w},x)=\frac{C(\mathbf{w},x)}{x}=\left[\left(\frac{\alpha_1}{\alpha_2}\right)^{\frac{\alpha_2}{E}}+\left(\frac{\alpha_2}{\alpha_1}\right)^{\frac{\alpha_1}{E}}\right]w_1^{\frac{\alpha_1}{E}}w_2^{\frac{\alpha_2}{E}}\gamma^{-\frac{1}{E}}x^{\frac{1}{E}-1}$$

in order to find out whether it is increasing or not

$$\frac{\partial \mathrm{LRAC}}{\partial x}=\left[\left(\frac{\alpha_1}{\alpha_2}\right)^{\frac{\alpha_2}{E}}+\left(\frac{\alpha_2}{\alpha_1}\right)^{\frac{\alpha_1}{E}}\right]w_1^{\frac{\alpha_1}{E}}w_2^{\frac{\alpha_2}{E}}\gamma^{-\frac{1}{E}}\frac{1-E}{E}x^{\frac{1-E}{E}-1}.$$

If

$$1-E>0\Rightarrow\frac{\partial AC}{\partial x}>0\Rightarrow E=\alpha_1+\alpha_2<1$$

when we have decreasing returns to scale the LRAC's are increasing and viceversa.

And the following is the Long Run Marginal Cost Curve:

$$\mathrm{LRMC}=\frac{\partial C(\mathbf{w},x)}{\partial x}=\left[\left(\frac{\alpha_1}{\alpha_2}\right)^{\frac{\alpha_2}{E}}+\left(\frac{\alpha_2}{\alpha_1}\right)^{\frac{\alpha_1}{E}}\right]w_1^{\frac{\alpha_1}{E}}w_2^{\frac{\alpha_2}{E}}\gamma^{-\frac{1}{E}}\frac{1}{E}x^{\frac{1}{E}-1}$$

then

$$\frac{\partial \mathrm{LRMC}}{\partial x}=\left[\left(\frac{\alpha_1}{\alpha_2}\right)^{\frac{\alpha_2}{E}}+\left(\frac{\alpha_2}{\alpha_1}\right)^{\frac{\alpha_1}{E}}\right]w_1^{\frac{\alpha_1}{E}}w_2^{\frac{\alpha_2}{E}}\gamma^{-\frac{1}{E}}\frac{1}{E}\frac{1-E}{E}x^{\frac{1-2E}{E}}$$

if

$$1-E>0\Rightarrow\frac{\partial MC}{\partial x}>0\Rightarrow E<1$$

when we have decreasing returns to scale are decreasing the LRMC's are increasing.

7.1.10 Applying the Duality

Assume a given function such as

$$\Phi(w, x) = x\, w_1^{a}\, w_2^{1-a}$$

we should find out whether it is a cost function coming from a profit maximising behaviour. In other words, what can we know about the corresponding technology?

For Φ (**w**, x) to be a cost function of a given technology it must be satisfied that

1. There is an homogeneous cost function of degree one in the inputs prices:

   Φ (**w**, x) is H (1) in w.

   That is to say

   $$\Phi(tw, x) = x\, t^{a}\, w_1^{a}\, t^{1-a}\, w_2^{1-a} = t\, x\, w_1^{a}\, w_2^{1-a} = t\, \Phi(w, x).$$

2. The cost function is continuous and increasing for $\forall\, x > 0$ and $\forall\, w \geq 0$:

   Φ (**w**, x) ≥ 0, $\forall\, x > 0$, $\forall\, w \geq 0$.

   If and only if $w \geq 0$, it is satisfied that $\Phi \geq 0$.
3. On the cost functions it is possible to obtain the input demand functions provided that

   $$\frac{\partial \Phi}{\partial w_i} \geq 0.$$

   Therefore, we have that

   $$\left.\begin{aligned} \frac{\partial \Phi}{\partial w_1} &= a\, x\, w_1^{a-1}\, w_2^{1-a} \\ \frac{\partial \Phi}{\partial w_2} &= (1-a)\, x\, w_1^{a}\, w_2^{-a} \end{aligned}\right\},$$

   if $w_1 \geq 0$ and $w_2 \geq 0 \Rightarrow$ it is always satisfied that $a \leq 1$.
4. The cost function Φ (**w**, x) is concave in w, therefore

   $$H = \begin{vmatrix} \dfrac{\partial^2 \Phi}{\partial w_1^2} & \dfrac{\partial^2 \Phi}{\partial w_1 \partial w_2} \\ \dfrac{\partial^2 \Phi}{\partial w_2 \partial w_1} & \dfrac{\partial^2 \Phi}{\partial w_2^2} \end{vmatrix}$$

   must be negative semidefinite, i.e., $(-1)^n H^n \geq 0$, main n-order minor, therefore,

$$H_1 = \frac{\partial^2 \Phi}{\partial w_i^2} \leq 0.$$

and $H \geq 0$,

$$\frac{\partial^2 \Phi}{\partial w_2^2} = (1-a)(-a)x\, w_1^a w_2^{-a-1} \; [\text{when } 0 \leq a \leq 1]$$

$$\frac{\partial^2 \Phi}{\partial w_1^2} = a(a-1)w_1^{a-1-1} w_2^{1-a} x = a(a-1)w_1^{a-2} w_2^{1-a} x \; [\text{when } 0 \leq a \leq 1]$$

$$\left.\begin{aligned} \frac{\partial^2 \Phi}{\partial w_1 \partial w_2} &= a(1-a)w_1^{a-1} w_2^{1-a-1} x \\ \frac{\partial^2 \Phi}{\partial w_2 \partial w_1} &= (1-a)a\, w^{a-1} w_2^{-a} x \end{aligned}\right\}$$

are equal.
Then, we have that the Hessian is

$$H = \begin{vmatrix} a(a-1)w_1^{a-2} w_2^{1-a} x & a(1-a)w_1^{a-1} w_2^{-a} x \\ a(1-a)w_1^{a-1} w_2^{-a} x & -a(1-a)x\, w_1^a w_2^{-a-1} \end{vmatrix} =$$

$$= a^2(a-1)^2 w_1^{a-2+a} w_2^{1-a-a-1} x^2 - a^2(1-a)^2 w_1^{2a-2} w_2^{-2a} x^2 = 0,$$

which means that $H = 0$. Therefore, the concavity of the function Φ (**w**, x) is satisfied.

Since these four properties are satisfied the function Φ (**w**, x) is a cost function of a particular technology due to the integrability problem.

This is how the production function of the "convexified" technology is obtained:

Φ (**w**, x) = C (**w**, x)

by Shephard's Lemma we have

$$\hat{y}_1 = \frac{\partial \Phi}{\partial w_1} = a\, w_1^{a-1} w_2^{1-a} x = a\left(\frac{w_2}{w_1}\right)^{1-a} x$$

$$\hat{y}_2 = \frac{\partial \Phi}{\partial w_2} = (1-a)w_1^a w_2^{-a} x = (1-a)\left(\frac{w_1}{w_2}\right)^{a} x.$$

In this two equations w_2 / w_1 is eliminated and an x function in y_1 and y_2 is obtained. Rearranging:

$$\frac{y_1}{a\,x} = \left(\frac{w_2}{w_1}\right)^{1-a} \rightarrow \frac{w_2}{w_1} = \left(\frac{y_1}{a\,x}\right)^{\frac{1}{1-a}}$$

$$\left(\frac{w_2}{w_1}\right)^{a} = \frac{(1-a)x}{y_2} \rightarrow \frac{w_2}{w_1} = \left[\frac{(1-a)x}{y_2}\right]^{\frac{1}{a}}$$

$$\left(\frac{y_1}{a\,x}\right)^{\frac{1}{1-a}} = \left(\frac{(1-a)x}{y_2}\right)^{\frac{1}{a}} \Rightarrow \left(\frac{y_1}{a\,x}\right)^{a} = \left(\frac{(1-a)x}{y_2}\right)^{1-a}$$

then

$$y_1^a y_2^{1-a} = a^a (1-a)^{1-a} x^{a+(1-a)} = a^a (1-a)^{1-a} x$$

Therefore, the production function is

$$x = a^{-a} (1-a)^{a-1} y_1^a y_2^{1-a}$$

With $\gamma = a^{-a}\,(1\text{-}a)^{a-1}$, we have a Cobb-Douglas production function with constant returns to scale.

$$x = \gamma\, y_1^{\,a}\, y_2^{\,1-a}.$$

7.2 The CES Production Function

$$x = x\,(\,y_1, \ldots y_r\,) = A\,[\alpha_1\, y_1^{\,\varphi} + \alpha_2\, y_2^{\,\varphi} + \ldots + \alpha_r\, y_r^{\,\varphi}]^{V/\varphi}.$$

7.2.1 The Marginal Rate of Technical Substitution (MRTS)

Assume only two inputs

$$x = A\left[\alpha_1\, y_1^{\varphi} + \alpha_2\, y_2^{\varphi}\right]^{\frac{V}{\varphi}},$$

then we have

$$\text{MRTS} = \frac{\dfrac{\partial x}{\partial y_1}}{\dfrac{\partial x}{\partial y_2}} = \frac{f_1}{f_2} = \frac{\text{MP}_1}{\text{MP}_2}$$

$$\frac{\partial x}{\partial y_1} = A\frac{V}{\varphi}\left[\alpha_1 y_1^{\varphi} + \alpha_2 y_2^{\varphi}\right]^{\frac{V-\varphi}{\varphi}} \alpha_1 \varphi y_1^{\varphi-1} = V\alpha \frac{A\left[\alpha_1 y_1^{\varphi} + \alpha_2 y_2^{\varphi}\right]^{\frac{V}{\varphi}}}{\alpha_1 y_1^{\varphi} + \alpha_2 y_2^{\varphi}} y^{\varphi-1} =$$

$$= V\alpha_1 x \frac{y_1^{\varphi-1}}{\alpha_1 y_1^{\varphi} + \alpha_2 y_2^{\varphi}}$$

Analogously, the marginal product of the input y_2 is:

$$\frac{\partial x}{\partial y_2} = V\alpha_2 x \frac{y_2^{\varphi-1}}{\alpha_1 y_1^{\varphi} + \alpha_2 y_2^{\varphi}},$$

therefore,

$$MRTS = \frac{\alpha_1}{\alpha_2}\left(\frac{y_1}{y_2}\right)^{\varphi-1}$$

which depends only on the input proportion since $x(y_1, y_2)$ is homothetic.

7.2.2 Returns to Scale

The function $x(y_1, y_2)$ is homogeneous of degree V:

$$x(ty_1, ty_2) = A\left[\alpha_1 t^{\varphi} y^{\varphi} + \alpha_2 t^{\varphi} y_2^{\varphi}\right]^{\frac{V}{\varphi}} = A\left[t^{\varphi}\left(\alpha_1 y_1^{\varphi} + \alpha_2 y_2^{\varphi}\right)\right]^{\frac{V}{\varphi}} =$$

$$= t^V A\left(\alpha_1 y_1^{\varphi} + \alpha_2 y_2^{\varphi}\right)^{\frac{V}{\varphi}} = t^V x(y_1, y_2).$$

If $V<1$, then, we have decreasing returns to scale. Moreover, if $V=1$, we have constant returns to scale.

7.2.3 The Elasticity of Substitution

The advantage of this type of production function is that it presents a constant elasticity of substitution, but it is non-unitary, unlike in the Cobb-Douglas.

$$\sigma = \frac{d\ln\left(\frac{y_2}{y_1}\right)}{d\ln MRTS} = \frac{d\left(\frac{y_2}{y_1}\right)}{dMRTS}\frac{MRTS}{\frac{y_2}{y_1}}$$

since,

$$MRTS = \frac{\alpha_1}{\alpha_2}\left(\frac{y_1}{y_2}\right)^{\varphi-1} \Rightarrow \left(MRTS\frac{\alpha_2}{\alpha_1}\right)^{\frac{1}{1-\varphi}} = \frac{y_2}{y_1},$$

then

$$\frac{d\left(\frac{y_2}{y_1}\right)}{dMRTS}=\frac{1}{1-\varphi}\left(MRTS\frac{\alpha_2}{\alpha_1}\right)^{\frac{1}{1-\varphi}-1}\frac{\alpha_2}{\alpha_1}=\frac{1}{1-\varphi}MRTS^{\frac{\varphi}{1-\varphi}}\left(\frac{\alpha_2}{\alpha_1}\right)^{\frac{1}{1-\varphi}}$$

$$\sigma=\frac{1}{1-\varphi}MRTS^{\frac{\varphi}{1-\varphi}}\left(\frac{\alpha_2}{\alpha_1}\right)^{\frac{1}{1-\varphi}}\frac{MRTS}{\frac{y_2}{y_1}},$$

and we have

$$\sigma=\frac{1}{1-\varphi}\frac{y_1}{y_2}\left(MRTS\frac{\alpha_2}{\alpha_1}\right)^{\frac{1}{1-\varphi}}$$

$$\sigma=\frac{1}{1-\varphi}.$$

7.2.4 The Output Supply Function and Input Demand Functions

The behaviour of a competitive firm, which maximises goods, can be described as:

$$\max\Pi = P\,A\left[\alpha_1 y_1^{\varphi}+\alpha_2 y_2^{\varphi}\right]^{\frac{V}{\varphi}}-w_1 y_1-w_2 y_2.$$

From the first-order conditions we have that, it must be satisfied that

$$MRTS=\frac{\alpha_1}{\alpha_2}\left(\frac{y_1}{y_2}\right)^{\varphi-1}=\frac{w_1}{w_2},$$

or analogously,

$$\left(\frac{y_1}{y_2}\right)^{\varphi-1}=\left(\frac{y_2}{y_1}\right)^{1-\varphi}=\frac{w_1}{w_2}\frac{\alpha_2}{\alpha_1}\Rightarrow\frac{y_2}{y_1}=\left(\frac{w_1}{w_2}\frac{\alpha_2}{\alpha_1}\right)^{\frac{1}{1-\varphi}},$$

then,

$$\frac{y_2}{y_1}=\left(\frac{w_1}{w_2}\frac{\alpha_2}{\alpha_1}\right)^{\sigma}\Rightarrow y_2=\left(\frac{w_1}{w_2}\frac{\alpha_2}{\alpha_1}\right)^{\sigma}y_1,$$

From which we obtain

$$\frac{\alpha_2}{\alpha_1}\frac{y_2}{y_1}=\frac{\alpha_2}{\alpha_1}\left(\frac{w_1}{w_2}\frac{\alpha_2}{\alpha_1}\right)^{\sigma}=\left(\frac{w_1}{w_2}\right)^{\sigma}\left(\frac{\alpha_2}{\alpha_1}\right)^{\sigma+1}.$$

Moreover,

$$\left(\frac{y_2}{y_1}\right)^{\varphi} = \left(\frac{w_1}{w_2}\frac{\alpha_2}{\alpha_1}\right)^{\sigma\cdot\varphi} = \left(\frac{w_1}{w_2}\frac{\alpha_2}{\alpha_1}\right)^{\sigma-1},$$

Therefore,

$$\frac{\alpha_2 y_2^{\varphi}}{\alpha\ y_1^{\varphi}} = \frac{\alpha_2}{\alpha_1}\left(\frac{w_1}{w_2}\frac{\alpha_2}{\alpha_1}\right)^{\sigma-1} = \left(\frac{w_1}{w_2}\right)^{\sigma-1}\left(\frac{\alpha_2}{\alpha_1}\right)^{\sigma}.$$

In addition we have,

$$\frac{\alpha_2 y_2^{\varphi} + \alpha_1 y_1^{\varphi}}{\alpha_1 y_1^{\varphi}} = \frac{\alpha_2 y_2^{\varphi}}{\alpha_1 y_1^{\varphi}} + 1 = \left(\frac{w_1}{w_2}\right)^{\sigma-1}\left(\frac{\alpha_2}{\alpha_1}\right)^{\sigma} + 1.$$

From the production function we have

$$\alpha_2 y_2^{\varphi} + \alpha_1 y_1^{\varphi} = \left(\frac{x}{A}\right)^{\frac{\varphi}{V}} = \left[\left(\frac{w_1}{w_2}\right)^{\sigma-1}\left(\frac{\alpha_2}{\alpha_1}\right)^{\sigma} + 1\right]\alpha_1 y_1^{\varphi},$$

solving x:

$$x = A\,\alpha_1^{\frac{V}{\varphi}}\, y_1^{V}\left[\left(\frac{w_1}{w_2}\right)^{\sigma-1}\left(\frac{\alpha_2}{\alpha_1}\right)^{\sigma} + 1\right]^{\frac{V}{\varphi}}.$$

The first-order conditions for the maximisation of goods are

$$\left.\begin{aligned} \frac{P\alpha_1 V x\, y_1^{\varphi-1}}{\alpha_1 y_1^{\varphi} + \alpha_2 y_2^{\varphi}} &= w_1 \\ \frac{P\alpha_2 V x\, y_2^{\varphi-1}}{\alpha_1 y_1^{\varphi} + \alpha_2 y_2^{\varphi}} &= w_2 \end{aligned}\right\}.$$

By substituting x into the previous equation, we obtain the demand functions of the inputs y_1 and y_2 and the supply function of the output. Thus, by substituting x in the profit equation and applying the first-order conditions for the profit maximisation, we obtain

$$\Pi = px - w_1 y_1 - w_2 y_2$$

$$\Pi = p\,A\alpha_1^{\frac{V}{\varphi}}\, y_1^{V}\left[\left(\frac{w_1}{w_2}\right)^{\sigma-1}\left(\frac{\alpha_2}{\alpha_1}\right)^{\sigma} + 1\right]^{\frac{V}{\varphi}} - w_1 y_1 - w_2 y_2$$

$$\frac{\partial \Pi}{\partial y_1} = 0 = \frac{P\,V}{y_1} x - w_1 = 0,$$

from which:

$$\frac{P\,V\,x}{y_1} = w_1 \Rightarrow \frac{P\,V\,x}{w_1} = y_1 \Rightarrow \frac{P\,V\left[A\alpha_1^{\frac{V}{\varphi}}\, y_1^{V}\left[\left(\frac{w_1}{w_2}\right)^{\sigma-1}\left(\frac{\alpha_2}{\alpha_1}\right)^{\sigma}+1\right]^{\frac{V}{\varphi}}\right]}{w_1} = y_1$$

$$y_1 = \left[\frac{P\,V\left[A\alpha_1^{\frac{V}{\varphi}}\left[\left(\frac{w_1}{w_2}\right)^{\sigma-1}\left(\frac{\alpha_2}{\alpha_1}\right)^{\sigma}+1\right]^{\frac{V}{\varphi}}\right]}{w_1}\right]^{\frac{1}{1-\sigma}}$$

Therefore,

$y_1 = y_1\,(w_1, w_2, P)$.

Analogously, we now have the classic demand for the input y_2 for a CES function. Therefore, we must take into account that the production function can be expressed only depending on y_2 since

$$\frac{\alpha_2\, y_2^{\varphi} + \alpha_1\, y_1^{\varphi}}{\alpha_2\, y_2^{\varphi}} = 1 + \frac{\alpha_1\, y_1^{\varphi}}{\alpha_2\, y_2^{\varphi}} = \left(\frac{w_2}{w_1}\right)^{\sigma-1}\left(\frac{\alpha_1}{\alpha_2}\right)^{\sigma} + 1$$

from which

$$\alpha_2\, y_2^{\varphi} + \alpha_1 y_1^{\varphi} = \left(\frac{x}{A}\right)^{\frac{\varphi}{V}} y_2^{V}\left[\left(\frac{w_2}{w_1}\right)^{\sigma-1}\left(\frac{\alpha_1}{\alpha_2}\right)^{\sigma} + 1\right]\alpha_2\, y_2^{\varphi},$$

solving x:

$$x = A\,\alpha_2^{\frac{V}{\varphi}}\, y_2^{V}\left[\left(\frac{w_2}{w_1}\right)^{\sigma-1}\left(\frac{\alpha_1}{\alpha_2}\right)^{\sigma} + 1\right]^{\frac{V}{\varphi}},$$

by substituting the value of x in the profit equation and applying the first-order conditions for the profit maximisation we have:

$$\frac{\partial \Pi}{\partial y_2} = 0 = \frac{P\,V}{y_2} x - w_2 = 0,$$

from which

$$\frac{P V x}{w_2} = y_2$$

$$y_2 = \left[\frac{P V A \alpha_2^{\frac{V}{\varphi}} \left[\left(\frac{w_2}{w_1} \right)^{\sigma-1} \left(\frac{\alpha_1}{\alpha_2} \right)^{\sigma} + 1 \right]^{\frac{1}{\varphi}}}{w_2} \right]^{\frac{1}{1-V}}$$

therefore,

$$y_2 = y_2 \,(w_1, w_2, P)$$

On the other hand, the good supply function can be obtained by substituting the demand functions of the inputs (y_1, y_2) previously obtained in the production function

$$x = A\left[\alpha_1 y_1^{\varphi} + \alpha_2 y_2^{\varphi}\right]^{\frac{V}{\varphi}}$$

since the production function represents a profit maximisation technology in equilibrium, which can be expressed as

$$x = A\, \alpha_1^{\frac{V}{\varphi}} y_1^{V} \left[\left(\frac{w_1}{w_2} \right)^{\sigma-1} \left(\frac{\alpha_2}{\alpha_1} \right)^{\sigma} + 1 \right]^{\frac{V}{\varphi}},$$

a function which depends only on y_1. Therefore, the supply function is

$$x = A\, \alpha_1^{\frac{V}{\varphi}} \left[\frac{P V A \alpha_1^{\frac{V}{\varphi}} \left[\left(\frac{w_1}{w_2} \right)^{\sigma-1} \left(\frac{\alpha_2}{\alpha_1} \right)^{\sigma} + 1 \right]^{\frac{V}{\varphi}}}{w_1} \right]^{\frac{V}{1-V}} \left[\left(\frac{w_1}{w_2} \right)^{\sigma-1} \left(\frac{\alpha_2}{\alpha_1} \right)^{\sigma} + 1 \right]^{\frac{V}{\varphi}}$$

therefore,

$$x = x\,(w_1, w_2, P).$$

7.2.5 The Cost Function and Input Conditioned Demand Functions

The rational behaviour of the firm can be expressed as follows:

$$\left.\begin{array}{l}\min w_1 y_1 + w_2 y_2 = C \\ \text{s.to } x = A\left[\alpha_1 y_1^{\varphi} + \alpha_2 y_2^{\varphi}\right]^{\frac{v}{\varphi}}\end{array}\right\}.$$

From the first-order conditions we have that, in equilibrium

$$\frac{w_1}{w_2} = \frac{\alpha_1}{\alpha_2}\left(\frac{y_1}{y_2}\right)^{\varphi-1} = \frac{\alpha_1}{\alpha_2}\left(\frac{y_2}{y_1}\right)^{\frac{1}{\sigma}}.$$

Therefore,

$$\frac{y_2}{y_1} = \left(\frac{w_1}{w_2}\frac{\alpha_2}{\alpha_1}\right)^{\sigma} \Rightarrow \frac{w_1 y_1}{w_2 y_2} = \left(\frac{w_1}{w_2}\right)\left(\frac{y_1}{y_2}\right) = \left(\frac{y_2}{y_1}\right)^{\frac{1}{\sigma}}\frac{\alpha_1}{\alpha_2}\frac{y_1}{y_2},$$

and,

$$\frac{w_1 y_1}{w_2 y_2} = \left(\frac{y_2}{y_1}\right)^{\frac{1}{\sigma}-1}\frac{\alpha_1}{\alpha_2} \Rightarrow \frac{w_1 y_1 + w_2 y_2}{w_2 y_2} = \left(\frac{y_2}{y_1}\right)^{-\varphi}\frac{\alpha_1}{\alpha_2} + 1,$$

from which we obtain

$$\frac{C}{w_2 y_2} = \left(\frac{y_1}{y_2}\right)^{\varphi}\frac{\alpha_1}{\alpha_2} + 1 = \frac{\alpha_1 y_1^{\varphi} + \alpha_2 y_2^{\varphi}}{\alpha_2 y_2^{\varphi}} = \frac{\left(\frac{x}{A}\right)^{\frac{\varphi}{v}}}{\alpha_2 y_2^{\varphi}}.$$

Solving y_2

$$C\left(\frac{x}{A}\right)^{-\frac{\varphi}{v}} = \frac{w_2}{\alpha_2} y_2^{1-\varphi},$$

then,

$$y_2 = \left[C\left(\frac{x}{A}\right)^{-\frac{\varphi}{v}}\frac{\alpha_2}{w_2}\right]^{\frac{1}{1-\varphi}} = C^{\sigma}\left(\frac{x}{A}\right)^{-\frac{1}{v}\left(\frac{\varphi}{1-\varphi}\right)}\left(\frac{\alpha_2}{w_2}\right)^{\sigma}.$$

Therefore, it can be written that

$$w_2 y_2 = C^{\sigma}\left(\frac{x}{A}\right)^{\frac{-\varphi\sigma}{v}}\alpha_2^{\sigma} w_2^{1-\sigma}.$$

Likewise,

$$w_1 y_1 = C^{\sigma}\left(\frac{x}{A}\right)^{\frac{-\varphi\sigma}{V}} \alpha_1^{\sigma} w_1^{1-\sigma}.$$

In conclusion, the cost of producing “x” units of a particular output is

$$C(\mathbf{w},x) = w_1 y_1 + w_2 y_2 = C^{\sigma}\left(\frac{x}{A}\right)^{\frac{-\varphi s}{V}} a_1^{\sigma} w_1^{1-\sigma} + C^{\sigma}\left(\frac{x}{A}\right)^{\frac{-\varphi\sigma}{V}} a_2^{\sigma} w_2^{1-\sigma}$$

$$[C(\mathbf{w},x)]^{1-\sigma} = \left(\frac{x}{A}\right)^{\frac{-\varphi\sigma}{V}} \left[\alpha_1^{\sigma} w_1^{1-\sigma} + \alpha_2^{\sigma} w_2^{1-\sigma}\right]$$

then, we have

$$C^{1-\sigma} = \left(\frac{x}{A}\right)^{\frac{1-\sigma}{V}} \left(\alpha_1^{\sigma} w^{1-\sigma} + \alpha_2^{\sigma} w_2^{1-\sigma}\right)$$

The long-run cost functions is

$$C(\mathbf{w},x) = \left(\frac{x}{A}\right)^{\frac{1}{V}} \left(\alpha_1^{\sigma} w_1^{1-\sigma} + \alpha_2^{\sigma} w_2^{1-\sigma}\right)^{\frac{1}{1-\sigma}}.$$

The input conditioned demand functions are obtained by applying Shephard’s Lemma

$$\frac{\partial C}{\partial w_1} = \hat{y}_1 = \left(\frac{x}{A}\right)^{\frac{1}{V}} \left(\frac{1}{1-\sigma}\right) \left(\alpha_1^{\sigma} w_1^{1-\sigma} + \alpha_2^{\sigma} w_2^{1-\sigma}\right)^{\frac{1}{1-\sigma}-1} \alpha_1^{\sigma}(1-\sigma) w_1^{-\sigma}$$

$$\hat{y}_1 = \left(\frac{x}{A}\right)^{\frac{1}{V}} \left(\frac{\alpha_1}{w_1}\right)^{\sigma} \left(\alpha_1^{\sigma} w_1^{1-\sigma} + \alpha_2^{\sigma} w_2^{1-\sigma}\right)^{\frac{\sigma}{1-\sigma}}.$$

Analogously,

$$\hat{y}_2 = \hat{y}_2(\mathbf{w},x) = \left(\frac{x}{A}\right)^{\frac{1}{V}} \left(\frac{\alpha_2}{w_2}\right)^{\sigma} \left(\alpha_1^{\sigma} w_1^{1-\sigma} + \alpha_2^{\sigma} w_2^{1-\sigma}\right)^{\frac{\sigma}{1-\sigma}}.$$

7.2.6 The LRAC and LRMC

$$LRAC = \frac{C(\mathbf{w},x)}{x} = \frac{\left(\frac{x}{A}\right)^{\frac{1}{V}} \left(\alpha_1^{\sigma} w_1^{1-\sigma} + \alpha_2^{\sigma} w_2^{1-\sigma}\right)^{\frac{1}{1-\sigma}}}{x}.$$

If $Z = \alpha_1^{\sigma} w_1^{1-\sigma} + \alpha_2^{\sigma} w_2^{1-\sigma}$, then,

$$LRAC = x^{\frac{1-V}{V}} A^{-\frac{1}{V}} Z^{\frac{1}{1-\sigma}}$$

Therefore, the LRAC curve has the following slope:

$$\frac{\partial LRAC}{\partial x} = \frac{1-V}{V} x^{\frac{1-V}{V}-1} A^{-\frac{1}{V}} Z^{\frac{1}{1-\sigma}}.$$

If we have constant returns to scale, then

$$\frac{\partial LRAC}{\partial x} = 0$$

and if we have increasing returns to scale, then

$$\frac{\partial LRAC}{\partial x} < 0.$$

$$LRMC = \frac{\partial C(\mathbf{w}, x)}{\partial x} = \frac{1}{V} x^{\frac{1-V}{V}} \left(\frac{1}{A}\right)^{\frac{1}{V}} Z^{\frac{1}{1-\sigma}}$$

$$\frac{\partial LRMC}{\partial x} = \frac{1}{V}\left(\frac{1-V}{V}\right) x^{\frac{1-2V}{V}} \left(\frac{1}{A}\right)^{\frac{1}{V}} Z^{\frac{1}{1-\sigma}}.$$

If we have constant returns to scale,

$$\frac{\partial LRMC}{\partial x} = 0$$

and with increasing returns to scale, then

$$\frac{\partial LRMC}{\partial x} < 0.$$

7.2.7 Applying the Duality

Assume the following function:

$$\Phi(w, x) = x\left[w_1^{-1} + w_2^{-1}\right]^{-1},$$

what can we know about the technology with respect to this "assumed" cost function?

For Φ (**w**, x) to be a cost function coming from a profit maximisation behaviour, the following properties must be satisfied:

1. The cost function Φ (**w**, x) must be homogeneous of degree one in w:

$$\Phi(tw,x)=x\left[(w_1t)^{-1}+(w_2t)^{-1}\right]^{-1}=x\left[t^{-1}\left(w_1^{-1}+w_2^{-1}\right)\right]^{-1}=$$

$$=tx\left[w_1^{-1}+w_2^{-1}\right]^{-1}=t\Phi(\mathbf{w},x).$$

The property is satisfied.

2. The cost function must be continuous and increasing for $\forall x>0$ and $\forall w\geq 0$:

$\Phi(\mathbf{w}, x)\geq 0, \forall \mathbf{w}\geq 0.$

since

$$\Phi(\mathbf{w},x)=\frac{x}{\frac{1}{w_1}+\frac{1}{w_2}},\quad \forall \mathbf{w}\geq 0.$$

3. The cost function must yield the input demand functions provided

$$\frac{\partial\Phi}{\partial w_1}=x(-1)\left[w_1^{-1}+w_2^{-1}\right]^{-2}(-1)w_1^{-2}=\frac{x}{w_1^2\left(\frac{1}{w_1}+\frac{1}{w_2}\right)^2}\geq 0$$

$$\frac{\partial\Phi}{\partial w_2}=x(-1)\left[w_1^{-1}+w_2^{-1}\right]^{-2}(-1)w_2^{-2}=\frac{x}{w_2^2\left(\frac{1}{w_1}+\frac{1}{w_2}\right)^2}\geq 0.$$

The property is satisfied.

The cost function Φ (w, x) must be concave in w, i.e., its Hessian must be negative semidefinite.

$$\frac{\partial^2\Phi}{\partial w_1\partial w_2}=xw_1^{-2}(-2)\left[w_1^{-1}+w_2^{-1}\right]^{-3}(-1)w_2^{-2}=2xw_1^{-2}w_2^{-2}\left(w_1^{-1}+w_2^{-1}\right)^{-3}$$

$$\frac{\partial^2\Phi}{\partial w_2\partial w_1}=xw_2^{-2}(-2)\left[w_1^{-1}+w_2^{-1}\right]^{-3}(-1)w_1^{-2}=2xw_1^{-2}w_2^{-2}\left(w_1^{-1}+w_2^{-1}\right)^{-3}$$

$$\frac{\partial^2\Phi}{\partial w_1^2}=x(-2)w_1^{-3}\left(w_1^{-1}+w_2^{-1}\right)^{-2}+(-2)x\left(w_1^{-1}+w_2^{-1}\right)^{-3}(-1)w_1^{-2}w_1^{-2}=$$

$$=-2xw_1^{-3}\left(w_1^{-1}+w_2^{-1}\right)^{-2}+xw_1^{-4}\left(w_1^{-1}+w_2^{-1}\right)^{-3}$$

$$\frac{\partial^2\Phi}{\partial w_1^2}=2xw_1^{-3}\left(w_1^{-1}+w_2^{-1}\right)^{-2}\left[w_1^{-1}\left(w_1^{-1}+w_2^{-1}\right)^{-1}-1\right].$$

Analogously, we obtain

$$\frac{\partial^2 \Phi}{\partial w_2^2} = 2xw_2^{-3}\left(w_1^{-1} + w_2^{-1}\right)^{-2}\left[w_2^{-1}\left(w_1^{-1} + w_2^{-1}\right)^{-1} - 1\right].$$

On the other hand we have:

$$w_1^{-1}\left(w_1^{-1} + w_2^{-1}\right)^{-1} - 1 = \frac{1}{w_1}\frac{1}{\dfrac{1}{w_1} + \dfrac{1}{w_2}} - 1 = \frac{1}{1 + \dfrac{w_1}{w_2}} - 1 = \frac{w_2}{w_1 + w_2},$$

which is negative for any $w \geq 0$.

Then, the main first-order minors are always non-positive. As far as the main second-order minor, i.e., the Hessian, is concerned, we have

$$H = \begin{vmatrix} \dfrac{\partial^2 \Phi}{\partial w_1^2} & \dfrac{\partial^2 \Phi}{\partial w_1 \partial w_2} \\ \dfrac{\partial^2 \Phi}{\partial w_2 \partial w_1} & \dfrac{\partial^2 \Phi}{\partial w_2^2} \end{vmatrix} = \frac{\partial^2 \Phi}{\partial w_1^2}\frac{\partial^2 \Phi}{\partial w_2^2} - \frac{\partial^2 \Phi}{\partial w_2 \partial w_1}\frac{\partial^2 \Phi}{\partial w_1 \partial w_2} =$$

$$= 4x^2 w_1^{-3} w_2^{-3}\left(w_1^{-1} w_2^{-1}\right)^{-4}\left[w_1^{-1}\left(w_1^{-1} + w_2^{-1}\right)^{-1} - 1\right] \cdot$$

$$\cdot\left[w_2^{-1}\left(w_1^{-1} + w_2^{-1}\right)^{-1} - 1\right] - 4x^2 w_1^{-4} w_2^{-4}\left(w_1^{-1} + w_2^{-1}\right)^{-6} =$$

$$= 4x^2 w_1^{-3} w_2^{-3}\left(w_1^{-1} w_2^{-1}\right)^{-4}\frac{w_2}{w_1 + w_2}\frac{w_1}{w_1 + w_2} - 4x^2 w_1^{-4} w_2^{-4}\left(w_1^{-1} + w_2^{-1}\right)^{-6} =$$

$$= 4x^2 w_1^{-3} w_2^{-3}\left(w_1^{-1} w_2^{-1}\right)^{-4}\left[\frac{w_1 w_2}{\left(w_1 + w_2\right)^2} - w_1^{-1} w_2^{-1}\left(w_1^{-1} + w_2^{-1}\right)^{-2}\right].$$

Then, we have

$$H = 4x^2 w_1^{-3} w_2^{-3}\left(w_1^{-1} + w_2^{-1}\right)^{-4} 0 = 0.$$

Therefore, it is satisfied that $H \geq 0$, so that Φ (**w**, x) satisfies all the properties necessary to have a cost function of a given technology. From the Hotelling Theorem we have

$$\frac{\partial \Phi}{\partial w_1} = \hat{y}_1 = x(-1)\left[w_1^{-1} + w_2^{-1}\right]^{-2}(-1)w_1^{-2} = xw_1^{-2}\left(w_1^{-1} + w_2^{-1}\right)^{-2}.$$

Analogously, we obtain

$$\hat{y}_2 = xw_2^{-2}\left(w_1^{-1} + w_2^{-1}\right)^{-2},$$

rearranging,

$$y_1 = \frac{x}{w_1^2}\left(\frac{1}{w_1}+\frac{1}{w_2}\right)^{-2} = \frac{x}{w_1^2\left(\frac{w_1+w_2}{w_1 w_2}\right)^2} = \frac{x\,w_2^2}{(w_1+w_2)^2}$$

$$y_2 = \frac{x\,w_1^2}{(w_1+w_2)^2}.$$

Raising to 1/2 we have

$$y_1^{\frac{1}{2}} = x^{\frac{1}{2}}\frac{w_2}{w_1+w_2}$$

$$y_2^{\frac{1}{2}} = x^{\frac{1}{2}}\frac{w_1}{w_1+w_2}$$

and with the addition of both expressions

$$y_1^{\frac{1}{2}} + y_2^{\frac{1}{2}} = x^{\frac{1}{2}}\left[\frac{w_2}{w_1+w_2}+\frac{w_1}{w_1+w_2}\right] = x^{\frac{1}{2}}\frac{w_1+w_2}{w_1+w_2} = 1,$$

then,

$$x = \left(y_1^{\frac{1}{2}} + y_2^{\frac{1}{2}}\right)^2,$$

which corresponds to a technology with an elasticity of substitution $\sigma = 2$ and constant returns to scale, $V = 1$.

Recommended Reading

Gravelle, H., Rees, R.: Microeconomics, 3rd ed. Longman Group UK Limited 1994
Mas-Collel, A., Whinston, M. D., Green, J. R.: Microeconomic theory. New York: Oxford University Press 1995
Varian, H.: Microeconomic Analysis, 3rd ed. W.W. Norton & Company 1992

8 Study on Econometric Applications: Production and Cost Functions

In order to estimate the production functions of a particular industry the measurements of the inputs and outputs used by its different plants are needed. Unlike the utility function, which is not observed, the production objective function, either output or profit maximisation, or cost minimisation, is directly observed.

It is possible to estimate empirically production and cost functions of just one output or two or more outputs for different combinations of inputs. The functional specifications to be estimated can be either uniequational or as an alternative, a production function or cost function system can be estimated with factor-share equations or cost-share equations respectively. It is also possible to propose a profit function with a series of net supply functions expressed in terms of profit shares. The systems to be used may correspond to productive technologies either of just one output or of two or more.

The real problem when estimating these functions is to find the specification of a functional form, which would properly account for the productive process. That is to say, to specify the relationship between inputs and outputs.

A procedure would be to directly propose a production or cost function and to directly obtain the corresponding estimations. For example, a Cobb-Douglas or a CES.

Alternatively, a flexible functional form can be proposed without putting any restriction and then the different hypotheses of homogeneity, symmetry, separability, additivity, etc., checked, which could lead us to a particular functional form.

On the other hand, it has been previously stated that factor demands, supply and other functions also characterise the technology to be studied. Therefore, it is necessary to state that for factor demands we can use the procedures of demand for only one good or service and alternatively, the estimation of systems of demand for more than two goods, with the only particularity that they are considered inputs here. With regards to product supplies, the steps to be followed in their estimation are again similar to those stated for the demands. In spite of this, it is most common to estimate production and cost functions, which are the most genuine with respect to supply.

8.1 Production Functions

The most common production functions are those of only one product among which we find the Leontief functional forms. Cobb-Douglas, CES, Liu and Hildebrand and Translog, which are the simplest functional forms, are also the most restrictive ones. Therefore, the Leontief production function is

$$x = \min\left\{\frac{y_i}{\beta_i}\right\}; \left(\beta_i > 0\right); \left(j = 1,\ldots,n\right)$$

where 'x' represents the quantity of the output, 'y' is the input and β is an always positive parameter. This production function has a null elasticity of substitution.

The economic particularity of the Leontief production function is that it can only occur with a fixed share of the productive factors.

A functional form less restrictive than the former is the Cobb-Douglas, which is of the type:

$$x = \gamma \prod_{i=1}^{n} y_i^{\alpha_i}; \left(\gamma > 0, \alpha_i > 0\right)$$

where x and y represent as above and where γ and α are parameters to be estimated taking into account that the sum of the different α estimated provides the degree of homogeneity and determines whether the corresponding industry presents constant, increasing or decreasing returns to scale, considering $\Sigma\ \alpha_i > 1$, $\Sigma\ \alpha_i = 1$ or $\Sigma\ \alpha_i < 1$. Finally, parameter γ represents efficiency.

The Cobb-Douglas production function presents the particularity of a constant and unitary elasticity of substitution.

The functional form CES only requires a constant elasticity of substitution with respect to Cobb-Douglas with the expression

$$x = \gamma\left[\sum_{i=1}^{n} \delta_i y_i^{-\rho}\right]^{-\upsilon/\rho}$$

$$\left(\upsilon, \delta_i, \gamma > 0; \Sigma\delta_i = 1; \rho \geq -1\right)$$

where γ is an efficiency parameter, υ represents the degree of homogeneity and, therefore, if $\upsilon > 1$, $\upsilon = 1$ or $\upsilon < 1$ it will account for increasing, constant or decreasing returns to scale.

The functional form of Liu and Hildebrand, with variable elasticity of substitution, is useful in the case of a production function with two factors:

$$x = \gamma(1-\delta)y_1^{-\rho} + \left(y_1^{-m\rho} y_2^{-(1-m)\rho}\right)^{-1/\rho}$$

$$\left(0 < m < 1; \rho \geq -1; \upsilon < \delta < 1; \gamma > 0\right).$$

This production function becomes a Cobb-Douglas if $\delta = 1$, and a CES if $m = 0$.

As well as being flexible and little restrictive, one of the most complex functional forms is Translog with the following expression for three factors:

$$\log x = \alpha_0 + \beta_1 \log y_1 + \beta_2 \log y_2 + \beta_3 \log y_3 +$$
$$+\frac{1}{2}\gamma_{11}(\log y_1)^2 + \frac{1}{2}\gamma_{22}(\log y_2)^2 + \frac{1}{2}\gamma_{33}(\log y_3)^2$$
$$+\delta_{12}\log y_1 \log y_2 + \delta_{13}\log y_1 \log y_3 + \delta_{23}\log y_2\ y_3$$

This production function allows us to check, from a flexible form, whether technology adjusts more adequately to a Liu and Hildebrand, a CES or a Cobb-Douglas.

8.2 Application III for Production Functions: Analysis of the Returns to Scale, Elasticities of Substitution and Behaviour of Shipping Production

The empirical analysis of production functions can be directed at least in two different ways, which may have the same results. Firstly, we may directly assume a particular and flexible production function, and then test the different restrictions stage by stage, in order to find the most suitable functional form. An alternative way would be to assume cost, profit or input conditioned demand functions, which, after satisfying the corresponding duality theorems must provide the same information as the production function. Therefore, if the production integrability problem allows us to change from a cost function -for instance- to a production function, the technology can be perfectly detected from such a cost function.

In this study, I will use the former method in which a flexible functional form such as the logarithmic transcendental or translog is directly assumed, which allows us to execute different parametrical tests of the various properties of the production technology. This choice requires information about the amount of output and of productive input. Some interesting results can be obtained from this function, such as the input elasticities of substitution, the returns to scale of the production function, the marginal products of inputs, the output elasticities and different economic hypotheses.

8.2.1 The Model

As said before, the functional form chosen to estimate the production function will be the translog, which can be written as:

$$\log Q = \alpha_0 + \beta_L \log L + \beta_K \log K + \beta_E \log E +$$
$$+\frac{1}{2}\gamma_{LL}(\log L)^2 + \frac{1}{2}\gamma_{KK}(\log K)^2 + \frac{1}{2}\gamma_{EE}(\log E)^2 +$$
$$+\delta_{LK}\log L \log K + \delta_{LE}\log L \log E + \delta_{KE}\log K \log E \quad (8.1)$$

where Q, L, E and K represent the amounts of output, labour, energy and capital respectively. Functional form (8.1) is, by definition, an approximation made from a second-order Taylor series, to any arbitrary point of the technological space. This functional form does not impose homotheticity, unitary elasticity of substitution or input linear separability. On the other hand, homogeneity of degree one will be assumed for prices, which means that (8.1) must be estimated along with the following restrictions in (8.2):

$$\beta_L + \beta_K + \beta_E = 1$$
$$\gamma_{LL} + \delta_{LE} + \delta_{LK} = 0$$
$$\gamma_{KK} + \delta_{LK} + \delta_{KF} = 0$$
$$\gamma_{EE} + \delta_{LE} + \delta_{KE} = 0. \tag{8.2}$$

In this kind of production model, (8.1) and (8.2) are usually estimated along with two share equations in order to increase the efficiency of the estimation. It is a matter of indiference which equation is to be excluded. Share equations are given by:

$$S_L = \frac{\partial \text{ Log } Q}{\partial \text{ Log } L} = \beta_L + \gamma_{LL} \text{ Log } L + \delta_{LK} \text{ Log } K + \delta_{LE} \text{ Log } E$$

$$S_K = \frac{\partial \text{ Log } Q}{\partial \text{ Log } K} = \beta_K + \gamma_{KK} \text{ Log } K + \delta_{LK} \text{ Log } L + \delta_{KE} \text{ Log } E$$

$$S_E = \frac{\partial \text{ Log } Q}{\partial \text{ Log } E} = \beta_E + \gamma_{EE} \text{ Log } E + \delta_{LE} \text{ Log } L + \delta_{KE} \text{ Log } K\ . \tag{8.3}$$

As well as homogeneity of degree one in prices -assumed here-, positive monotonicity restrictions and strict quasi-concavity guarantee that the production function is well-behaved. Monotonicity does not have to be assumed, and can be tested once the production function has been estimated by verifying the positive sign of the various marginal products of inputs. On the other hand, the strict quasi-concavity requires that the marginal rates of substitution be decreasing (that is to say, that the principal minors of the relevant bordered Hessian must alternate in sign) and can be tested for the functional form estimated.

On the other hand, the output elasticities of the factors labor (ε_L), energy (ε_E) and capital (ε_k), can be estimated from function (8.1) and (8.3) as follows:

$$\varepsilon_L = S_L;\ \varepsilon_K = S_K \text{ and } \varepsilon_E = S_E. \tag{8.4}$$

Once we know the different values of the output elasticities of the factors in (8.4), the following returns to scale of production can be obtained:

$$\varepsilon_L + \varepsilon_K + \varepsilon_E = \varepsilon \tag{8.5}$$

If value ε is higher, equal or lower than the unit the returns to scale obtained will be increasing, constant or decreasing.

The Allen-Uzawa elasticities of substitution of factors can be obtained as follows:

$$\sigma A_{ij} = [\ \delta_{ij} + S_i\ S_j] \,/\, S_i\ S_j;\ i \neq j \tag{8.6}$$

where $\sigma A_{i,j}$ is the input elasticity i with respect to input j.

Once we have obtained the values of equation (8.6) the demand-price elasticities for the production factors are calculated as follows,

$$E_{ij} = S_i \, \sigma A_{ij} \, ; \text{ for all } i = j \text{ or } i \neq j \text{ and } E_{ij} \neq E_{ji} \quad (8.7)$$

8.2.2 Data

The data have been obtained from the records of the companies in various Registers of business companies, for 1992. Further information obtained from the companies themselves and other institutions such as the associations of ship owners, shipping agents and shipbuilders, as well as from the association of the Merchant Navy officers, has been added to these data. The number of litres of fuel has been obtained dividing the total cost of fuel by the average price of fuel-oil paid by each ship in 1992. Analogously, in order to estimate the capital, I have calculated the dead weight tonnage (DWT) in each ship, which actually measures the cargo capacity of each ship, so we have something which is not either the typical capital stock which corresponds with the amount of equipment, or the flow of goods or services which correspond with the depreciation generated in the ship by the cargo of each goods -corrected by its corresponding stowage factor-. The amount of labour is estimated through the number of workers of each company. To measure the output, I have applied the number of tons of general cargo goods transported by each company that year.

All the data have been obtained from 41 companies, of which 27 are dry cargo companies with ships of less than 16,000 DWT, 2 are transoceanic regular line companies and the 12 remaining are national coastal trade regular line companies. Thus, the dry cargo sector with less than 16,000 DWT is covered in 86.3% of its tons, the transoceanic regular lines in 76.81% and the national coastal trade regular line sector in 81.42%. The sum of these three sectors provides what we might call the "general cargo" sector of maritime transportation.

8.2.3 Empirical Results

The translog production function estimated appears in table 8.1. From this estimation I have carried out the tests of hypotheses of linear homogeneity in the prices as shown in Table 2. As can be observed, the assumption of such a hypothesis is not rejected at the 0.01 level. In table 8.2 other restrictions such as homotheticity, homogeneity and homogeneity and unitary elasticity of substitution (linear separability of inputs) are tested. In view of the results of these tests all these hypotheses are rejected.

From table 8.1 we can estimate the corresponding returns to scale taking the average value of 1.32 for all the companies, which provides the sector with increasing returns to scale and, therefore, the companies exert power of the market, and do not make optimal use of the productive capacity.

The Allen-Uzawa elasticities of substitution -in table 8.3- present low average values; there is little scope for substitution between the factors labour, capital and energy.

Table 8.1. Coefficients estimated for translog production function

	Coefficients
α_0	- 0.7114
	(- 1.2321)
β_L	0.0523
	(2.3127)
β_K	0.1729
	(4.5126)
β_E	0.8758
	(12.3210)
γ_{LL}	0.1612
	(2.3410)
γ_{KK}	0.1431
	(1.9320)
γ_{EE}	0.0617
	(2.3421)
δ_{LK}	0.0143
	(4.2120)
δ_{LE}	0.0180
	(6.2750)
δ_{KE}	0.0025
	(0.7891)
Log likelihood	273.512
S.E. dependent variable	1.472
S.E. regression	0.162

Note: t-Student statistics within brackets.

Table 8.2. Tests of likelihood rate

			Critical Values		
	χ^2 calculated	Number of restrictions	10%	5%	1%
Homotheticity	21.31	3	4.60	5.99	9.21
Homogeneity	9.86	3	6.25	7.81	11.34
Unitary elasticity of substitution	65.24	3	6.25	7.81	11.34
Homotheticity and unitary elasticity of substitution	88.22	5	9.23	11.07	15.08
Homogeneity and unitary elasticity of substitution (Cobb-Douglas Technology)	108.34	6	10.64	12.59	16.81

Table 8.3. Allen-Uzawa elasticities

	Labour	Capital	Energy
Labour	-0.852145	- 0.029830	0.071560
Capital	-0.029830	-1.023145	0.610234
Energy	0.071560	0.610234	-0.921310

Table 8.4. Own price and cross elasticities for inputs demands

	Labour	Capital	Energy
Labour	-0.413126	0.281320	0.223254
Capital	0.314520	-0.627810	0.193185
Energy	0.216852	0.210815	-0.281876

8.3 Cost Function

Similarly, we will deal with production functions here. That is to say, the most usual cost functional forms will be put forward, from the most simple and restrictive to the most complex and flexible.

Leontief cost function is of the type

$$C(x, \mathbf{w}) = \sum_{i=1}^{n} \beta_i w_i x$$

where C (x, **w**) represents the costs of the quantity of output x produced, with the prices of the inputs **w**, and β_i is a parameter to be estimated.

A more complex cost function than the former is that of the generalised Leontief technology or an approximation (local) of an arbitrary or Diewert cost function with the expression

$$C(x, \mathbf{w}) = x \sum_{i=1}^{n} \sum_{j=1}^{n} \beta_{ij} w_i^{1/2} w_j^{1/2} ; \left(\beta_{ij} = \beta_{ji}\right)$$

where x, w_i, w_j represent as above and where β_{ij} is a symmetrical parameter to be estimated if $\beta_{ij} = 0$ for $i \neq j$, The cost function becomes the Leontief one described above.

Cobb-Douglas cost function for two factors is

$$C(x, \mathbf{w}) = \gamma w_1^{\alpha} w_2^{\beta} x$$

or else

$$\log C(x, \mathbf{w}) = \log \gamma + \alpha \log w_1 + \beta \log w_2 + \log x$$

The logarithmic transcendental cost function (Translog) is one of the most flexible functional forms, and it is of the type

$$\log C(x, \mathbf{w}) = \alpha_0 + \sum_{i=1}^{n} \alpha_i \log w_i + \frac{1}{2} \sum_{i=1}^{n} \sum_{j=1}^{n} \gamma_{ij} \log w_i \log w_j +$$

$$+ \delta_0 \log x + \sum_{i=1}^{n} \alpha_i \log w_i \log x + \frac{1}{2} \delta_{00} (\log x)^2$$

The following restrictions must be necessarily verified in this function so that it is homogeneous in the prices

$$\sum_{i=1}^{n}\alpha_i = 1 \;;\gamma_{ij} = \gamma_{ji} \;;\sum_{i=1}^{n}\gamma_{ij} = 0;\sum_{i=1}^{n}\delta_i = 0.$$

The symmetry condition is sometimes also required

$$\sum_{i=1}^{n}\gamma_{ij} = \sum_{j=1}^{n}\gamma_{ji} = 0.$$

8.4 Other Empirical Functions

In this section, other empirical functions, which may be possibly estimated and also characterise a certain technology, will be mentioned.

Thus, the factor demands of a Leontief function are

$$y_i(\mathbf{w}, x) = \beta_i\, x\,;\, (i = 1,\ldots, n)$$

where n is the number of factors.

The factor demands of a Cobb-Douglas function have the general form

$$y_i(\mathbf{w}, x) = \frac{\alpha_i}{w_i} x \prod_{i=1}^{n}\left(\frac{w_i}{\alpha_i}\right)^{\alpha_i};\,(i = 1,\ldots n).$$

The factor demands of a generalised Leontief function are of the type

$$y_i(\mathbf{w}, x) = x\sum_{j=1}^{n}\beta_{ij}\left(\frac{w_i}{w_j}\right)^{1/2};\,(i, j = 1,\ldots n).$$

The factor conditioned demands of the Translog function are

$$y_i(\mathbf{w}, x) = s_i(\mathbf{w}, x);\,(i = 1,\ldots n)$$

where S_i is the relative share of y_i in the costs of production. The reason for this is that applying the Shephard's Lemma we have

$$\frac{\partial \log C(\mathbf{w}, x)}{\partial \log w_i} = \frac{w_i y_i(\mathbf{w}, x)}{C(\mathbf{w}, x)} = s_i(\mathbf{w}, x).$$

This expression can still be given in linear terms as follows

$$s_i(\mathbf{w}, x) = \alpha_i + \sum\gamma_{ij}\log w_i + \delta_i \log x;\,(i = 1,\ldots, n).$$

This is a factor relative share function in the total costs, which is also linear in the parameters (α_i, γ_{ij}, δ_i).

The technology can also be characterised by means of a profit Translog function as follows:

$$\log \Pi(\mathbf{q}, y_k) = \alpha_0 + \sum_{i=1}^{s} \alpha_i \log q_i + \frac{1}{2} \sum_{i=1}^{s} \sum_{j=1}^{s} \gamma_{ij} \log q_i \log q_j +$$
$$+ \sum_{i=1}^{s} \sum_{j=s+1}^{n} \delta_{ij} \log q_i \log y_k + \sum_{j=s+1}^{n} \beta_j \log y_{kj} +$$
$$+ \frac{1}{2} \sum_{j=s+1}^{n} \sum_{m=s+1}^{n} \lambda_{jm} \log y_{kj} \log y_{km}$$

where $\mathbf{q}$ represents a vector with the input and output prices and variable y_{ki} represents the amounts of fixed inputs.

The homogeneity of degree one in $\mathbf{q}$ requires

$$\sum_{i=1}^{s} \alpha_i = 1; \sum_{i=1}^{s} \delta_{ij} = 0; (j = s+1, \ldots n)$$
$$\sum_{j=1}^{s} \gamma_{ij} = 0; (i = 1, \ldots, s)$$

and symmetry requires

$$\gamma_{ij} = \gamma_{ji}; (i, j = 1, \ldots, s)$$
$$\lambda_{jm} = \lambda_{mj}; (j, m = s+1, \ldots, n).$$

On the other hand, the homogeneity of degree one in y implies the existence of constant returns to scale

$$\sum_{i=s+1}^{n} \beta_i = 1; \sum_{j=s+1}^{n} \delta_{ij} = 0; (i = 1, \ldots, s)$$
$$\sum_{m=s+1}^{n} \lambda_{jm} = 0; (j = s+1, \ldots, n).$$

Besides, by applying Hotelling's theorem to the profit function we can obtain the factor demand from which it is possible to derive the following profit share functions:

$$s_i(\mathbf{q}, y_k) = \frac{\partial \log \Pi(\mathbf{q}, y_k)}{\partial \log \mathbf{q}}; (i = 1, \ldots, s),$$

that is to say

$$s_i(\mathbf{q}, y_k) = \alpha_i + \sum_{j=1}^{s} \gamma_{ij} \log q_j + \sum_{j=s+1}^{n} \delta_{ij} \log y_{kj}.$$

8.5 Application IV for Cost Functions: Elasticities of Substitution and Behaviour of Shipping Costs[1]

The wish to know the business reaction to the relative prices of production factors has led to studies of cost and production functions. The elasticity of substitution, formulated by Hicks in 1932 (Ferguson, 1979), is the key concept provided by such a function. In Allen (1938) extended the concept of elasticity of substitution to multiproduct technologies, generating a new concept which carries his name in the economics literature. Subsequently, according to this, there have been some contributions on constant elasticity of substitution production functions, such as the work by Arrow et al. (1961). However, more recent studies question the accuracy of the Allen elasticity of substitution, since it is a one-factor one-price elasticity and is a derived demand elasticity divided by a share proportion. Thus, other authors state that the Morishima elasticity (Blackorby and Russell, 1981) provides some information about economics more relevant than Allen's. Blackcorby and Russell (1989) point out the need to assume both of these elasticities of substitution, and warn seriously against the use of the Allen elasticities of substitution when multifactor technologies are being studied.

Maritime transport is managed in Spain by private companies (although there are also some public firms), which provide passenger and goods transport service. Transport prices are fixed mainly by the market.

In the present section, we estimate cost functions for Solid Bulk shipping transport by 34 private firms for 1991. The functional form used is the Translog drawn by Christensen, Jorgensen and Lau (1973). We also estimate the Allen and Morishima elasticities of substitution, and compare and interpret the results as well.

8.5.1 Model

The present model is based upon Keeler's (1974) research and Caves et al. (1981).

It is assumed that the production function has only one output and three inputs. The shipping of solid bulk is multiproduct as regards goods, services, departures and arrivals, timetables and so on. For this reason, the production function must have a vector of products. There are also many other factors, but the availability of data forces us to consider only three. It is also assumed that the prices of production input are exogenous.

Due to these two assumptions: product homogeneity and exogeneity of input prices; it is possible to represent a transformation surface of combinations of the three production factors in order to obtain the output implicitly:

$$\phi\,(Q, K, L, E) \tag{8.8}$$

Function ϕ in (8.8) represents variable Q of the output , K of the capital, L of the labour and E of the energy.

[1] This research has been done with the collaboration of J. Baños-Pino and A. Rodríguez.

If ϕ meets the good behaviour conditions (monotonicity, quasi-concavity and homogeneity of degree-one), we can apply Shepard's Lemma and obtain the satisfactory combinations of inputs and products from the cost function derivatives with respect to the factor prices.

In other words, there is a dual cost function:

$$C = \psi\,(Q, m, w, e) \tag{8.9}$$

where m, w and e are the prices of the respective inputs and C the output production costs.

In order to estimate cost function (8.9) we can test several functions, of which the most common ones are: Cobb-Douglas, CES, Diewert and Translog. Following the Okun principle we choose the Translog, the function which postulates the least number of restrictions and which is the most flexible one. Moreover, through it we can show the particular functions mentioned above.

The Translog cost specification used is:

$$\begin{aligned}
\mathrm{Ln}C &= \alpha_0 + \alpha_Q \mathrm{Ln}\,Q + \frac{1}{2}\alpha_{QQ}(\mathrm{Ln}\,Q)^2 + \beta_L \mathrm{Ln}\,w + \beta_K \mathrm{Ln}\,m + \\
&+ \beta_E \mathrm{Ln}\,e + \frac{1}{2}\gamma_{LL}(\mathrm{Ln}\,w)^2 + \frac{1}{2}\gamma_{KK}(\mathrm{Ln}\,m)^2 + \frac{1}{2}\gamma_{EE}(\mathrm{Ln}\,e)^2 + \\
&+ \delta_{LK}(\mathrm{Ln}\,w)(\mathrm{Ln}\,m) + \delta_{LE}(\mathrm{Ln}\,w)(\mathrm{Ln}\,e) + \delta_{KE}(\mathrm{Ln}\,m)(\mathrm{Ln}\,e) + \\
&+ \rho_{LQ}(\mathrm{Ln}\,w)(\mathrm{Ln}\,Q) + \rho_{KQ}(\mathrm{Ln}\,m)(\mathrm{Ln}\,Q) + \\
&+ \rho_{EQ}(\mathrm{Ln}\,e)(\mathrm{Ln}\,Q);
\end{aligned} \tag{8.10}$$

In this kind of cost model, (8.10) is usually estimated along with two share equations in order to increase the efficiency of the estimation. It is a matter of indifference which equation is to be excluded. Share equations are given by:

$$S_L = \frac{\partial\ \mathrm{Ln}\,C}{\partial\ \mathrm{Ln}\,w} = \beta_L + \gamma_{LL}\ \mathrm{Ln}\,w + \delta_{LK}\ \mathrm{Ln}\,m + \delta_{LE}\ \mathrm{Ln}\,e + \rho_{LQ}\ \mathrm{Ln}\,Q$$

$$S_K = \frac{\partial\ \mathrm{Ln}\,C}{\partial\ \mathrm{Ln}\,m} = \beta_K + \gamma_{KK}\ \mathrm{Ln}\,m + \delta_{LK}\ \mathrm{Ln}\,w + \delta_{KE}\ \mathrm{Ln}\,e + \rho_{KQ}\ \mathrm{Ln}\,Q$$

$$S_E = \frac{\partial\ \mathrm{Ln}\,C}{\partial\ \mathrm{Ln}\,e} = \beta_E + \gamma_{EE}\ \mathrm{Ln}\,e + \delta_{LE}\ \mathrm{Ln}\,w + \delta_{KE}\ \mathrm{Ln}\,m + \rho_{EQ}\ \mathrm{Ln}\,Q$$

The following restrictions guarantee that equation (8.10) presents homogeneity of degree one in the input prices,

$$\beta_L + \beta_K + \beta_E = 1$$

$$\rho_{LQ} + \rho_{KQ} + \rho_{FQ} = 0$$

$$\gamma_{LL} + \delta_{LE} + \delta_{LK} = 0$$

$$\gamma_{KK} + \delta_{LK} + \delta_{KF} = 0$$

$$\gamma_{EE} + \delta_{LE} + \delta_{KE} = 0.$$

The Allen elasticities of substitution σA_{ij} between factors are defined as follows (Uzawa,1962):

$$\sigma A_{ij} = \frac{C\left(\dfrac{\partial^2 C}{\partial P_i \partial P_j}\right)}{\left(\dfrac{\partial C}{\partial P_i}\dfrac{\partial C}{\partial P_j}\right)}$$

where C are the costs and P_i and P_j are the input prices (P_i, P_j:m, w, e).

For the Translog cost function, Allen partial elasticities of substitution (Blackorby and Russell, (1989) can be estimated as shown,

$$\sigma A_{ij} = \frac{\left(\delta_{ij} + S_i S_j\right)}{S_i S_j}; \text{ with } \quad i \neq j$$

where δ_{ij} refers to parameters in (8.10): δ_{LK}, δ_{LE}, δ_{KE} However, variables S_i and S_j account for the different shares: S_L, S_K and S_E.

As regards multiple factors, the Morishima elasticities σ M_{ij} are defined as follows (Blackorby and Russell,1989):

$$\sigma M_{ij} = \frac{\partial \operatorname{Ln}\left(\dfrac{C_i}{C_j}\right)}{\partial \operatorname{Ln}\left(\dfrac{P_i}{P_j}\right)}$$

where C_i and C_j account for the production costs with the respective factors i and j; and P_i and P_j account for the prices of factors m, w and e.

For the Translog cost function, the Morishima elasticities of substitution can be obtained from the following expressions (Blackorby and Russell,1989):

$$\sigma M_{ij} = \left(\frac{\delta_{ij}}{S_i}\right) - \left(\frac{\gamma_{jj}}{S_j}\right) + 1$$

$$\sigma M_{ji} = \left(\frac{\delta_{ij}}{S_j}\right) - \left(\frac{\gamma_{ii}}{S_i}\right) + 1$$

where $\delta_{ij} = \delta_{ji}$ and σ $M_{ij} \neq \sigma$ M_{ji}. This means that, unlike the Allen elasticity of substitution, which verifies that σ $A_{ij} \neq \sigma$ A_{jj} the Morishima elasticity is not symmetrical, which can be interpreted as follows: the various relative prices of factors provide different elasticities of substitution depending on the price (i^{th} or j^{th}) of the modified factor.

8.5.2 Data

The data used comes from the official statistics of the Ministry of Transport as well as Private Companies' Memoranda.

The output variable has been approximated by the indicator tons of goods transported. By adding different outputs (as many as possible departures and arrivals in the port network, and for the different timetables) we can see the great heterogeneities in the amount of services. However, such aggregation depends on the availability of data.

Three inputs have been considered: labour, capital and energy. The price of labour will be represented by (w), that of capital by (m), and the price of input energy will be (e).

Finally, the total costs C, consist of the amount of the factors used, multiplied by their respective prices.

8.5.3 Empirical Results

A Translog model has been used with degree one homogeneity in prices. The results of the estimation are shown in table 8.5.

Moreover, an analysis has been carried out on the optimal behaviour of the cost function. The results obtained give evidence of well behaved since the cost function tested satisfies the following conditions:

1 monotonicity in factor prices;
2 homogeneity of degree one with respect to factor prices;
3 quasi-concavity with respect to input prices.

In table 8.6 the following conditions have been tested: homotheticity, homogeneity, unitary elasticity of substitution, homotheticity and unitary elasticity of substitution, and homogeneity and unitary elasticity of substitution (Cobb-Douglas technology).

The Allen and Morishima elasticities of substitution have been estimated from the coefficients of the estimation in table 8.5. In tables 8.7, 8.8, 8.10 and 8.11, we show the elasticities obtained by this procedure. The estimations of the Allen and Morishima elasticities of substitution give evidence that factors are all substitutive but not complementary between themselves.

The comparison between elasticities supports the results of previous works such as Blackorby and Russell (1989) and MacMillan et al. (1991); the Allen elasticities overestimate substitution relationships.

Table 8.5. Coefficients estimated for translog cost function*

	Coefficients eq. without restrictions	Coefficients homothetic cost function
α_0	-0.2862	-0.2725
	(-3.1660)	(-2.9610)
α_Q	0.1800	-0.0352
	(1.2840)	(-0.3670)
α_{QQ}	0.9761	0.8496
	(3.1950)	(2.9060)
β_L	0.3476	0.3486
	(24.2070)	(22.2120)
β_K	0.3212	0.3196
	(19.9060)	(17.8730)
β_E	0.3311	0.3316
	(26.8370)	(26.6350)
γ_{LL}	0.1156	0.1221
	(10.2090)	(10.5570)
γ_{KK}	0.0852	0.0884
	(4.6950)	(4.7510)
γ_{EE}	0.1160	0.1126
	(6.7790)	(6.6310)
δ_{LK}	-0.0424	-0.0489
	(-3.9520)	(-4.4320)
δ_{LE}	-0.0732	-0.0731
	(-7.1840)	(-7.2040)
δ_{KE}	-0.0427	-0.0394
	(-2.8050)	(-2.5610)
ρ_{LQ}	-0.0440	-
	(-1.8060)	
ρ_{KQ}	0.0655	-
	(2.4060)	
ρ_{EQ}	-0.0215	-
	(-1.0070)	
Log likelihood	70.450	67.910
S.E. dependent variable	0.476	0.476
S.E. regression	0.449	0.472

Note: * (Statistics t-student within brackets). The variables are estimated according to the deviations from the geometrical average. This transformation reduces multicolineality problems.

Table 8.6. Tests of likelihood rate

			Critical Values		
	χ^2 calculated	Number of restrictions	10%	5%	1%
Homotheticity	5.08	2	4.60	5.99	9.21
Homogeneity	11.66	3	6.25	7.81	11.34
Unitary elasticity of substitution	65.24	3	6.25	7.81	11.34
Homotheticity and unitary elasticity of substitution	58.12	5	9.23	11.07	15.08
Homogeneity and unitary elasticity of substitution (Cobb-Douglas Technology)	67.36	6	10.64	12.59	16.81

Table 8.7. Allen elasticities

	Labour	Capital	Energy
Labour	-0.947916 (0.099566)	0.617550 (0.096721)	0.349394 (0.090562)
Capital	0.617550 (0.096721)	-1.251722 (0.167601)	0.610234 (0.138934)
Energy	0.349394 (0.090562)	0.610234 (0.138934)	-0.955222 (0.153745)

Table 8.8. Morishima elasticities (for the system without restrictions)

	Labour	Capital	Energy
Labour	0	0.615138 (0.081975)	0.435243 (0.030213)
Capital	0.528038 (0.059755)	0	0.522264 (0.083699
Energy	0.437588 (0.052123)	0.612730 (0.080906)	0

Table 8.9. Own price and cross elasticities for factor demands (system without restrictions)

	Labour	Capital	Energy
Labour	-0.319736 (0.033584)	0.203223 (0.031829)	0.116564 (0.030213)
Capital	0.208302 (0.032624)	-0.411915 (0.055695)	0.203585 (0.046351)
Energy	0.117852 (0.030547)	0.200815 (0.045720)	-0.318679 (0.051292)

Table 8.10. Allen elasticities (for the homothetic system without restrictions)

	Labour	Capital	Energy
Labour	-0.891055	0.558675	0.349874
	(0.101702)	(0.099604)	(0.090242)
Capital	0.558675	-1.222267	0.640775
	(0.099604)	(0.171868)	(0.140236)
Energy	0.349874	0.640775	-0.985771
	(0.090242)	(0.140236)	(0.152560)

Table 8.11. Morishima elasticities (for the homothetic system)

	Labour	Capital	Energy
Labour	0	0.586070	0.445594
		(0.079770)	(0.074556)
Capital	0.489000	0	0.542644
	(0.060695)		(0.083021)
Energy	0.418570	0.613087	0
	(0.052528)	(0.081989)	

Table 8.12. Own price and cross elasticities for factor demands (homothetic system)

	Labour	Capital	Energy
Labour	-0.300556	0.183848	0.116724
	(0.034304)	(0.032778)	(0.030106)
Capital	0.188444	-0.402222	0.213774
	(0.033597)	(0.056558)	(0.046785)
Energy	0.118014	0.210865	-0.328870
	(0.030439)	(0.046149)	(0.050897)

8.5.4 Summary and Conclusions

The behaviour of the costs of private firms for 1991 has been studied in this section. The Translog function with the restriction of homogeneity of degree one in factor prices has been analysed and acceptable results have been obtained for the output tons of goods. The cost function estimated has a good behaviour since it satisfies the conditions of monotonicity, quasi concavity and homogeneity of degree one in factor prices.

The homotheticity hypothesis can only be rejected in a 10% so that the homothetic cost function is also estimated.

It has been tested in both cases that all the direct price elasticities and the Allen elasticities of substitution are always negative. Therefore, the cost function is monotonic in the factor prices.

Moreover, the matrix of the Allen elasticities of substitution is negative semi-definite in the average value of the data, so that the cost function is quasi-concave.

The comparison between elasticities support the results in previous research since it can be seen that the Allen elasticities of substitution with respect to the Morishima elasticities overestimate both substitution and complementary relationships.

Basic References

Gravelle, H., Rees, R.: Microeconomics, 3rd ed. Longman Group UK Limited 1994

Henderson, J.M., Quandt, R.E.: Microeconomic Theory. A Mathematical Approach. 3rd ed. New York: Mc Graw-Hill Book Company, Inc. 1985

Madden, P.: Concavity and Optimization in Microeconomics. Basil Blackwell, Ltd. Oxford, U.K. 1986

Sher, N., Pinola, L.: Microeconomic Theory. Elsevier, North Holland Inc. 1980

Silberberg, E.: The Structure of Economics. A Mathematical Analysis, 2nd ed. Singapore: Mc Graw-Hill Publishing Company 1991

Varian, H.: Microeconomic Analysis. 3rd ed. USA: W. W. Norton & Company 1992

References and Further Reading

Arrow, K. J.; Chenery, H. B.; Minhas, B. S., Solow, R. W.: Capital-Labour Substitution and Economic Efficiency. Review of Economics an Statistics 43, 225-254 (1961)

Atkinson, S., Halvorsen, R.: The relative efficiency of public and private firms in a regulated environment: the case of U.S. electric utilities. Journal of Public Economics 29, 281-94 (1986)

Blackorby, C., Russell, R.: The Morishima Elasticity of Substitution: Symmetry, Constancy, Separability, and Its Relationship to the Hicks and Allen Elasticities. Review of Economic Studies 48, 147-158 (1981)

Blackorby, C., Russell, R.: Will the Real Elasticity of Substitution Please Stand Up? (A Comparison of the Allen/Uzawa and Morishima Elasticity of Substitution). American Economic Review 79, 882-888 (1989)

Carbajo, J.C., De Rus, G.: Railway Transport Policy in Spain. Journal of Transport Economic and Policy, May, 209-215 (1991)

Caves, D., Christenson, L., Swanson, J.: Productivity Growth, Scale Economies and Capacity Utilisation in US Rail-roads 1955-1974. American Economic Review 5, 994-1002 (1981)

Cornes, R.: Duality and modern economics. Cambridge University Press 1992

Coto-Millán, P.: Recent History of OPEC: An Analysis through the functions of demand. Working Paper. University of Oviedo, Department of Economics, 1989

Coto-Millán, P.: Determinants of Private Demand for Sea transport in Relation to the International Market: An Empirical Approach. Working Paper. University of Oviedo, Department of Economics 1990

Coto-Millán, P.: The sea transport of coal and iron ore: recent evolution and perspective (I) and (II). Newsletter of EIMS 15 and 16, 32-36 and 39-43. (1991)

Coto-Millán, P.:The sea transport of cement: recent evolution and perspective. Newsletter of EIMS, 18; 33-37 (1992)

Coto-Millán, P.: Internal and External Trade according to transportation Means in Spain (1974-1986), (I), (II) and (III). Newsletter of EIMS, 21, 22 and 23; 17-23, 17-23 and 17-22 (1993)

Coto-Millán, P.: Viability Plans of the Spanish Merchant Marine. The restructuring of the shipping sector for the Single Market. Newsletter of EIMS, 17, 45-47 (1993)

Coto-Millán, P.: National Air and road Passenger Transport Competition in Spain. Working Paper. University of Cantabria, Department of Economics 1994

Coto-Millán, P.: Scale of Economies, Elasticities of Substitution and Behaviour of the Railway Transport. University of Cantabria, Department of Economics 1994

Coto-Millán, P.: The conditioned demands of Spanish sea Transport 1975-1990. International Journal of Transport Economics XXII, 3, 325-346 (1995)

Coto-Millán, P.: Intermodal Competition on Inter-Urban Rail: Theoretical and Empirical Microfoundations. International Journal of Transport Economics, XXIII, 3, 379-382 (1996)

Coto-Millán, P.: Maritime Transport Policy in Spain (1974-1995). Transport Policy. Unit of Transport Studies, Oxford University 3, 37-41 (1996)

Coto-Millán, P.: Returns to Scale, Elasticities of Substitution and Behaviour of General Cargo Shipping Companies Productions. Working Paper. University of Cantabria, Department of Economics 1997

Coto-Millán, P. et al.: Intercity Public Transport in Spain 1980-1988: Elasticities, Prices, Income and Time series. Working Paper. University of Cantabria, Department of Economics 1994

Coto-Millán, P., Baños-Pino, J.: Derived Demands for "General Cargo" shipping in Spain, 1975-1992, an Economic Approach. Applied Economics Letters 3, 175-178 (1996)

Coto-Millán, P., Baños-Pino, J., Rodríguez, A.: Returns to Scale, Elasticities of Substitution and Behaviour of Solid Bulk Shipping Companies Costs. Working Paper. University of Cantabria, Department of Economics 1997

Coto-Millán, P., Carrascal, U.: Estimating Engel Curves for Transport expenditures: evidence from UK household budget data. International Journal of Transport Economics 25-3, 379-80 (1998)

Coto-Millán, P., Carrascal, U.: An Almost Ideal Demand System for Transport Consumer Behaviour. Working Paper. University of Cantabria, Department of Economics 1997

Coto-Millán, P., Baños-Pino, J., Inglada, V.: Marshallian Demands of Intercity Passenger Transport in Spain: 1980-1992. An Economic Analysis. Transportation Research: Part E: Logistics and Transportation Review 33-2, 79-96 (1997)

Coto-Millán, P., Baños-Pino, J., Inglada, V.: Railway Inter-City Passenger Transport in Spain: A Cointegration Analysis. Transport Research (8th WCTR Selected Proceedings) 1998

Christensen, L. R., Jorgeson, D. W., Lau, L. J.: Transcendental Logarithmic Production Frontiers. Review of Economics and Statistics 55, 28-45 (1973)

Eakin, B. K., Kniesner, T.: Estimating a non-minimum cost function for hospitals. Southern Economic Journal 54-3, 583-597 (1988)

English, M., Grosskopf, S., Hayes, K., Yaisawarng, S.: Output allocative and technical efficiency of banks. Journal of Banking and Finance 17, 349-366 (1993)

Färe, R., Grosskopf, S.: A distance function approach to price efficiency. Journal of Public Economics 43, 123-126 (1990)

Farrell, M. J.: The measurement of productive efficiency. Journal of the Royal Statistical Society Serie A 120, 253-281 (1957)

Ferguson, C. E.: The Neoclasical Theory of Production & Distribution. Cambridge University Press 1979

Greene, W. H.: Maximum likelihood estimation of econometric frontier functions. Journal of Econometrics 13, 27-53 (1980)

Grosskopf, S., Hayes, K.: Local public sector bureaucrats and their input choices. Journal of Urban Economics 33, 151-166 (1993)

Grosskopf, S., Hayes, K., Hirschberg, J.: Fiscal stress and the production of public safety: a distance function approach. Journal of Public Economics 57, 277-296 (1995)

Jacobsen, S.: On Shephard's duality theorem. Journal Economic Theory 4, 458-464 (1972)

Keeler, T. E.: Railroads Costs, Returns to Scale and Excess Capacity. Review of Economics Statistics 61, 201-208 (1974)

Lovell, C. A. K.: Discussants' comments on Berger et al. and English et al. Journal of Banking and Finance 17, 367-370 (1993)

McMillan, M. L., Amoako-Tuffour, J.: Demands for Local Public Sector Outputs in Rural and Urban Municipalities. American Journal of Agricultural Economics 73, 313 – 325 (1991)

Nash, C. A.: Economics of Public Transport. Ed. Longman 1982

Pindyck, R. S.: Interfuel Substitution and the Industrial Demand for Energy: An International Comparison. Review of Economics and Statistics 61, 69-179 (1979)

Shephard, R. W.: Cost and Production Functions. Princeton University Press 1953

Uzawa, H.: Production Functions with Constant Elasticities of Substitution. Review of Economic Studies 29, 291-299 (1962)

Williamson, O.: Managerial discretion and business behaviour. American Economic Review 53, December, 1032-1057 (1963)

PART III: UNCERTAINTY

9 Utility, Production and Uncertainty

9.1 Introduction

A rational individual can choose under conditions of certainty, as we have assumed up until now, or under conditions of uncertainty, as we shall see in this chapter. The key issue is how to order the different alternatives in the presence of uncertainty in accordance with the individual's preferences. This issue has had three different responses throughout the history of the development of utility. Here they will be summarised in three stages. Later, we shall address a situation in which the company produces under conditions of uncertainty. To end this chapter, we shall set out the main critiques of expected-utility theory and connect such critiques with the theory of limited rationality.

9.2 First Stage in the Development of Utility Theory Under Conditions of Uncertainty: the Principle of Expected Value

A rational consumer lives in a world of uncertainty, not certainty, as we have assumed up until now. To represent consumer choice, $\{x_1, x_2, ..., x_n\}$, with the likelihood of each choice, $\{P_1, P_2, ..., P_n\}$, we shall use the lottery concept L:

$$L \equiv (x_1, x_2, ..., x_n; p_1, p_2, ..., p_n)$$

Let us assume that choices $\{x_1, x_2, ..., x_n\}$ are mutually exclusive, i.e., if x_1 is chosen and not x_2 or any of the other choices:

$$p_1 + p_2 + ... + p_n = 1$$

For example, let us look at the following game: if we roll a die and get a 1, a 3, a 5 or a 6, then we toss a coin. If we get tails we win nothing, if we get heads we get 100$; if, however, we roll a 2 or a 4, then we get 200$. This game can be represented as a lottery:

$$L \equiv (200, Y; 1/3, 2/3)$$

where $Y \equiv (100, 0; 1/2, 1/2)$
i.e.:

$L \equiv \{200, (100; 0;1/2;1/2); 1/3, 2/3)\}$

or, put another way:

$L \equiv (200, 100, 0; 1/3, 1/3, 1/3)$

At this first stage of the theory, the response to how to order the various alternatives in line with the individual's preferences is as follows: the individual will try to maximise the expected value of the different lotteries, that is, of $\overline{X} = \sum_i p_i x_i$.

But it was soon shown that this expected-value criterion was insufficient. For instance, let us look at a game in which there are 10 numbers, and each is sold at 50$. The lottery prize is 600$. In this game, the probability of winning is 10%, i.e., 60$, so the expected value of the game is 60$, which is greater than the 50$ needed to buy a number. According to the expected-value criterion, all individuals would should take part in the game. However, this criterion does not take into account that individuals are different – some are risk-lovers while others are risk-averse. Another example is the following lottery:

$L \equiv (1, 2, 4, 8, \ldots; 1/2; 1/4; 1/8; \ldots)$

The expected value of which is:

$$\overline{X} = \sum_i x_i p_i = \left[1\left(\frac{1}{2}\right) + 2\left(\frac{1}{4}\right) + 4\left(\frac{1}{8}\right) + 8\left(\frac{1}{16}\right) + \ldots\right] = \frac{1}{2} + \frac{1}{2} + \frac{1}{2} + \ldots + \frac{1}{2} = \infty$$

i.e., the expected value $\overline{X}$ is infinite, but nobody would be prepared to pay more than a reasonable amount to take part in this lottery, more than 20$ for instance.

This last example, which pointed out the defects of the expected-value principle, is now known as the 'St Petersburg paradox'.

9.3 Second Stage in the Development of Utility Theory Under Conditions of Uncertainty: the Principle of Expected Utility

The "St Petersburg paradox" was posited by Nicolas Bernouilli when in 1713 he sent several colleagues the following problem: "Peter tosses a coin and carries on doing so until it shows up heads. He agrees to pay Paul one ducat if it shows heads on the first throw, two ducats if on the second, four if on the third throw, eight if on the fourth, and so on, such that for every additional throw the number of ducats owed doubles. Let us suppose we try to determine Paul's expected winnings. Put another way, what is the maximum payment Paul should make to take part in the game?"

This is the lottery posited above:

$L \equiv (1, 2, 4, \ldots; 1/2; 1/4; 1/8; \ldots)$

with an expected value of:

$$\overline{X} = \left(\frac{1}{2}\right)1 + \left(\frac{1}{4}\right)2 + \left(\frac{1}{8}\right)4 + \left(\frac{1}{16}\right)8 + \ldots = \infty$$

Gabriel Cramer and Daniel Bernouilli proposed a response to ordering the lotteries. A valuation of a game should not be done simply based on its consequences (x_1, x_2, ..., x_n), but in accordance with the utility that each of such consequences is expected to provide. Thus, although the expected value is the same for everyone, the expected utility is different for each individual, depending on his attitude to risk. Utility will be different for a risk-lover and for a risk-avoider. The expected utility, $\overline{U}$, can now be represented as:

$$\overline{U} = \sum_i U(x_i)p_i$$

where $U(x_i)$ is the utility assigned by the agent to result x_i of the lottery, and p_i is the probability that x_i will come about.

$U(x_i)$ is a cardinal utility function with a finite mathematical expectation.

Cramer, to solve the paradox, assumes that the utility function is bounded and thus makes the expected utility finite. On that basis, he finds a secure-wealth value, Z_0, the utility of which is equal to the expected utility of a lottery, i.e.:

$$U(W + Z_0) = U(W + x_1)p_1 + U(W + x_2)p_2 + \ldots$$

where W is initial wealth, and x_i, p_i are defined as for all the previous lotteries. Hence, if

$$U(x_i) = Lnx_i$$

and the individual's initial wealth is 50,000 ducats, the maximum amount to be paid for taking part in the paradox lottery is about 9 ducats.

Therefore, under the Bernouilli-Cramer criterion, individuals should choose lotteries on the basis of expected utility, which is bounded, as opposed to traditional utility, which is not.

9.4 Third Stage in the Development of Utility Theory Under Conditions of Uncertainty: Von Neumann-Morgenstern Utility Function

Until von Neumann and Morgenstern (1944) recovered the notion of expected utility, the theory remained unknown for almost two hundred years. Von Neumann and Morgenstern's postulate is as follows.

Let the set of possible lotteries be L, and Z and Q are two lotteries belonging to set L, such that the lottery:

$$\beta Z + (1 - \beta)Q \in L$$

where β is any probability. This means that L is a set analogous to the consumption universe of neo-classical theory, but now the set of possible results is finite, as L contains the probabilistic mixes of all possible lotteries.

Von Neumann and Morgenstern defined rational behaviour as that which fits the following axioms:

Axiom I on ordering.
The individual's preferences must be reflexive, complete and transitive with respect to L.

Axiom II on continuity.
Let Z, Q and R be three lotteries belonging to L. If Z is preferred to Q and Q is preferred to R, then a probabilistic mix of Z and R exists that is indifferent to Q, always provided that there exists a probability β verifying that:
$\beta Z + (1-\beta)R$ is indifferent to Q

Axiom III on independence.
Let Z and Q be two lotteries belonging to L. If Z is preferred to Q, then a probabilistic combination of Z and any other prospect, R, also belonging to L, will be preferred to a combination with the same probabilities of Q and R. That is to say: if Z is preferred to Q, then, $\beta Z + (1-\beta)R$ is preferred to $\beta Q + (1-\beta)R$.

With the above axioms, we can make the following proposition:

Proposition I. If the relationship "at least as preferred as" verifies the axioms of ordering, independence and continuity, then there exists a utility function $U(Z) = U(P_1, P_2, ..., P_n)$ that assigns to each lottery $Z \in L$ a real number.

Of these axioms, independence is perhaps the most novel. It assumes, among other things, the absence of relations of complementarity or substitutability. With these axioms, von Neumann and Morgenstern proved that a utility function exists for the above axioms which we shall call the NM utility function. This function is 'cardinal' insofar as it preserves the ordering of preferences up to a linear transformation: if $U(x_i)$ is the function NM, then $W(x_i) = a + bU(x_i)$ represents the same preferences, where (a, b) are real numbers and b>0. The expected-utility function allows us to establish a direct relationship between the function from NM and individuals' attitudes: risk-loving or risk-averse.

Hence, let the lottery be:

$$L \equiv (x_1, x_2; p, 1 - p)$$

and a utility function

$$U(x_i)$$

like that represented in figure 9.1

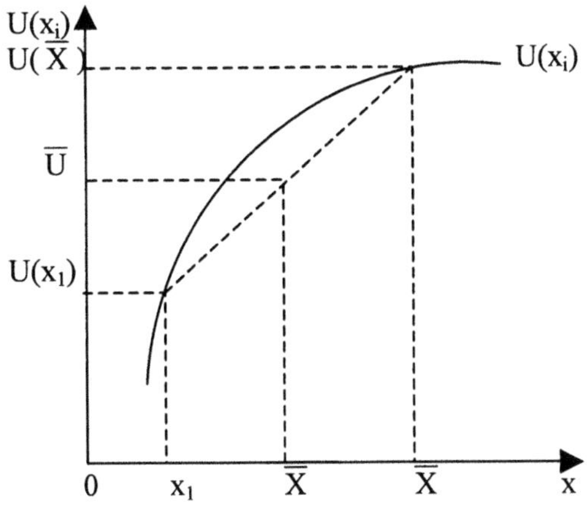

Fig. 9.1

The expected value of the lottery is $\overline{X}$ and the expected utility value (the expected utility) is $\overline{U}$. The certain utility of the lottery, Ec(L), is a certain amount that provides the same utility as the act of playing.

9.5 Individuals' Attitudes to Risk

It is assumed that the most widespread attitude among individuals is to be risk-averse. How can the degree of risk aversion be measured? Risk aversion is equivalent to the concavity of the utility curve in figure 9.1. If the curve were convex, the individual would be risk-loving, as in figure 9.2, while a straight line represents risk neutrality, also shown in figure 9.2 as the straight line joining points A and B.

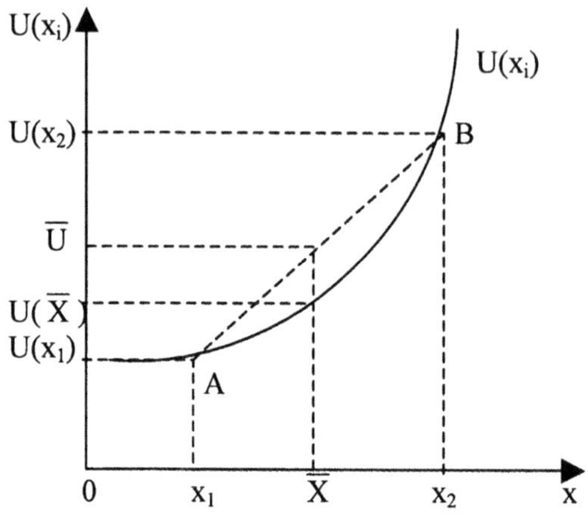

Fig. 9.2

In this case the individual prefers playing to receiving with certainty the expected value of the lottery, as in figure 9.2

$$\bar{U} > U(\bar{X})$$

To dissuade the individual from playing, he would have to be given an amount greater than the expected value of the lottery:

$$Ec(Z) > \bar{X}$$

In the case of risk neutrality, we would have:

$$\bar{U} = U(\bar{X})$$

$$Ec(Z) = \bar{X}$$

In 9.2 the curve $U(x_i)$ would be the straight line AB.

On the basis of these postulates, Arrow and Pratt proposed a risk-aversion index:

$$r(x) = - U''(x) / U'(x)$$

The greater the concavity of the utility function at point X, the higher the index.

9.6 Production and Uncertainty

Let us assume a competitive company which accepts market price p for a perishable product x, whose production costs are:

$$C(x) = C_F + C_V (x)$$

where C_F is the fixed cost and $C_V (x)$ is the variable cost.

If we assume that marginal costs, MC(x), are increasing, then the profit function is:

$$\pi(x) = px - C_F - C_V(x)$$

Uncertainty in production springs from the fact that the company must determine its optimum production volume before knowing the product sale-price. Let the price be a random variable of which we know the distribution function $\Phi(p)$, with the expectation of p being $E(p) = \bar{p}$. If we assume that $E(p) > 0$, therefore $\bar{p} > 0$ and $\bar{p} > MC(x)$ for $x = 0$.

The company will now try to maximise the expected utility of its profits, which are valued according to a concave utility function $U(\pi(x))$, i.e.:

$$\underset{x}{\text{Max}}\ U(x) = \text{Max}\ E[U(\pi(x))]$$

The first-order condition is:

$$E[U'(\pi(x))p] = C'(x)\ E[U'(\pi(x))]$$

Subtracting from both members $\bar{p}\,E[U'(\pi)]$ we obtain[1]:

$$(C'(x) - \bar{p})\ E[U'(\pi)] = E[U'(\pi)(p - \bar{p})] < 0$$

hence

$$C'(x) < \bar{p}$$

That is to say, the production volume of this risk-averse competitive company will be lower under conditions of uncertainty than under certainty conditions.

9.7 Critiques of the Theory of Expected Utility and the Theory of Limited Rationality

The above axioms propounded by von Neumann and Morgenstern were soon questioned. The reason for that is that empirical evidence, provided by studies of groups of people, violates the axioms of independence and transitivity.

9.7.1 Violation of the Axiom of Independence

Let us assume that all lotteries allow three consequences $\{x_1, x_2, x_3\}$, and we additionally posit the hypothesis $x_1 < x_2 < x_3$, such that the subject's preferences can be expressed as a map of indifference curves. The lottery can be represented as:

$$(x_1, x_2, x_3; p_1, p_2, p_3)$$

where $p_1 + p_2 + p_3 = 1$, hence $p_2 = 1 - p_3 - p_1$.

[1] U is concave, U' is decreasing in x, y in P; further, π (p) is increasign in P, and $E[U'(\pi)\ (p - \bar{p})] < 0$.

If we have three lotteries, L_1, L_2, L_3, they can be characterised by the probabilities p_1 and p_3, corresponding to x_1 and x_3. That is:

$$L_1 \equiv (p_1, p_3);\ L_2 \equiv (p_1^*, p_3^*);\ L_3 \equiv (p_1^{**}, p_3^{**})$$

which allows a two-dimensional representation, as in figure 9.3, of all the lotteries possible within the right-angled triangle OAB.

Along OA, $p_3 = 0$; along OB, $p_1 = 0$; and along AB, $p_2 = 0$. As $x_1 < x_2 < x_3$, then:

$$U(x_1) < U(x_2) < U(x_3)$$

This means that individuals' preferences increase in the direction of the arrows in figure 9.3

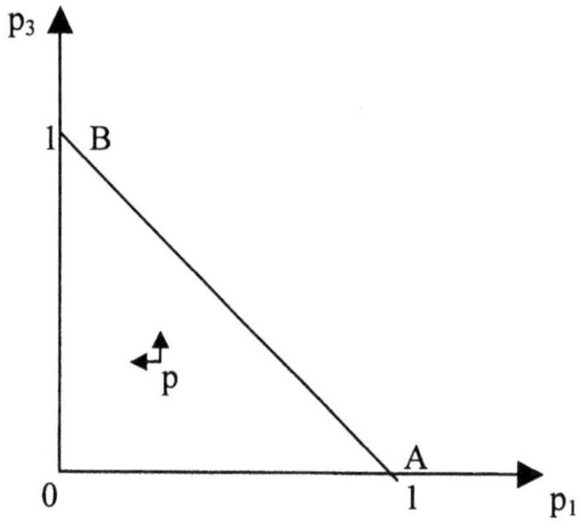

Fig. 9.3

Since the utility level must be constant on any indifference curve, then:

$$p_1U(x_1) + p_2U(x_2) + p_3U(x_3) = \overline{U}$$

where $\overline{U}$ is the constant utility; and now substituting $p_2 = 1 - p_3 - p_1$ and denominating $U(x_1) = U_1$, $U(x_2) = U_2$ y $U(x_3) = U_3$, we have:

$$p_1U_1 + (1 - p_1 - p_3)U_2 + p_3U_3 = \overline{U}$$

$$p_1U_1 + U_2 - U_2p_1 - U_2p_3 + p_3U_3 = \overline{U}$$

$$(U_3 - U_2)p_3 + (U_1 - U_2)p_1 = \overline{U} - U_2$$

$$(U_3 - U_2)p_3 = \overline{U} - U_2 + (U_2 - U_1)p_1 \tag{9.1}$$

where the only variables are p_1 and p_3, as x_1, x_2, x_3 are always the same and U_1, U_2, U_3 are constant. This means that the equation (9.1) is a straight-line equation like:

$p_3 = \alpha + \beta p_1$

where

$$\alpha = \frac{(\overline{U} - U_2)}{(U_3 - U_2)} \text{ and } \beta = \frac{(U_2 - U_1)}{(U_3 - U_2)}$$

For its part, α is the value of the utility level, $\overline{U}$, and β is a constant. Therefore, the independence axiom requires that the indifference curves be parallel straight lines, like those shown in figure 9.4, where preferences grow in the direction of the arrow.

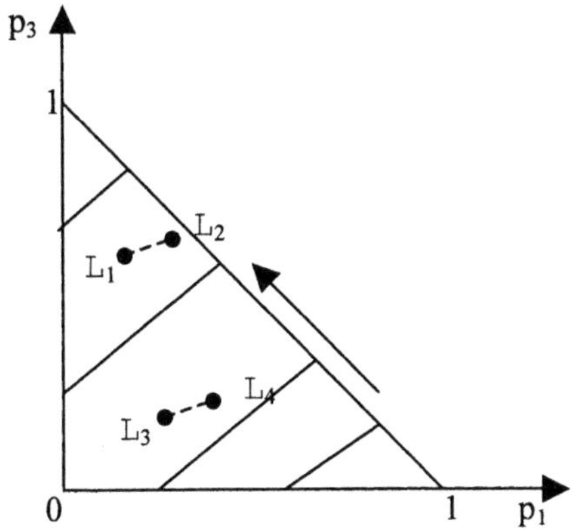

Fig. 9.4

Applying the above, if lottery L_1 is preferred to lottery L_2, then L_3 must be preferred to L_4; and conversely, if L_2 is preferred to L_1, L_4 must be preferred to L_3.

However, Maurice Allais tested the independence axiom and found that experiment did not verify it. Allais proposed the following experiment offering two lotteries:

$L_1 \equiv$ receive 100 million

$$L_2 \equiv \begin{cases} \text{receive 500 million with a probability of 10\%} \\ \text{receive 100 million with a probability of 89\%} \\ \text{receive nothing with a probability of 1\%} \end{cases}$$

Now, each individual is asked to choose between lottery L_1 and L_2.

Next, each individual in the previous experiment is asked to choose between the following lotteries:

$$L_3 \equiv \begin{cases} \text{receive 100 million with a probability of 11\%} \\ \\ \text{receive nothing with a probability of 89\%} \end{cases}$$

$$L_4 \equiv \begin{cases} \text{receive 500 million with a probability of 10\%} \\ \text{receive nothing with a probability of 90\%} \end{cases}$$

The results of this game present a structure similar to that shown in figure 9.4. That is, if in the first game an individual prefers L_1 to L_2, then in the second he will choose L_3 as preferable to L_4. But if the individual chooses L_2 over L_1, in the second game he must choose L_4 as better than L_3. However, the experimental results found by, for instance, Kahneman and Tversky (1979), show that on experimenting with 72 people on these games, 82% chose L_1 for the first game, while 83% chose L_2 in the second. In the same study – Kahneman and Tversky – many other examples are offered of experiments that violate the independence axiom.

To solve this important problem, one solution is to propose that the indifference straight-lines be inclined like the rods of a fan, i.e., as in figure 9.5.

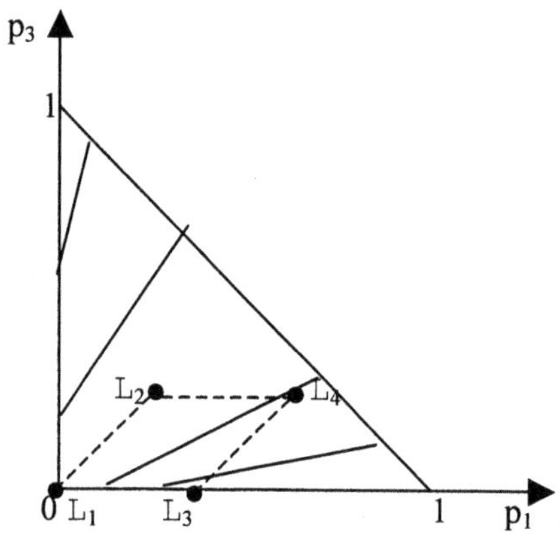

Fig. 9.5

In this case, the Allais paradox could be explained. To reach this result, we must start off with the theory of expected utility and demand that the preference index be linear in the probabilities, i.e.:

$$U(L) = \Sigma p_i U(x_i)$$

Now, however, we must start off with the following utility function.

$$V(L) = \Sigma \pi(p_i) U(x_i)$$

where $\pi(p_i)$ is a non-linear function. Suitably choosing $\pi(p_i)$ we obtain the result in figure 9.5.

The functions $\pi(p_i)$ represent the subjective effect of p_i on the individual. This approach is called "subjective expected utility theory".

9.7.2 Violation of the Transitivity Axiom

Experiments also showed that there were systematic violations of the transitivity axiom. To explain this behaviour, Lichtenstein and Slovic (1971, 1973) defined ‚reverse preference' for the following example: "two bets are offered to an individual, one of which is highly likely to garner a modest sum of money (bet L_1), while the other offers a small chance of winning a large sum of money (bet L_2)".

The result of Grether and Plott's (1979) experiments on 148 people was that 127 people choose L_1 while 71 people (and not 21 as expected) assign a greater pecuniary value (a higher certain equivalent) to bet L_2.

If the bets are:

$$L_1 \equiv (X, o; p_1, 1 - p_1)$$

$$L_2 \equiv (Y, o; p_1, 1 - p_1)$$

where $p_1 > p_2$, and $Y > X$.

If $(X_0 + X, X_0; p_1, 1 - p_1)$ is indifferent to $X_0 + Ec\ (L_1)$ by the definition of certain equivalent.

On the other hand, $(X_0 + Y, X_0; p_2, 1 - p_2)$ is indifferent to $X_0 + Ec\ (L_2)$, also by the definition of certain equivalent.

And if in the experiments individuals choose bet L_1, this means that $(X_0 + X, X_0; p_1, 1 - p_1)$ is preferred to $(X_0 + Y, X_0; p_2, 1 - p_2)$.

The fulfilment of the transitivity axiom means that $X_0 + Ec\ (L_1)$ must be preferred to $X_0 + Ec\ (L_2)$. That is, $Ec\ (L_1) > Ec\ (L_2)$.

However, the experiments show that $Ec\ (L_2) > Ec\ (L_1)$.

How can the experimental results be explained?

The response of theory has been to try to develop a new ‚rationality theory'. Simon (1959, 1972) has critiqued the concept of rationality in economics. He refers to the concept of limited rationality implying that individuals have limited information and assessment ability. Even if individuals have all the information available, they are unable to process it adequately. Simon suggests that limited rationality can be useful in two types of decision model.

The first model attempts to simplify a very complex situation into a relatively simple one in order to make a decision. For example, an individual decides to invest his money and, from a whole set of possible investments, reduces his decision to two alternatives: an electricity company or an investment fund. Thus, the ‚better' decision approximates an optimum decision.

The second model tries to reduce a very complex situation to a simpler one on the criterion of a certain degree of satisfaction. Logically, that degree of satisfaction must be below optimum. However, over time, if the framework is stable and choices proceed in succession, it is to be expected that individuals will review their degree of satisfaction until achieving optimum.

Loomes and Sugden (1982), Fishburn (1982) and Bell (1982) proposed the "Regret Theory". This theory consists of assuming that individuals tend to compare their current situation with the situations they would have been in if they had made a different decision in the past. If they realise that they are worse off than they might have been if they had taken another decision, they feel regret, while if the contrary is the case they rejoice.

References

Bell, D. E.: *Regret in Decision Making under Uncertainty.* Operations Research 30, 961-981 (1982)

Fishburn, P. C.: Nontransitive Measurable Utility. *Journal of Mathematical Psychology* 26, 31-67 (1982)

Gravelle, H., Rees, R.: *Microeconomics.* Longman Group Limited 1981

Grether, D. M., Plott, C. R.: Economic Theory of Choice and the Preference Reversal Phenomenon. *American Economic Review* 69, 623-638 (1979)

Kahneman, D., Tversky, A.: *Prospect Theory: an Analysis of Decision under Risk.* Econometrica 47 (2), 263-291 (1979)

Lichtenstein, S., Slovic, P.: Reversals of Preference between Bids and Choices in Gambling Decisions. *Journal of Experimental Psychology* 89, 46-55 (1971)

Lichtenstein, S., Slovic, P.: Response-Induced Reversals of Preference in Gambling: an Extended Replication in Las Vegas. *Journal of Experimental Psychology* 101, 16-20 (1973)

Loomes, G., Sugden, R.: Regret Theory: an Alternative Theory of Rational Choice under Uncertainty. *Economic Journal* 92, 805-824 (1982)

Segura, J.: *Análisis Microeconómico.* 3ª ed. Alianza Universidad Textos 1994

Simon, H. A.: Theories of Bounded Rationality. Chap. 8 in McGuire, Radner, R. (eds.) *Decision and Organisation.* North-Holland, Amsterdam 1972

Simon, H. A.: Theories of Decision-Making in Economics and Behavioural Science. *American Economic Review* vol. XLIX nº 3 (1959)

Varian, H.: *Microeconomic Analysis.* 3rd ed. Norton & Company 1992

Contributions to Economics

Nikolaus Thumm
Intellectual Property Rights
2000. ISBN 3-7908-1329-X

Max Keilbach
Spatial Knowledge Spillovers and the Dynamics of Agglomeration and Regional Growth
2000. ISBN 3-7908-1321-4

Alexander Karmann (Ed.)
Financial Structure and Stability
2000. ISBN 3-7908-1332-X

Joos P. A. van Vugt/Jan M. Peet (Eds.)
Social Security and Solidarity in the European Union
2000. ISBN 3-7908-1334-6

Johannes Bröcker/Hayo Herrmann (Eds.)
Spatial Change and Interregional Flows in the Integrating Europe
2001. ISBN 3-7908-1344-3

Kirstin Hubrich
Cointegration Analysis in a German Monetary System
2001. ISBN 3-7908-1352-4

Nico Heerink et al. (Eds.)
Economic Policy and Sustainable Land Use
2001. ISBN 3-7908-1351-6

Friedel Bolle/Michael Carlberg (Eds.)
Advances in Behavioral Economics
2001. ISBN 3-7908-1358-3

Volker Grossmann
Inequality, Economic Growth, and Technological Change
2001. ISBN 3-7908-1364-8

Thomas Riechmann
Learning in Economics
2001. ISBN 3-7908-1384-2

Miriam Beblo
Bargaining over Time Allocation
2001. ISBN 3-7908-1391-5

Peter Meusburger/Heike Jöns (Eds.)
Transformations in Hungary
2001. ISBN 3-7908-1412-1

Claus Brand
Money Stock Control and Inflation Targeting in Germany
2001. ISBN 3-7908-1393-1

Erik Lüth
Private Intergenerational Transfers and Population Aging
2001. ISBN 3-7908-1402-4

Nicole Pohl
Mobility in Space and Time
2001. ISBN 3-7908-1380-X

Pablo Coto-Millán (Ed.)
Essays on Microeconomics and Industrial Organisation
2002. ISBN 3-7908-1390-7

Mario A. Maggioni
Clustering Dynamics and the Locations of High-Tech-Firms
2002. ISBN 3-7908-1431-8

Ludwig Schätzl/Javier Revilla Diez (Eds.)
Technological Change and Regional Development in Europe
2002. ISBN 3-7908-1460-1

Alberto Quadrio Curzio/Marco Fortis (Eds.)
Complexity and Industrial Clusters
2002. ISBN 3-7908-1471-7

Friedel Bolle/Marco Lehmann-Waffenschmidt (Eds.)
Surveys in Experimental Economics
2002. ISBN 3-7908-1472-5

Pablo Coto-Millán
General Equilibrium and Welfare
2002. ISBN 7908-1491-1

Wojciech W. Charemza/Krystyna Strzala (Eds.)
East European Transition and EU Enlargement
2002. ISBN 3-7908-1501-2

Natalja von Westernhagen
Systemic Transformation, Trade and Economic Growth
2002. ISBN 3-7908-1521-7

Josef Falkinger
A Theory of Employment in Firms
2002. ISBN 3-7908-1520-9

Engelbert Plassmann
Econometric Modelling of European Money Demand
2003. ISBN 3-7908-1522-5

Reginald Loyen/Erik Buyst/Greta Devos
Struggeling for Leadership: Antwerp-Rotterdam Port Competition between 1870–2000
2003. ISBN 3-7908-1524-1

GPSR Compliance

The European Union's (EU) General Product Safety Regulation (GPSR) is a set of rules that requires consumer products to be safe and our obligations to ensure this.

If you have any concerns about our products, you can contact us on ProductSafety@springernature.com

In case Publisher is established outside the EU, the EU authorized representative is:

Springer Nature Customer Service Center GmbH
Europaplatz 3
69115 Heidelberg, Germany

Batch number: 10725973

Printed by Printforce, the Netherlands